500

Re,

THE POLITICS OF PROCRUSTES

After this Theseus killed a man called Procrustes, who lived in what was known as Corydallus in Attica. This person forced passing travellers to lie down on a bed, and if any were too long for the bed he lopped off those parts of their bodies which protruded, while racking out the legs of the ones who were too short. This was why he was given the name of Procrustes [The Racker].
Diodorus Siculus, The Library of History (IV 59, 5)

The Politics of Procrustes
Contradictions of enforced equality

ANTONY FLEW

Professor of Philosophy
University of Reading

Prometheus Books
1203 Kensington Avenue
Buffalo, New York 14215

1981

Published 1981 by Promethus Books
1203 Kensington Avenue, Buffalo, New York 14215

Copyright © 1981 by Antony Flew

ISBN 0 87975 150 9

Printed in Great Britain

Contents

Acknowledgements

None of the chapters which follow is a straight reprint of anything published before. But several do recycle fragments of material previously published elsewhere; while Chapters IV and V, together constituting rather less than a quarter of the whole, are more or less drastically revised and rewritten versions of earlier articles.

I am therefore glad to thank the several publishers and editors concerned for their permission to reuse whatever has been reused. The sources thus put under very various levels of tribute are as follows: 'Who are the Equals?', in *Philosophia* (Ramat-Gan, Israel) for 1980; 'Wants or Needs, Choices or Commands', in Ross Fitzgerald (Ed.) *Human Needs and Politics* (Rushcutters Bay, N.S.W.: Pergamon, 1977); 'The Profit Motive', in *Ethics* for 1976, published by the University of Chicago Press; 'Equality *or* Justice?', in P.A. French (Ed.) *Midwest Studies in Philosophy: Vol. III Studies in Ethical Theory* (Morris, Minn.: Minnesota UP, 1978); 'The Procrustean Ideal', in *Encounter* (London) for 1978; 'Selfishness and the Unintended Consequences of Intended Action', in D.J. Den Uyl and D.B. Rasmussen (Eds) *Freedom and Reason: Essays on the Thought of Ayn Rand* (Urbana, Ill.: Illinois UP, 1980); 'What Is A Right?', in *The Georgia Law Review* for 1979; and 'Intended Conduct and Unintended Consequences', in R. Duncan and M. Weston-Smith (Eds) *Lying Truths* (Oxford: Pergamon, 1979).

I also wish to thank some others for assistance of different kinds: Michael Ivens and the Foundation for Business Responsibilities, for commissioning what have in the event turned out to be preliminary drafts for Chapters II and VI; Christopher Coope of the University of Leeds and David Cooper of the University of Surrey, for showing me typescripts, which had not by my time of writing been published, and from which I was able to make some appropriations not otherwise acknowledged; and colleagues and students in institutions too numerous to mention, for criticising various drafts read as papers. Finally I thank Joan Morris, Secretary to the Department of Philosophy in the University of Reading, for transforming my legible but unlovely manuscript into a typescript making what I had written look vastly better than it did before; and, perhaps, than it is.

CHAPTER I

Prologue

> Philosophers today never compose useful articles,
> organise conventions, honour the gods, comfort the
> afflicted, arbitrate in civil disputes, counsel the young
> (or anyone else), or give any thought in what they write
> to considerations of the public good. *Aelius Aristides:*
> *Oration on the Four*

The present book could be submitted in evidence to support a plea
of 'Not Guilty' against at least the first and last of these perennial
charges. For its several chapters both examine and assail presuppositions and implications of two master notions in the
contemporary climate of opinion, two notions which in their main
connections and ramifications have a claim to be called –
borrowing one of the finest phrases of *The German Ideology* – 'the
illusion of the epoch' (Marx and Engels 1846, p.51). Equality
(and it is usually equality without prefix or suffix) seems to be
accepted almost everywhere as self-evidently and without qualification good. Of course sincere devotion to any ideal of equality is
by no means universal. But lip service is very widely both
expected and given; open dissidents are made to feel outsiders and
reactionaries.

Socialism too is in the same way respectable and required.
Certainly it is not and never was true that 'we are all socialists
now', if that is to be construed as involving a conscious and
articulate commitment. But everywhere the dominant assumptions
appear to be socialist assumptions: that the collectively controlled
and collectively owned is legitimate, that whatever is public must
be public spirited and in the public interest; whereas the privately
controlled and privately owned is selfish, unruly and always
fundamentally illegitimate. Public service employment, as it is so
often flatteringly described, is seen as somehow inherently

virtuous; whereas to work, as it is said, only for your own or for someone else's private profit is to be either an exploiter or exploited. Dr Johnson pronounced once, in the time of his glory, that there were few ways in which a man could be more innocently employed than in making money through commerce and industry; today too many of his compatriots appear to regard such harmless necessary activity as at best an indecency.

Certainly we do have a good deal of evidence that precise egalitarian prescriptions and actual socialist institutions are rather less popular with the vulgar than among the opinion-forming intelligentsia. (Compare, for instance, Schumpeter, Chapter XIII and passim, with Harris and Seldon 1963 and 1979.) The present book, however, is not primarily and immediately concerned either with particular policies or with the institutional expression of egalitarian and socialist ideas. Instead it is going to pick out and to take issue with some of the assumptions behind these concepts as they are presented in their most intellectually formidable form through the works of political philosophers, sociologists and economists.

Nevertheless the book will not upon that account become remote from the general battle of ideas, the outcome of which must surely play a large part in determining whether Britain's accelerating decline is to be reversed; or whether, well before this century is out, we are to see the firm establishment of Ingsoc – an English Socialism not too unimaginably far removed from the slum totalitarianism of George Orwell's last appalling nightmare *1984*. For whatever else may be wrong with *The General Theory of Employment, Interest and Money*, the author was dead right in one claim: 'The ideas of economists and political philosophers . . . are more powerful than is commonly understood. Indeed, the world is ruled by little else . . . Madmen in authority, who hear voices in the air, are distilling their frenzy from some academic scribbler of a few years back' (Keynes, p.383).[1] So the hope is that any rectification of ideas which have captivated so many of our intellectuals will in the not too distant future spread out into broader circles.

1 What is to be done

Section 2 of the present chapter tries to clear up some of the confusion to be found around and about the notion of socialism. Preliminaries thus complete, Chapter II distinguishes would-be factual claims about human equalities from three ideals. These are not merely distinguishably different. There is also reason to believe that the third, and currently most fashionable, is ultimately incompatible with both the first and the second. This is an ideal neither of equal liberty for all to pursue whatever each individually holds to be good, nor of fair and equal competition to secure scarce opportunities, but of equality of condition. Sometimes, as in an Israeli Kibbutz, this third ideal is voluntarily accepted and self-imposed. But normally nowadays it is something to be enforced upon others by political power and social engineering. It is this drive for the collective and compulsory imposition of equality which, as the prefatory motto makes clear, is best described as Procrustean.

This raises an urgent question. By what right do such equalisers labour to impose their ideal upon anyone other than themselves? (Indeed we cannot help noticing, nor should we, that the equalising labours of many rather conspicuously underdeprived egalitarians are directed at almost everyone else but themselves!) The answer offered is that equality, in this present understanding, is the categorical imperative of (social) justice. So Chapter III, with special reference to the enormous and enormously influential book of John Rawls, argues that any identification of equality with justice is totally wrong; the Procrusteans ought frankly to eschew the propaganda advantages of proclaiming themselves enforcers of justice, and instead urge us all to abandon that whole backward-looking business in favour of their own fine, fresh and forward-looking aims. Chapter IV goes on to elucidate the degrading assumptions about the nature of man necessarily presupposed by this misrepresentation of equality of outcome as the requirement of justice. In a word, Rawls and others find that they have to maintain that nothing which can differentiate one human being from another, including even individual actions and abstentions from action, are really either parts of us or truly ours.

Chapter V examines the notions of want and need, and the logical relations between these notions, in order to show why the idea of need possesses so strong an appeal to all who would like to be members of a power élite providing what and only what they by their superior judgement determine to be best for all those subject to them. Here and elsewhere it is emphasised that 'the illusion of the epoch' serves as the uniting and justifying ideology of certain social groups. In a word again, the Procrustean ideal has, as it is bound to have, the most powerful attraction for those already playing or hoping in the future to play prominent or rewarding parts in the machinery for its enforcement.

Finally, Chapters VI and VII try to sort out a great entanglement of invalid arguments and false assumptions. These combine to undermine the legitimacy of any pluralist, private, and freely competitive economic arrangements. Such undermining once achieved, the way is open to the fully socialist society in which everything is collectively owned and controlled, with state monopolies providing for their dependents what and only what the various ruling élites determine to be fitting. What will in fact be thus determined may or may not turn out to be equality between all those who are so dependent. But as between those who give and those who receive the commands in any such command economy there can of course be no equality at all.

2 Socialism, social democracy, and democratic socialism

This might well be described as a book of philosophical essays on equality and socialism. Why the two topics are conjoined in a single volume should become clearer as we proceed. But it has to be said at once that the linkage is not a straight matter of definition. Although many socialists are egalitarians, in some interpretation, believing that socialism is a necessary if not the sufficient condition for realising the sort of equality they favour, it is, I shall argue, altogether wrong to conclude, in the words of an enormously distinguished revisionist, Professor Arthur Lewis: 'Socialism and nationalisation of property are now commonly identified, but this is as great an error as the identification of socialism and the extended state . . . . Socialism is about equality. A passion for equality is the one thing that links all socialists; on all others they are divided' (Lewis, p.10).

With regard to equality, fundamental distinctions will be made in the immediately subsequent chapters. But the word 'socialism' is bound to appear in those too. So it is now necessary both to explain and to justify the usage to be followed throughout. 'Socialism', then, is always taken to mean public or common, and therefore normally state, ownership and direction of – in the hallowed words of the original Clause IV of the Constitution of the UK Labour Party – 'all the means of production, distribution, and exchange'; which presumably embraces the production, distribution and exchange of health, education, and welfare services as well as

– what shall we say? – corporeal goods.

What Professor Lewis might truly and usefully have said, but in fact did not say, is that progressive nationalisation – the establishment, that is, of state-owned and normally monopolistic corporations – is not the only way of moving towards a socialist society. Especially in the USA substantial moves in that direction have taken two very different forms: first, a great leap forward in the proportion of GNP passing through and spent by federal and other lesser public hands; and, second, an enormous increase in regulation and in regulatory agencies – such as OSHA (the Occupational Safety and Health Agency) and EPA (the Environmental Protection Agency).

(i) Certainly present usage of the word 'socialism' is far removed from that suggested by Margaret Cole in the 'Socialism' article of the standard Edwards *Encyclopaedia of Philosophy*; although it is substantially what George Lichtheim in *A Short History of Socialism* is strong to recommend, if not wholly consistent in observing.

(a) In what is supposed to be, and usually is, an authoritative work of reference Margaret Cole proposes four defining characteristics supposedly common to all those properly admitted into the socialist fold. These are the beliefs: first, 'that the existing system of society and its institutions should be condemned as unjust and morally unsound'; second, 'that there can be created a different form of society with different institutions, based on moral values which will tend to improve mankind instead of, as now, corrupt it'; third, that what is required is 'a fundamental transformation of society amounting to a revolution'; and, finally, that any truly socialist movement must be internationalist.

Two separately sufficient reasons for dismissing any definition on these lines are: first, that the first three criteria proposed together yield no hint of what the positive characteristics of a socialist society must be, or of what negative features are essential to the non-socialist; and, second, that such general references to 'the existing system of society' – without any specifications limiting these to particular times and particular places – have the uncovenanted effect of making socialism essentially unattainable. Such a lifelong activist as Margaret Cole could not have been willing to live with these implications had her Editor shown her what they are.

Towards the end of the *Short History* the author at last

emphasises, what he ought to have made quite clear from the beginning, that 'the only reasonable description of socialism is one that centres on common or social ownership' (Lichtheim, p.341). However, like so many others, he also has times when, finding some aspect or expression of actual socialism not altogether to his taste, he refuses to accept an unacceptable face as the authentic visage of the real thing. For instance: 'in Burma, Indonesia and Egypt' the work of 'ruling political élites', which without doubt did nationalise the greater part of all three economies, is discounted, inasmuch as they 'attempted to industrialise and modernise the societies under their control along state-capitalist lines' (*Ibid.*, p.290). Yet, unless some peculiar meaning is specially stipulated for that last phrase, anyone who adopts Lichtheim's correctly conventional criterion for socialism becomes thereby committed to rejecting all talk of 'state-capitalism' as self-contradictory and without sense.

(b) Whatever may or may not be or have been appropriate in other countries or at other times, there is no question but that in Britain today it darkens counsel to employ the word 'socialism', or to pretend to employ it, without requiring satisfaction of that most familiar and traditional criterion, collective ownership and public control. For it is in precisely this understanding that one of the two great parties of government has been for more than sixty years, and still is, both in theory and in practice, socialist. Although in some of the decades since World War II the denials have been quite frequent, coming both from party spokespersons addressing outside audiences and from wiseacre political commentators, still this remains as true as it is important – as obviously true as it is obviously important.

A few years ago no less an authority than the then Prime Minister, James Callaghan, reassured the House of Commons: since 'this party has always stood for a mixed economy and not a totally controlled economy, that must be the basis on which our economic policy proceeds' (Hansard, for 3 May 1976). Nevertheless, if he is to be construed as asserting more than that total socialism has never been on the immediate agenda, his statement was quite simply false. When in 1918 the categorically and totally socialist Clause IV was written into the constitution of the Labour Party as its official statement of intent, nothing was said about mixing a private and pluralist with a public and monopolistic sector. Yet it is this Clause IV and this clause alone which has without fail been printed on every membership card for at least as long as Callaghan himself has belonged to the party; and it still is. Nor have the amendments actually accepted at the 1959 conference done anything to limit the scope of the ultimate and totally socialist commitment.

Again – remembering that the Labour Party in Britain began and remains a creature of the labour unions, which both provide eighty or ninety per cent of the funds and cast eighty or ninety per cent of the votes at the conferences – we have to notice that similar clauses are included among the constitutional aims of both the general Trades Union Congress (TUC) and most older individual unions. For instance: Rule 2.4 of the reputedly 'moderate' or 'right-wing' General and Municipal Workers' Union (GMWU) speaks of sponsoring members of parliament 'pledged to collective ownership . . . of the means of production, distribution and exchange'. Rule 3 of the National Union of Mineworkers (NUM) commits it 'to join with other organisations for the purpose of and with the view to the complete abolition of capitalism'. And so on, down a very long roll. (By the way: it should surely be seen as an outrage, of a kind which most liberally minded persons like to believe both distinctive of and peculiar to totalitarian countries, that for so many in Britain today membership in such specifically political, partisan organisations has become a condition of employment.)

Confronted by these constitutional facts, as in fact people rather rarely are, some may try to dismiss them as 'mere theology'. What really matters, they will suggest in their most worldly-wise manner, is who are the office-seekers and office-holders, and what is actually done; not factitious platforms or wildly whirling manifestos, which every insider thinks that he knows are adopted and issued only in order to recruit the innocents and to hold the support of the fundamentalists.

Without accepting such wholesale cynicism, by all means let persons and parties be judged by their deeds, not their words. But here we still get the same verdict. For, although the drive on towards complete socialism is sometimes stronger and sometimes weaker, every Labour parliament makes at least some moves in that direction, whether absolutely massive or relatively miniscule; and always, if it should come to a question of reversing any such move, then at once the whole party is solidly united. Left and right together, all insist that nothing which has once fallen into the hands of the impersonal and collective 'people' may ever be sold again to private individual persons; so that any reversal actually achieved is at the first opportunity itself reversed.

But now, if you keep taking steps always in the same direction, then, however short the steps and however often you stop or are stopped, there can be no doubt either about where you are going or about your eventual arrival at that destination. In this understanding at any rate the Fabians have always been right to underline 'the inevitability of gradualness'! So, once seized of the realities of this ratchet railway, we cannot but concede – in terms of an old Leninist distinction expressing a quite unLeninist conclusion – that the Labour Party is not only subjectively but also objectively socialist.

(ii) In recent years more and more commentators have been suggesting that, on the contrary, the greater part of the front bench leadership and of the whole parliamentary party neither is now nor ever has been any more truly socialist than the majority of rank and file Labour voters. Constitutional commitments and all the conference rhetoric notwithstanding, the real leaders are said never to have had any (subjective) intention to move to that end.

Still more recently the expression 'social democrat' has been reintroduced into domestic British political usage. Its intended meaning appears to be fairly definite in a negative direction. Social democrats, it is said, reject full socialism in favour of a predominantly private and pluralist economy. On the positive side they are always taken to believe in generous and extensive state provision of health, education and welfare services; and that, apparently, is all there is to it. Yet, surely, if British Conservatives are to be kept out of the club, and in particular if – as those who are giving renewed currency to the term 'social democrat' would insist – such notorious bogeypersons as Sir Keith Joseph and Mrs Margaret Thatcher are to be blackballed, then some further and more exclusive membership requirement has got to be added?

(a) Certainly Chancellor Schmidt and the adult majority of the Social Democratic Party of Germany are social democrats in this present sense, rather than (democratic) socialists. For at Bad Godesberg in 1959, the year in which our Labour Party rejected a move to limit its commitment to total public ownership of 'the means of production, distribution and exchange', its German brother, with equal decisiveness, repudiated socialism in favour of the triumphantly successful 'social market economy' of Ludwig

Erhard. One confusing consequence is that one at least of the main present and founding members of the second Socialist International is thus now unequivocally non-socialist.

A further danger of confusion lies in the historic fact that all the older parties still bearing the Social Democratic name were in origin Marxist. So Lenin's world-shattering coup in October 1917 was made by one fraction of the Russian Social-Democratic Workers' Party, and against what must by the usage just now explained be rated the social democratic government of Kerensky. As a final twist of paradox, notice too that the largest element in what all the British and American media labelled 'the right-wing alliance' victorious in the 1979 elections in Portugal is called the Social Democratic Party; a name which, by the two criteria specified above, is without doubt entirely appropriate.

(b) But in this understanding it would seem that most of what is called the centre and the right of the parliamentary Labour Party is not, and never has been, even subjectively social democratic. Some people hark back to what they think of as the golden days when Clement Attlee was Leader. Certainly many things were different then, and perhaps better. But there is no reason for thinking that Attlee was not originally chosen as, or that he later ceased to be, a socialist.

In a book published in 1937 he wrote: 'The evils that capitalism brings about differ in intensity in different countries, but the root cause of the trouble once discerned, the remedy is seen to be the same. . . . The cause is private property, the remedy is public ownership' (Attlee, p.15). In 1945 he led his party to its greatest electoral victory. This was on a manifesto, *Let us Face the Future*, proclaiming: 'The Labour Party is a socialist party and proud of it. Its ultimate purpose is the establishment of the socialist common-wealth of Great Britain.' At the 1946 conference he said, and the deeds of his administration conformed to these words: 'We are resolved to carry out as rapidly and energetically as we can the distinctive side of Labour's programme; our socialist policy, our policy of nationalisation.'

In a later generation C.A.R. Crosland was widely taken to be the very model of a modern social democrat. Yet even in his last book, *The Conservative Enemy*, he actually rejects only 'the continuous proliferation of state monopolies on the existing pattern'. For him 'the object' still is '*generally* to increase the area of public ownership . . . it is sufficient to extend public investment in any direction. . . . This is the rationale behind the various proposals for public share-buying' (Crosland 1962, pp.47-8: italics original).

Crosland's lost leader Hugh Gaitskell, borrowing a forgotten phrase from Lenin's announcement of his own strictly temporary New Economic Policy, bravely though without success tried to persuade the 1959 party conference to limit the commitment of Clause IV, and to confine old-look state monopoly nationalisation to 'the commanding heights of the economy'. But he too insisted that any investment incomes must as such constitute immoral unearnings. Thus in a Fabian Tract of 1956 Gaitskell made the completely unhesitant and categorical assertion: 'The existence of unearned income is wrong in itself no matter how it is distributed' (p.6). So, like Crosland in his last years, he would have had to score himself as a democratic socialist rather than a social democrat: which, in the present understanding, are entirely different things. (Surely, I have to interject in parentheses, Gaitskell must have been thinking only of that investment income which remains individual and private as opposed to collective and public? For wherever capital is productively employed the fruits of its employment have to go somewhere!)

(c) Everyone appears to agree that those variously described as the moderates, the right, or the social democrats within the Labour Party have been and are half-hearted and ineffective in their resistance to the rise in the seventies of the hard left. I suggest that one neglected reason why is that most of the people involved not merely have to pretend to be, but in truth themselves are, socialists. For example, the so-called moderates of the Manifesto Group derive their *nom de guerre* from the 1974 manifestos. But these contained proposals for what the future Chancellor Denis Healey at the 1973 conference characterised as 'a massive extension of nationalisation'; and yet the members of the Manifesto Group have supported and continue to support these and other purely socialist measures, both on their election platforms, and in the division lobbies of the House of Commons. So any claim to moderation on their behalf has still to refer to their socialism. (In any case what sense does it make to say that someone is a moderate without prefix or suffix, as opposed to a moderate this or an extreme that?)

One consequence is that the dispute within the Labour Party between left and right has to be, not about the direction of travel,

but about how fast and how far to try to go. Here the most effective
argument for caution has been undercut by the experience of the
two 1974 elections. These showed, if this was not obvious
already, that, so long as Britain maintains the first-past-the-post
electoral system, it is just not true to say that the Labour Party
cannot get elected if it commits itself to a fast-lane socialist
immediate programme; and in Britain there are then, of course, no
effective constitutional limits upon what legislation can be passed
even by a single vote majority in the House of Commons. We here
live, as the present Lord Chancellor has put it, under 'an elective
despotism'.

CHAPTER II

Four Kinds of Equality

It is evident that, barring major physical catastrophe,
war, or some other massive cause of deflection of
current social interests, the idea of equality will be
sovereign for the rest of this century in just about all
circles concerned with the philosophical bases of
public policy . . . . In the past, unifying ideas tended to
be religious in substance. There are certainly signs that
equality is taking on a sacred aspect among many
minds today, that it is rapidly acquiring dogmatic
status, at least among a great many philosophers and
social scientists. *Robert Nisbet*

The motto of this chapter is taken from the first paragraph of a
Review Essay, greeting – though one could not say welcoming –
John Rawls's book *A Theory of Justice* 'as the long-awaited
successor to Rousseau's *Social Contract*, and as the rock on
which the Church of Equality can properly be founded in our time'
(Nisbet 1974, pp. 103 and 107). That the words in the motto are
true scarcely calls for proof. It will, nevertheless, be worthwhile in
Section 1 of this chapter to mount a long parade of passages
showing how widely nowadays it is assumed to be just obvious that
equality is a good in itself, even the overriding and supreme good.
For it is easy to overlook something which pervades the whole
climate of opinion in which we live, even when that something
might astonish visitors from other times or other places. The same
passages will also serve to indicate some very practical commitments springing from, or conflicting with, various theoretical
principles to be examined later.

The remaining sections of the chapter (2-5) deal with the 'Four
Kinds of Equality' mentioned in its title. The first kind is
concerned with what are supposed to be matters of fact, with
assertions that something *is* the case. The other three are proposed

ideals of how things *ought* to be.

Of the three ideals, or sorts of ideal, the first, the most ancient, and the most difficult to define, is sometimes seen as a secular version of something believed to be common to the three great traditions of Mosaic theism. Judaism, Christianity, and Islam are popularly presented as teaching the Brotherhood of Man under the Fatherhood of God, with the apparent consequence that all human souls are of equal value in the eyes of their Creator.

The second ideal is customarily called equality of opportunity, although it would be more apt to speak of open competition for scarce opportunities: this was, in the French Revolution of 1789, 'La carrière ouverte aux talents'.

The third ideal, and the one to which so many of our political intellectuals today profess allegiance, is best characterised as equality of outcome or equality of result. (In the French Revolution this ideal was briefly represented by Gracchus Babeuf, and his ill-starred Conspiracy of the Equals: see Talmon, Part III.)

1 The most manifest of goods?

Let us begin with three introductory indicators that equality of some sort has gained wide acceptance as a good in itself. They come from very various sources, and their authors might well disclaim concern 'with the philosophical bases of public policy'.

The first was collected from a leading London daily newspaper, *The Guardian.* Confronted by every sort of danger and decline, the editorialist, who presumably knows his readers, struck this clarion keynote for a New Year: 'Nearly all of us want to get through 1975 with the least damage to social equality' (30 December 1974).

The second is the first paragraph of a letter sent by the North West Thames Regional Health Authority to the heads of all its departments and divisions, concluding with the words: 'Will you please ensure that each member of your staff is aware of this.' This paragraph was printed, and the significance of the whole letter discussed by Bernard Levin, in *The Times* of London, under the bitter headline: 'Sense takes a holiday and envy stays at home' (7 July 1978). Itself headed 'Unpaid Leave (other than compassionate)' the complete paragraph read: 'The grant of unpaid leave is not normally approved because *it could be held to be unfair* to those staff who cannot afford the financial diminution while favouring those who can' (italics supplied).

The third of these introductory indicators is again a letter, this time from a Rural Dean to his old Oxford college. Featured in the *Christ Church Record* for 1977 it cannot be reproduced in full. It was protesting the supposed scandal that Christ Church, along with many other ancient foundations in Oxford and Cambridge, still nominates clerics to several Church of England benefices (i.e., livings). The anonymous Rural Dean – shall we, in the spirit of 1789, think of him as Père Egalité? – urged as the sufficient reason for abolishing this curious institution the fact that Christ Church is still able and willing to supply to the incumbents of its livings some good things which, as he put it, 'are denied to others'.

(i) If we turn now to the academics, we can see that equality is indeed 'acquiring dogmatic status'. The Professor of Social and Administrative Studies within that same University of Oxford recently edited a volume of papers 'chosen to illustrate the approach and the achievement of the human sciences in theory and research concerning the ancient problem of nature and nurture' (Halsey, 1977, p.1). In a long, frequently technical Introduction to his often correspondingly technical selections he takes it for granted that any reduction of inequality – inequality without prefix or suffix – is beyond dispute a manifest good (*Ibid.*, p.25). Immediately identifying this good with (not justice but) 'social justice', he then plain cannot understand how opposition to his favoured measures for the enforcement of equality might sometimes spring from something other than 'malevolence' (*Ibid.*, p.8).

(a) Consider next a major Harvard contribution to the sociology of education. Towards the end of an extended research report, entitled simply *Inequality*, Christopher Jencks remarks: 'The reader should by now have gathered that our primary concern is with equalising the distribution of income' (p.261). That they should. For though Jencks is far too scrupulous a social scientist to permit what he deprecatingly calls private 'prejudices and obsessions' to distort published findings, he quite properly has no hesitation about making his ideals evident (p.v). He even hints that he might someday feel bound to go beyond even the most drastic rearrangement of incomes. There are, for instance, pages where he toys with the notion of 'cognitive equality' – a condition in which, universalised, no one would know more than anyone else (pp.64 and 109). Then at the end, after reflecting that social engineering may in the event turn out to be harder and less effective than genetic engineering, he insists: 'Most educators and laymen evidently feel that an individual's genes are his, and that they entitle him to whatever advantages he can get from them. . . . For a thoroughgoing egalitarian, however, inequality that derives from biology ought to be as *repulsive* as inequality that derives from early socialisation' (p.73: italics supplied).

In a Foreword to the British edition, Tyrrell Burgess commends *Inequality* to his fellow left-wing educationists. He praises Jencks and his colleagues for 'stating the liberal and radical assumptions about education and then testing them against the evidence.' Apparently these assumptions included the notion that equalising educational opportunity must go a long way towards equalising pay and status in the adult world; hence many 'liberal and radical' people, finding that this is not so, have been (surprisingly) surprised (*Ibid.*, pp.37, 91ff., 109 and 255). Wanting such eventual equalisation above all else, Jencks is frank in pointing the way to a command rather than a market economy (*Ibid.*, p.199); though he does neglect to specify that, if socialism is to serve his purpose, then all the commands will of course have to be issued either by Jencks himself or by those like-minded with him.

To Burgess 'The conclusion seems inescapable: reforming the schools will not bring about social change . . . .' He goes on: 'To almost any proposal for education we can now ask "did it survive the Jencks" test?'. And, if not, we can further ask "What explicit steps are proposed to fend off failure this time?" . . . A clue to the way we ought to do this can be found in the experience of the schools. Their failure as engines of social change . . . .' (*Ibid.*, pp.1 and 2). To Burgess, as to so many of his educationist colleagues, it is altogether obvious that an educational policy has to be a policy for eventual equalisation. (Here as elsewhere the toothless general expression 'social change' seems to be a code-name for moves only in that most desired direction.)

Educational failure becomes, therefore, failure in something quite other than the essential business of education as traditionally conceived; namely, teaching and learning. This tendency in what we should now hesitate to label educational thought is seen again in an article in the *Oxford Review of Education*, where the author, considering a thoroughly equalised society, lays it on the line: 'the role of education must largely be to maintain such a society once it has been attained' (Halsey 1975, p.10). A Professor of Education in the University of Leicester is similarly categorical. As reported in *The Times* he said: 'the objective should be equality' (27 September 1965).

The prime assumption that inequality is always in itself bad, so that equality must be correspondingly good, is revealed again and again in what their authors see as exposés of educational scandals. A recent issue of the *Times Educational Supplement* presented a 'Dismal Catalogue' (21 June 1978). This consisted in a list of ways in which immigrant children in a Redbridge school were not doing as well as their non-immigrant classmates. Nothing was said about the absolute performance levels of any of the children. For all we were told to the contrary everyone may have been achieving splendidly, albeit the immigrants less splendidly than the non-immigrants. The TES correspondent simply took it for granted that not doing as well as others is in and by itself sufficient reason to feel dismal.

Ivan Illych provides in *Deschooling Society* a second similar example. He reckons there to have clinched his case against schools by the end of Chapter 1; simply and solely by making out that schools benefit some so much more than others. Only in later chapters does he begin to deploy arguments which he hopes will show that even those doing best at school would have done better outside.

(b) Turning from education to economics, take a look at a little treatise on *Political Violence* published four or five years ago by a prestigious North American university press. The author, Ted Honderich, was at the time of writing a Reader in Philosophy in the University of London. He offers a qualified defence of political violence – but exclusively, of course, left-wing political violence: his opponents are wicked animals if they defend themselves. Honderich starts from what he insists upon presenting as the facts of inequality: 'the worst-off tenth now living in each of the developed societies will have considerably shorter lives than the individuals in the best-off tenth'; while 'On average males in Gabon die well before what is regarded as middle age in Britain.' Thus 'There arises the question of the possibility of any real change either in the inequalities of lifetime within developed societies, or in the inequalities of lifetime between developed and less developed societies' (Honderich, pp.4, 5 and 6).

It is only later, and as if as an afterthought, that he directs attention not only to the relativities but also to the absolute situation of the poor: 'the facts of inequality . . . claim our attention not only because they consist in *inequalities*. It is not merely that some people have less, but that they have *so little*, judged in an absolute rather than a comparative way'; and so 'What emerges . . . is that what we must have is a principle or a pair or a set of principles which give importance to the avoidance of both distress and inequality . . . . Obviously a perfect equality of suffering leaves much to be desired.'

Yes, he is certainly welcome to repeat that last sentence. But we must not let the chorus of agreement conceal a remarkable fact. It is in terms of two actual or putative evils, neither one reducible to the other, that he formulates his own negative neo-Utilitarianism: 'that we should always act in such a way as to produce *that state of affairs which most avoids inequality and distress*'. The manifesto is forthwith glossed: 'this attitude . . . is the fundamental part of the most common of all reflective moralities' (*Ibid.*, pp.10, 38 and 24: all italics original).

Whatever the merits of such a negative neo-Utilitarianism, a moment's thought about the implications of introducing inequality as a second bad, whether or not it is fully coequal with the first, must at once dispose of the suggestion that Honderich is merely reformulating classical Utilitarianism. For that spoke only of the greatest happiness of the greatest number. Concentrating upon the maximisation of aggregate satisfaction, it had nothing to say about equal distribution as a separate and independent good; although its spokespersons have sometimes suggested that equality may in fact be the best means by which to reach their sole supreme end.

For instance: in his 'Leading Principles of a Constitutional Code' Bentham himself said: 'The more remote from equality are the shares . . . the less is the sum of felicity produced by those shares' (Bentham, II, p.27: compare Jencks, p.9, and Quinton, pp.75-6). But this consideration, important thought it is, cannot support a separate principle of the badness of inequality as such. It offers, therefore, no obstacle to whatever incentive inequalities may in fact be necessary in order to achieve the supreme Utilitarian good.

By contrast, Honderich's own system, since it condemns all inequalities as in themselves bad, requires that such incentives be conceded only grudgingly, if at all – traded off after hard bargaining against whatever decrease in 'distress and suffering' they may make possible. For the same reason an adherent of this 'most common of all reflective moralities' must insist that, even in a society or a world in which no one was afflicted by 'deprivation, distress and suffering', it still would be bad if anyone became in any way better off than anyone else. And, furthermore, any such mean moralist must be committed to saying that it would even then be positively wrong for anyone to try to advance themselves beyond their fellows.

It would appear that Honderich himself both sees and relishes one consequence. This is that, unless those who are better off can justify their relative position as indirectly bettering the situation of the worse off, it is imperative to reduce their prosperity – and this whether or not that reduction makes the situation of the previous worse off absolutely better. For it is with longing that Honderich asserts: 'There are economies, as satisfactory as ours, which are without the rich' (*Ibid.*, p.85: it is, surely, remarkable both that he appears to find the state of the British economy otherwise satisfactory and that he forebears to name any of our rich-free peers.)

However, whether or not he is right to claim that his manifesto commitment 'is the fundamental part of the most common of all reflective moralities', there can be no doubt that there are plenty of egalitarians, perhaps especially in the public welfare world, for whom inequality is bad irrespective of the absolute position of those who are less equal than the others. Indeed many of these egalitarians give the impression that they are rather more concerned to abolish inequality than to abolish poverty. Certainly anyone who has in such circles argued for the adoption in Britain of the policies through which Ludwig Erhard unleashed the really quite unmiraculous 'German economic miracle' will be drearily familiar with the stock objection. It is protested that, even though this might both reverse our national economic decline and enable us to have – as the now so much richer Germans do – a higher-hung and more close-meshed safety net of public welfare provision, nevertheless such 'social market' economic policies, which include lower and less steeply progressive income taxation combined with friendly tax treatment for the capital gains of wealth-creating investment, must result in more of that evidently intolerable and altogether infamous thing – inequality.

This, rather than the poverty which involves actual 'distress and suffering', appears to be the prime concern of the former Director of the Child Poverty Action Group, since elected to Parliament in the Labour interest. Thus the free-spending and deeply compassionate Minister for Social Services in the 1970-74 Heath administration, Sir Keith Joseph, popularised the expression 'cycles of deprivation'. But Frank Field, continuing the discussion under the title *Unequal Britain*, prefers always to speak of 'cycles of inequality': indeed he never seems to notice that he is misreporting Sir Keith, who spoke always of poverty and absolute deprivation rather than of inequality.

In the same book, presenting mortality statistics, Field is unable to draw much satisfaction from the declines shown in all sections. It is, it would seem, the distribution of premature death across classes, rather than premature death itself, which constitutes the proper problem. Despite a reduction in infant mortality, he complains, 'the occupational and class differences remained stubbornly the same' (Field 1973, passim, and p.9). We should not be surprised to find, therefore, skimming his publisher's latest list, that – to coin a rather naughty phrase – Field has taken the lead in a rich hunt: 'Until now poverty studies have been exclusively concerned with studying the poor. This controversial book aims to change the whole debate about poverty in Britain by shifting the emphasis to a detailed examination of the rich.'

(c) In the previous two subsections we have not heard from any of those whose commitment to equality is grounded on a belief that it is either to be identified with, or is the fundamental dictate of, justice. Yet precisely this is what is most commonly assumed or asserted by those for whom, as Nisbet had it, 'equality is taking on a sacred aspect'.

Some years ago Lester Thurrow, Professor in the Massachusetts Institute of Technology and a chief economics adviser to Senator McGovern in his 1972 Presidential campaign, published what he saw as only an interim programme for the equalisation of wealth and income in the USA. In a later issue of the same journal another economist, Richard Posner, points out that this programme would be enormously disruptive, and complains, 'nowhere in his essay does Thurrow suggest a reason why a much greater equality of income and wealth would be a good thing for our society. He does not claim that society would be wealthier, or happier, or politically more stable as a result – and none of these conclusions is self-evident' (Posner, p.119).

This is both unfair to Thurrow, and inconsistent with Posner's own account of Thurrow's paper; which, as Posner truly says, 'argued that economic justice requires radical changes in the distribution of income and wealth in this country . . . ' (*Ibid.*, p.109). Thurrow does 'suggest a reason why a much greater equality of income and wealth would be a good thing': namely, that it would be more just. What he does not attempt is to demonstrate that justice prescribes such equality. Presumably to him, as to his compatriot in the Chair of Jurisprudence in the University of Oxford, this is one of those things which is plumb obvious: the rearrangement proposed is 'more equal and, therefore, more just' (Dworkin, p.232).

The final illustration in this subsection of illustrations comes from the last testament of a much more practical politician and a much more sophisticated political economist. Some months later he died in office as Britain's Foreign Secretary. In an address delivered in Central America, an address which is on that account aptly nicknamed his *Epistle to the Costa Ricans*, C.A.R. Crosland made it very clear that for him equality was a value, and that he here identified equality with justice: 'The standard of living of working class people, it is (rightly) said, can be improved much faster by economic growth than by any conceivable redistribution of existing income . . . . But this is not the point. For at least in the advanced industrialised countries, the argument for more equality is based not on any direct material gain to the poor, but on the claims of natural and social justice. And the question is: do these claims conflict with the need for incentives?' (Crosland 1975, p.6).[2]

(ii) The question of identifying equality with justice must wait till Chapter III. But there are two general clarifications to be made before we proceed to distinguish four kinds.

(a) The first point or pair of points is this. The contention that equality is for you a value, that you cherish it as good in itself, irrespective of consequences, is not refuted either by the fact that you are not committed to making people equal in every respect or by the fact that in those respects where you do advocate more, you nevertheless eschew complete equality. The first of these objections perhaps shows no more than that it is only equality in certain dimensions that you value. You might, for instance, value equality in income or wealth, without also valuing equality in natural gifts; and therefore going on to urge that the better endowed must be taxed in order to provide for the compensation of the less fortunate. So far the advocates of such genetic inheritance taxes have in fact been few: most mentions of ideas of this kind have occurred in satire. But note that those who pick and choose their egalitarianisms need to take a lot of care to ensure that the rationale for their own particular inclusions or exclusions includes and excludes all and only those dimensions of equality and inequality which they do themselves wish to include or to exclude. This, as we shall discover in the two following chapters, is much easier said than done.

The other objection, that you are not advocating complete equality, is likely to show only that for you equality is not an indefeasible good, nor the sole good. In that case the reason why you do not advocate it complete and perfect will presumably be that you expect always to have to make tradeoffs against some other value or values. Crosland, for example, in the first passage quoted at the end of the last paragraph but two, seems to have been thinking that whereas 'natural and social justice' obviously requires as near as may be perfect equality of incomes, some of this claim of justice will always have to be sacrificed to economic expediency.[3]

(b) The second point is that 'equality' is a relative word, carrying an essential reference either to another term or to other terms in a relationship. You value equality as such only when for you the fact that someone has or is going to have something is *a* reason, perhaps *the* reason why someone else should have the same, or some equivalent. To the extent that you are indeed an authentic egalitarian you are committed to saying that what various persons are to hold is to be determined primarily by reference to what other people have, rather than by reference to what those persons themselves both are or are not, and have or have not done.

One important consequence is that many demands and denunciations couched in egalitarian terms are in truth not egalitarian at all. In those cases the word 'equality' and its cognates are both redundant and misleading. Let us start with an artificial and undistracting example. Suppose that, in an English winter, someone proclaims that all equally ought to be free from head colds. Then his 'equally' is intrusive and superfluous. If he simply means that no one should have a cold, then the word 'equally' is redundant. It only has point and a meaning if the speaker in fact values equality as much as or more than freedom from colds; and so believes, not that as many colds as possible should be cured, but that, if colds cannot all be cured, then it is better that none should be rather than that we should in this respect tolerate inequality. This is a doctrine known to its enemies as that of the equality of misery. It is in Britain, unhappily, both quite widely accepted and deeply felt; although by no means so universal as some of our leading social engineers would wish.

Another immediate and usually neglected consequence is that those who do not accept equality as a value are not necessarily, and by that token, lovers of inequality as such. They very often reject both egalitarianism and inegalitarianism as direct objectives, because it seems to them perverse to lay such emphasis upon any mere relativities; to attend above all, that is, not to first-order goods and how to maximise them, but instead to second-order questions about who has more or less of one than another has. It is, therefore, although understandably tempting, wrong to label all those who do not recognise equality as a value, or who oppose policies for its enforcement, inegalitarians. You might as well argue that anyone who does not accept the classical Utilitarian thesis that the supreme good is the greatest happiness of the greatest number must, by that rejection, be committed to cherishing as the only alternative the maximum misery of the maximum number. Brian Walden was, however venially, dropping from his usual high level of accuracy and fairness when, shortly before withdrawing from the Parliamentary Labour Party to the lusher pastures of commercial television, he described some of our new Whigs as 'Jacobins of Inequality'.

A third corollary of the present main point, that equality is essentially relative, is that many policies and institutions occasionally classed as egalitarian, and which are indeed from time to time supported by authentic egalitarians, are by no means in themselves the real thing. For instance, there is nothing essentially egalitarian about a welfare state: it may well be concerned simply to ensure that no one falls below a certain level of welfare. It was, therefore, utterly wrong for one contributor to yet another volume on this sovereign notion to write: 'What the criterion of . . . economic equalisation requires is the establishment of the material conditions necessary for a generous measure of freedom of choice for all' (Schaar, p.242).

To provide such a minimum is by no means to enforce equality. It is not to insist that that minimum be at the same time the maximum; that the ceiling be screwed down onto the floor. Nor is it at all to determine what one should get by reference to what another has. Truly and distinctively egalitarian politics begins only when the provision has to be both uniform and monopolistic; equal, and the same for all. In itself and essentially it is not egalitarian to provide tax-supported schools open to everyone. But it is when you begin to crush all independent or various educational institutions, on the grounds that no one must do either better or worse than others, whether for themselves or for their children. With appropriate alterations the same applies to national health services, state retirement pensions, and the rest.

This being so, your genuine egalitarian has no business to respond to the challenge to justify his peculiar commitments by simply parading a concern that none shall fall below certain minimum levels of welfare; whether with or without some further, false suggestion that anyone rejecting his own Procrusteanism thereby reveals a Satanic callousness. Yet exactly and only this response was what I myself got in a recent private communication from a leading spokesperson: 'It *is* arguable [sic] that bad housing, squalor, pollution, ignorance, etc. are "good". But unless you are prepared to argue that case you must be an egalitarian . . . ' (Italics original).

Not long afterwards that same private correspondent, in his distinguished public capacity, contributed a centre-page feature article to *The Observer*, an old-established London Sunday newspaper. This article began by listing 'Britain's longer-term aims' as three: first, liberty 'the right to run one's life in one's own way without interference'; second, security 'a secure home to live in, medical care when we need it, and a reasonable income when we cannot work'; and, third, progress including 'the expectation that work will bring its reward'. These undoubtedly common aspirations were then without explanation, falsely, described as 'egalitarian aspirations'. The conclusion drawn – this too being in all probability equally false – was that the general public must share the author's professional devotion to 'equalising policies' and his corresponding revulsion from 'inequalities of earnings'. These inequalities are supposedly tolerable to him, if at all, only where 'required to keep the economy moving' (12 November 1978). To no one's surprise no answer was vouchsafed to the question: 'How then, if justice requires universal equalisation, is often unequal work "to bring its reward"?'

2 Facts of equality

The previous section did two things. First, it displayed illustrations
to show how widespread nowadays is the acceptance of equality
as a self-evident good – the clear mandate of (social) justice.
Second, it brought out two features of what it must be to pursue
equality as good in itself. The purpose of the present section is to
distinguish, on the one hand, actual or supposed facts about
human equalities and inequalities, from, on the other hand,
proposed norms or ideals. In the one case we have assertions that
such or such actually *is* so. In the other, claims that, however
things actually are, this is how they *ought* to be.

   (i) It is this categorical distinction which J.V. Stalin was
collapsing when in the thirties he told a group of US Senators:
'You believe that men are equal. I know that they are not.' No
doubt Stalin had at some time come across the American
Declaration of Independence, and the sentence in it which begins:
'We hold these truths to be self-evident, that all men are created
equal . . . .' No doubt he too, along with so many others nearer
home, failed to attend to its next two clauses. These spell out the
true content of the initial assertion: 'that they are endowed by their
Creator with certain inalienable rights, that among these are life,
liberty, and the pursuit of happiness.'

   A comment by Abraham Lincoln further illuminates the mind
of the Signers: 'The authors of that notable instrument . . . did not
intend to declare all men equal in all respects. They did not mean
to say that all men were equal in colour, size, intellect, moral
development, or social capacity. They defined with tolerable
distinctness in what respects they did consider all men created
equal – "certain inalienable rights, among which are life, liberty
and the pursuit of happiness".' Lincoln might well have added that
Thomas Jefferson himself – the man who, thanks to his 'peculiar
felicity of expression', was deputed to draft the Declaration –
certainly did not hold: either that all individual persons are in fact
born equal in temperament and talent; or even what the US
Department of Labour made so bold as to assert in 1965. They
then ruled, by their own sheer authority: 'Intelligence potential is
distributed among Negro infants in the same proportion and
pattern as among Icelanders or Chinese, or any other groups . . . .
There is absolutely no question of any genetic differential.'

   On the contrary: in *Notes on the State of Virginia*, his sole book, Jefferson sketches a programme for meritocratic secondary and tertiary education; a programme which assumes and asserts that talent is scarce, and unequally distributed. Every year in every neighbourhood primary school the 'best genius' is to be selected, to proceed to one of twenty 'grammar schools . . . to be erected in different parts of the country'. Next, from every grammar school cohort, after 'one or two years', the single 'best genius of the whole' is to be picked out. He – and it is here, I am afraid, the he which does not embrace she – is to be 'continued six years and the residue dismissed. By this means twenty of the best geniuses will be raked from the rubbish annually. . . . At the end of six years instruction, one half are to be discontinued (from among whom the grammar schools will probably be supplied with future masters); and the other half, who are to be chosen for the superiority of their parts and disposition, are to be sent . . . ' to study subjects of their own choice 'at William and Mary College' (Jefferson 1787, p.146).

The more sensitive subject of racial differences Jefferson discusses at greater length. He makes no scruple to concede that black slaves have been, and are being, monstrously wronged: this wrong, and the understandable black reaction to it, constitute his main reason for recommending, as the ultimate solution, not integration but emigration. Always too he emphasises the fundamental humanity, upon which the 'self-evident' claims to 'certain unalienable rights' are based. All the differences, he insists on another occasion, are minor 'by comparison with the faculty that gives man his unique dignity, that grounds his rights, that makes him self-governing' (Quoted by Wills, p.227). Nevertheless, after several bolder observations, some of which I should be reluctant to repeat, he advances 'as a suspicion only' the proposition 'that the blacks are . . . inferior to the whites in the endowments both of body and mind' (Jefferson 1787, p.143; and compare pp.137-42).

What all this shows is: in general, that there is indeed a difference of category between 'assertions that such and such actually *is* so' and 'claims that, however things actually are, this is how they *ought* to be'. In particular, it is clear that the Signers did not put their names to a declaration that all men in fact are, as it were, products of cloning. In the areas of our present interest, both the general and the particular point are often missed. For instance, the American authors of *The Hidden Injuries of Class* confront the evidence that IQ distribution is, in the statistical sense, 'normal'. It is all too much for them: 'If intelligence is distributed in this way, then what is the meaning of the phrase 'All men are created equal"?'

They therefore respond by abusing the innocent messengers of unwelcome news. Without either themselves presenting any argument to discredit such messages, or referring us to supposedly decisive demonstrations by others, they take their own blustering way to put down Arthur Jensen and H.J. Eysenck: 'The work of these men is so flimsy on scientific grounds that critics tend to lose sight of issues in the debate . . . .' But then, a paragraph or so later, it sounds as if there is some fear of what even the most impeccable and unflimsy investigations might or do reveal about the hereditary component in IQ and other psychological measures. Might not, do not, such investigations show – what after all our authors too know to be the truth – that people are born different in both talents and temperaments, that we are not completely creatures of our environments? For what has still to be investigated, and what remains legitimately controversial, is only and exactly how large and where the genetic components of performance are.

But our two present pained, almost pitiful egalitarians protest: 'Why should psychologists want to have such knowledge? . . . After all, the results can be perverted to destroy a fragile dream, only a few hundred years old, of equality among men.' Soon, however, they are showing somewhat less pathetically appealing collectivist teeth: 'The testing of ability acquires legitimacy in the eyes of its practitioners as the continuation of an old glorification of the individual apart from the social conditions into which he is born' (Sennett and Cobb, pp.59, 60, 61 and 62: and compare Chapter IV, below).

If your 'fragile dream' really is one of making people and their circumstances more uniform, then certainly you do have to recognise the facts of genetic diversity as a formidable practical obstacle. Yet in and by themselves genetic have no more power than any other facts to invalidate norms. The proposition that, as of now, people in this or that respect actually are unequal, does not entail, either that the situation calls for remedy, or that it does not. The facts themselves are neutral, and if anyone fears that they are going to be 'perverted' for evil purposes, then the right response is not to choke off the research, nor to suppress its findings, but to correct the perversions; an exercise for which, it has to be admitted, Sennett and Cobb do not on present showing appear to be qualified.

One once prevalent perversion was to argue: because, it is alleged, one racial or social group *is* on average superior in talent or temperament to another, therefore every member of the superior group *ought* to be in some way valued or preferred or rewarded over every member of the inferior. The argument is fallacious on two separate counts. In the first place – and this is the categorial contention which the entire present subsection has been labouring to establish – committed conclusions of value cannot be validly deduced from premises consisting in nothing but neutral and non-partisan statements of fact. In the second place, nothing about the individual quality of any particular member of a group follows from any general proposition stating the arithmetic mean value of that characteristic over the group as a whole. You yourself may be either a dwarf, or a giant, or neither; and yet still happen to belong to a group which is on average either very tall or very short or just plain middling. (Compare, for instance, Flew 1976a, Chapter 5).

(ii) Someone may ask how, if the prime contention of the previous subsection is correct, it could be proper for Jefferson to speak of 'the faculty that gives man his unique dignity, that grounds his rights, that makes him self-governing'. This straight question demands and deserves a direct and frank reply. The truth is that, if this grounding is an attempt to deduce claims to rights from neutral psychological facts alone, then it simply will not do; and the fine words of the Declaration are as ill-founded and as arbitrary as so much other talk of rights has been; and is. There is, however, no call for me to develop and defend a full substantive doctrine of rights here. But there are two reasons for saying something about the conceptual questions of what would be necessarily true of such entities. (For more about these conceptual questions see Flew 1980.) The first is the need to show that the objection put against Jefferson could be met. The second is to prepare the way for the account, in Section 3, of the first of three kinds of ideal of equality.

(a) One important preliminary is to state that the present discussion is of moral not of legal rights. There is no dispute about the existence, under various systems of positive law, of innumerable legal rights. The disputed issue is whether there are in addition moral rights; rights, that is, of a kind by reference to which the several prescriptions and proscriptions of any and every system of positive law may properly be, and indeed must be, examined and appraised. (Guided perhaps by 'a decent respect to the opinions of mankind' the Declaration itself misrepresents its most fundamental moral rights as, rather, legal rights under the Divine system of positive law.)

Anyone today who maintains the existence of such prior moral rights does so in conscious defiance of one of the most famous and most magisterial rulings of the Great Jeremy. For did he not, in the *Anarchical Fallacies*, deliver the judgment: 'Right is the child of law; from real laws come real rights, but from imaginary law, from "laws of nature", come imaginary rights. Natural rights is simple nonsense, natural and imprescriptable rights rhetorical nonsense, nonsense upon stilts' (Bentham, Vol.II, p.501)?

(b) The first conceptual point about moral rights is epitomised in an elegant coinage from Stanley Benn. Such a right, he wrote, 'is a normative resource' (Benn, p.64). A right is an entitlement; something of which the bearer ought not, at least against his will, to be deprived. But it is also of the essence that this entitlement be construed as in some fashion objective; independent of the capricious will of any particular individual or group.

This essential objectivity is, in a rather indirect and embarrassed way, acknowledged by the most prominent contemporary legal theorist to claim – perhaps instead we should say pretend – to be himself *Taking Rights Seriously*: 'A great many lawyers are wary of talking of moral rights, even though they find it easy to talk about what it is right or wrong for governments to do, because they suppose that rights, if they exist at all, are spooky sorts of things that men have in much the same sort of way that they have non-spooky things like tonsils' (Dworkin, p.139).

(c) A second conceptual point about moral rights is that they have to be grounded in – which is most emphatically not to say deduced from – some fact or facts about their bearers. Suppose that two bearers of rights are to be said to have different rights. Then this difference has to be accounted for by reference to some dissimilarity between what each of the two is, or has done, or has suffered. It is not, on the other hand, similarly essential, if two bearers of rights are to be said to have the same right, that this right should be similarly grounded in each case: 'Treat like cases alike' does not entail, 'Treat unlike cases unlike.'

Such truths are purely formal. They place no substantial

restriction upon the particular respects in which, if they are to have
the same or different rights, the bearers must either be or have been
either similar or different. That any rights must be grounded upon
some facts about their bearers is thus no more than a conceptual
truism, which should be quite undisputatious. What actual rights
there are, if any, and upon what particular facts these are
grounded, is a substantial matter of morals. As such it must no
doubt remain inherently contentious. It would be different if rights
were indeed deducible from their grounds, the grounds entailing
the availability of one normative resource and not another. For in
that case, the relevant facts about people being known, questions
of rights could be settled by the operations of a logical calculus.

This second conceptual truth about moral rights constitutes the
local special case of a much more general truth about all appraisal
and valuation. So in making both the particular and the general
point we are, as 'the implacable Professor' J.L. Austin used to say,
'looking not merely at words . . . but also at the realities we use
words to talk about. We are using a sharpened awareness of words
to sharpen our perception of the phenomena' (Austin 1970,
p.182).

The general truth is that in appraising and valuing – as opposed
to either just stating our likes and dislikes or simply reacting with
squeals of delight or howls of anger – we are engaged in an
essentially rational activity; albeit an activity which is, as far as
the present point is concerned, essentially rational only in the thin
sense that in it we necessarily commit ourselves to returning the
same verdicts in all other similar cases. Yet this is no trivial point,
to be dismissed as 'merely philosophical'. For if you want to
maintain that someone is endowed with some right, then you have
to be ready to specify what it is about that person which serves as
the ground for that right. That conceptual requirement carries a
more exciting consequence. By specifying the ground for the right
you commit yourself, by the very logic of the term, to allow that
anyone else satisfying the same specification must be by that token
endowed with the same right.

It was through this crisp, decisive logic that the Girondin
Marquis de Condorcet during the great French Revolution – like
Abigail Adams in the American – demonstrated the rights of
women. In an address *On the Admission of Women* he argued
that, since the agreed rights of man are grounded in our common
humanity, without reference to sex, therefore: 'Women, having

these same qualities, must necessarily possess equal rights';
adding, with his eyes on the opposition, that 'he who votes against
the rights of another . . . has thereby abjured his own.'

(d) Condorcet's second point is now also our third. But before
developing this we have to notice, and from the present context
dismiss, much of what is today common usage. No one, I think, in
Jefferson's generation would have been prepared to attribute
rights to anything not either actually or potentially capable of both
demanding its own and reciprocally respecting those of others. But
recently some people, admirably concerned to protect the surviving
redwoods of California, have been floating the notion of trees'
rights. Then in 1978, UNESCO, in what time it felt it could spare
from an obscurantist and destructive campaign to bring all news
media under the control of governments, adopted a Universal
Declaration of the Rights of Animals. This starts with a bold,
round declaration: 'all animals are born with an equal claim on life
and the same rights to existence.' After skirting, very understandably, the awkward issues of killing animals for luxury eating, it
concludes: 'any act involving mass killing of wild animals is
genocide.'[4]

For people too it is common practice nowadays to proclaim
moral rights to just about anything which the proclaimers believe,
or would like it thought that they believe, that it would be good for
everyone to have. Thus in 1948 the UN General Assembly
adopted a Universal Declaration of Human Rights. This is much
longer, and worse written, than the famous manifestos of the late
1700s. In the main it is longer through containing too many
wordily phrased rights to health, education, social security, and
the like. Among other things, it tells us: that 'Everyone, as a
member of society, has a right to social security . . . ' (Article 22);
that 'Everyone has the right to . . . periodic holidays with pay'
(Article 24); that 'Everyone has the right to a standard of living
adequate for the health and well-being of himself and of his family
. . . and the right to security in the event of unemployment,
sickness, disability, widowhood, old age or other lack of livelihood
in circumstances beyond his control' (Article 25); that 'Everyone
has the right to education. Education shall be free, at least in the
elementary and fundamental stages' (Article 26); and so on, and
on and on.

The emphasis in the classical declarations was on being left
alone, presumably to do the best you can for yourself and your

family. We could say that they demanded option as opposed to welfare rights. The contemporary concentration is upon what is to be provided, presumably by impersonal and anonymous public authorities. In terms of the previous contrast, it is now a matter of welfare rather than option rights. With option rights, rights and their corresponding duties can be perfectly reciprocal. My right to choose generates both your duty to respect that right and my duty to respect your parallel right. Just as the rights attach to all, so the corresponding duties fall unambiguously and universally on everyone alike. Nor would there appear to be any intractable problem of practicality. Option rights call only for non-interference, which is always possible. With welfare rights, however, there seems to be no room for similar reciprocities. Also, although these welfare rights too are stated to be universal – pertaining to all persons at all times and everywhere – they include demands which scarcely could be met in anything but a fairly prosperous modern industrial state (Cranston, pp.50-2).

So, whatever the independent merits of the several demands enshrined in such UN declarations, the fact remains that, if the word 'right' is to retain any distinctive point and purpose, then its employment has got to be restricted. We must not insist that, where a duty is owed, there must always be a correlative right to the performance of that duty. To maintain, for instance, that cruelty to the brutes is wrong there is no need to try to make out that they have rights to kindness. The crux, as Bentham urged in the *Principles of Morals and Legislation,* is not ' "Can they *reason?*" nor "Can they *talk?*" but ' "Can they *suffer?*" ' (XVII 4*n*: italics original).

Nor must we allow that there are universal rights to just anything, or to everything really important; however much we might like to see such generous universal provision – especially, one may be tempted to add, when it is to be made by persons unknown. Instead there has to be some rationale determining and limiting the possible content of anything which is to achieve the status of a universal moral right, a rationale somehow providing for both the objectivity and the groundedness essential to the concept. Such a rationale will surely have to centre on the notion of reciprocity, as Condorcet realised. We should, therefore, insist on this as a third essential for a distinctive and viable concept of basic moral rights. Certainly we know that reciprocity was very much in the minds of the American Founding Fathers also.

Jefferson, for instance, defends American blacks against the common charge of depraved lack of respect for the rights or property: 'That man in whose favour no laws of property exist, probably feels himself less bound to respect those made in favour of others. When arguing for ourselves, we lay it down as fundamental, that laws, to be just, must give a reciprocation of right: that, without this, they are mere arbitrary rules of conduct, founded in force, and not in conscience' (Jefferson 1787, p.142; and compare his *Collected Papers*, Vol.XIV, p.492). Again, in a quite separate tradition, a disciple once asked Confucius whether his rule of conduct might be epitomised in a single word: 'The Master replied, "Is not 'reciprocity' the word?" ' (*Analects*, XV, Section 23).

3 Ideals of equality: choice

The main thrust of Section 2 was to bring out the categorial difference between any facts (or supposed facts) about human equality, and ideals or norms. The first of the three different sorts of ideal of equality is certainly the oldest, as well as the hardest to characterise satisfactorily. Often it is said to be a secularisation of something common to all the great traditions of Mosaic theism (Williams, p.235). In the standard *Encyclopaedia of Philosophy*, edited by Paul Edwards, the article 'Equality' quotes *Galatians*: 'For ye are all the children of God by faith in Christ Jesus. For as many of you as have been baptised into Christ have put on Christ. There is neither Jew nor Greek, there is neither bond nor free, there is neither male nor female: for ye are all one in Christ Jesus' (III, 26-8).

It may well be that that has been the more influential passage. Yet it is not to be forgotten that *Romans*, another equally authoritative Pauline epistle, contains a most shattering suggestion of the unequal arbitrariness of sheer Omnipotence: 'Therefore hath he mercy on whom he will have mercy, and whom he will he hardeneth. . . . Hath not the potter power over the clay, of the same lump to make one vessel unto honour, and another unto dishonour? What if God, willing to show his wrath, and to make his power known, endured with much long suffering the vessels of wrath fitted for destruction: And that he might make known the riches of his glory on the vessels of mercy, which he had afore prepared unto glory, even us, whom he hath called, not of the Jews only, but also of the Gentiles?' (IX, 18 and 21-4).

(i) In a deservedly famous tract on *Equality*, first published in 1931, the Christian and socialist historian R.H. Tawney apologises for the vulgarity of citing 'The sage who defined his Utopia as a society in which any man can say to any other, "Go to Hell", but no man wants to say it, and no man need go when it is said . . . ' (p.177). Certainly it was an equality of our first sort which was, very rightly, being demanded and conceded when in 1964 the US Supreme Court struck down a sentence for contempt against Mary Hamilton, a black. She had refused to answer the Public Prosecutor of Alabama when he called her Mary and not, as he would have done had she been white, Miss Hamilton (Pole, pp.340-1).

But these are particular applications. To approach the general principle, consider in Immanuel Kant 'The Formula of the End in Itself'. After taking 'rational nature', or – as we would be more likely to say – personality, as 'something *whose existence* has *in itself* an absolute value' Kant's Categorical Imperative becomes: *'Act in such a way that you always treat humanity, whether in your own person or in the person of any other, never simply as a means, but always at the same time as an end'* (Kant, pp.90 and 91: italics and capitalisation original).

These formulations will not do. But they surely have a large part of the heart of the matter in them. One sufficient reason why they will not do was urged by Kant's admiring critic Schopenhauer. It is, strictly, incoherent to speak of 'ends in themselves'. There can no more be 'ends in themselves' unrelated to the persons whose ends they are, than there can be sisters in themselves, unrelated to any siblings of whom they are the sisters (Schopenhauer, p.95). But it remains that Kant was seized of the crucial importance of the facts: that we are all able to, and cannot but, form ends for ourselves; and that in giving to ourselves or to others our reasons for acting thus but not thus we are, however irrational those reasons, rational beings. (Never forget that only a being which is, in this primary and fundamental sense, rational as opposed to non-rational, can be, in the secondary and everyday sense, commendably rational – or, as the case may be, scandalously irrational. Even the most unreasonable of human beings are, that is to say, rational animals; because, though some of us actually are most irrational, we all are capable of rationality.)

From these necessary facts of our human nature nothing can be immediately deduced about how such creatures ought to treat one another. However – to borrow a characteristic concept from Kant

– 'as legislating members of the Kingdom of Ends' we ourselves can lay it down that all such rational agents are to be respected in their pursuit of their own chosen ends; or, in favourite words of a much more recent generation, their doings of their own things. Indeed, we cannot avoid doing so if we say or assume that we, as rational agents, possess these rights ourselves (Gewirth 1972, p.20). This is where the essential reciprocity of rights comes in. For, if people are implicitly or explicitly to presuppose that they themselves, when they are doing no harm to others, are not merely able but entitled to act without interference, then, it follows necessarily from this their own presupposition, that all other similar agents must possess these same normative resources. If I claim I have a right, on some ground, then I necessarily concede, by that same claim, a corresponding right to everyone else who satisfies that same condition.

The notion of equality enters here because no one can consistently claim such universal human rights for themselves except in so far as they at the same time concede to others the same rights, the same liberties. The content of such rights cannot but be in consequence the same for all. So, to Marxist and other enemies of liberty who here ask, 'Liberty, for whom?', the only defensible answer is 'Equal liberty for all'. The universal human rights and liberties of one person must end when, and only when, these would conflict with another person's corresponding rights and liberties. The 1945 Turkish constitution provides an agreeably unhackneyed illustration: 'Every Turk is born free and lives free. He has liberty to do anything which does not harm other persons. The natural right of the individual to liberty is limited only by the liberties enjoyed by his fellow citizens.' The practice presents every kind of problem. The principle is luminous.

Some key ideas in the previous two paragraphs come from Kant. But the American Declaration of Independence preceded the *Groundwork of the Metaphysics of Morals*. So let us take note that Jefferson improved upon both Locke and the more congenial Hutcheson (Wills, passim). Passages already quoted indicate that Jefferson both grasped that reciprocity must be of the essence of any arguable claims to universal human rights, and picked out 'the faculty that gives man his unique dignity . . . that makes him self-governing' as the characteristic of man 'that grounds his rights'. Maybe this still leaves us a long way from a clear and compelling doctrine. But it is a great deal more persuasive and forthcoming than, for instance, Locke's blunt offering in Section 6 of the *Second Treatise of Civil Government*. He just tells us, what sound Whigs are delighted to hear: that the Law of Nature 'which obliges everyone . . . teaches all Mankind, who will but consult it, that being all equal and independent, no one ought to harm another in his Life, Health, Liberty, or Possessions.'

(ii) This ideal of an equality of respect for all rational agents in their pursuit of their own chosen ends carries implications for government. Although it may not categorically require complete one-person-one-vote democracy in all areas, it certainly does demand some minimum of consent. This demand is not based on any false and silly doctrine that majorities are always, or usually, right. Collections of rational agents can be in their decisions as prejudiced, ill-informed, perverse and – in a word – irrational as their individual members! The point is that the decisions should be their own decisions. This just is what it is to respect people as choosers and pursuers of their own ends. It was put, simply yet magnificently, by the russet-coated Captain Rainborough during the Putney Debates of the New Model Army: 'Really I think that the poorest he that is in England hath a life to live as the greatest he; and therefore truly, Sir, I think it is clear, that every man that is to live under a government ought first by his own consent to put himself under that government; and I do believe that the poorest man in England is not at all bound to that government that he hath not had a voice to put himself under' (Firth, Vol.I, p.301).

Besides some minimum of consent to government, the same ideal clearly calls for limitations on what government does. Since the object is equal liberty for all, and the maximum for everyone, it cannot accept the doctrine of total popular sovereignty; that anything and everything goes, provided only that it is supported by a majority. It was a main part of the political wisdom of the makers of the US constitution, dedicated as they were to this ideal of liberty, to be almost obsessively aware of the danger that majorities in sovereign assemblies will exploit and oppress minorities, and will restrict liberties (Vieira, passim). That is why they created, as American conservatives love to say, not a democracy but a republic. That is the reason for most of the entrenchments, above all the entrenchment of the amendments known collectively as the Bill of Rights. It is also the reason why many in Britain who hold to the same ideal have recently begun to worry the ideas of writing the previously unwritten constitution, and/or in some other way entrenching a similar Bill of Rights. They speak, with feeling and reason, of the present sovereignty of the House of Commons as elective despotism; adding perhaps that – thanks to an electoral system giving most unequal value to votes for third party candidates – no government since World War II has come into office with even the slimmest majority of the votes cast in the previous general election.[5]

Although the unlimited sovereignty of majorities, like any other unlimited sovereignty, does threaten the maximum equal liberty of the present ideal, there are both necessary and contingent connections between democratic institutions and some particular liberties. The logically necessary connections are with those liberties without which it cannot be truly said that voting decisions were made and implemented freely. These must include effective guarantees against intimidation for both rival candidates and electors. Certainly too it has to be possible to get and to spread relevant information, to discuss issues with other people, and to organise opposition. It cannot be the case, for instance, as it is now in all the countries of the Socialist Bloc, that no private person is permitted to own and to operate so much as a duplicating machine.

But, besides whatever civil liberties are in this way logically necessary to the working of democratic institutions, there are also strong reasons to believe that some other liberties, and in particular economic liberties, are required as a matter of contingent fact. Can it really be nothing but a quirk of history that, among all the many countries that are as near as makes no matter fully socialist, there is not one where opposition parties are allowed to organise, and to contest elections? In Poland, I have myself heard all too experienced students of political geography ask: 'Where is there a socialist democracy?' They gave themselves the wry answer, 'On the moon.'

Certainly the Institute of Marxism-Leninism in Moscow is happy to recognise that, in a favourite Soviet phrase, 'it is no accident'. In 1971, with their eyes most immediately upon Chile and France, they sketched a programme for achieving, through 'United Front' or 'Broad Left' tactics, irreversible Communist domination: 'Having once acquired political power, the working class implements the liquidation of the private ownership of the means of production ... As a result, under socialism, there remains no ground for the existence of any opposition parties counter-balancing the Communist Party.'[6] In some countries wise readers will take note that the future one-party monopolists do not have to be called, nor to have been from the beginning organised as, a Communist Party.

The author of that well-nicknamed *Epistle to the Costa Ricans* made a similar point with equal emphasis: 'A mixed economy is essential to social democracy ... complete state collectivism is without question incompatible with liberty and democracy' (Crosland 1975, p.2). Unfortunately he gave no indication either there or elsewhere of the point, if any, at which he himself would have to leave a party committed by its constitution to 'the public ownership of all the means of production, distribution, and exchange', and in practice insisting relentlessly on ever more and never less state ownership and control of everything – except, of course, its own owners the labour unions. So it is to be presumed that Crosland was, for whatever reasons, at one with

> ... the virtuous young lady of Kent
> Who said that she knew what it meant
>   When men took her to dine
>   Gave her cocktails and wine;
> She knew what it meant – but she went.

4 Ideals of equality: opportunity

Whether or not the second sort of ideal can in any way be derived from the first, it is certainly both different and more limited in scope.

At the beginning of the chapter the suggestion was made that what has usually been meant by 'equality of opportunity' would be better described as open competition for scarce opportunities. The equality here lies in the sameness of the treatment of all the competitors in an open competition, and the only opportunity which is equal is precisely the opportunity to compete on these terms. Certainly in the French Revolution of 1789, when a cry was raised 'La carrière ouverte aux talents!', the drive was to open public appointments to competition from members of formerly excluded groups. Thus in that year, in the *Declaration of the Rights of Man and of the Citizen*, we read: 'The law is an expression of the will of the community ... it should be the same to all ... and all being equal in its sight, are equally eligible to all honours, places and employments, *according to their different abilities, without any other distinction than that created by their virtue and talents*' (Article VI: italics supplied – and compare Lloyd-Thomas 1977).

Such policies may of course be implemented, and often have been, not so much to benefit the newly enfranchised potential competitors, as to make the institutions to which they may now be recruited more efficient. For it seems obvious that completely open competition, with incentives to win, must, all other things being equal, be the most efficient means of ensuring that the best qualified and most competent people get the jobs needing such training and competence. Anyone who has ever visited Les Invalides in Paris will think here of those romantic portraits of meteoric military high achievers – 'Butcher's son, General of the Army at 24, Marshal of France 1802'; and so on. It is hard not to believe that this readiness to promote the talent wherever it was found must have been at least one of the reasons why for years the revolutionary armies smashed the best that the old dynasts could send against them.

For many others, perhaps most, efficiency has not been the only or the main consideration. They have seen equality of opportunity, in some understanding, as a good in itself, either simply as equality or else perhaps as being a particular aspect of universal justice.

(i) The first step towards clarity in this context is to spell out the reasons why it is so confusing to describe open competition for scarce opportunities as equality of opportunity. Someone has an opportunity to do something (or to have something) if, and only if, they can do (or have) that something, if they choose. I have an opportunity to visit Japan, if some organisation undertakes to pay my travel expenses, in return for my producing a paper or giving some lectures. The something in question also has to be thought of by the speaker or writer as being – like a trip to Japan – good. Only in sarcasm, or while contemplating the brute beastliness of senile decay or protracted terminal illness, could you say that someone had missed their earlier opportunities to get themselves killed in action.

It follows that to offer two people equal opportunities must be, in a literal interpretation, to offer them either the same or arguably equivalent opportunities. A father would be doing this to his two daughters if he invited both of them to join him on some jaunt; or if, knowing their different tastes, he offered Harriet a week on a climbing course and Joanna a week at a riding school.

But in an open competition for scarce opportunities the only equality, as was said above, lies in the sameness of the treatment of all competitors and potential competitors. The only opportunities are the opportunities to compete; and, of course, whatever other opportunities are won in the competition by the successful but not the unsuccessful competitors. In a newspaper competition, for instance, one of the prizes may be the opportunity to spend an all-expenses-paid fortnight in Benidorm; an opportunity which some fastidious winners might be reluctant to take. The necessarily equal opportunities here are precisely and only the opportunities to compete.

Ideals of equality of opportunity, literally understood, would by contrast come close to ideals of equality of outcome. The difference, presumably, would have to be that an egalitarian in such a sense is more of a liberal – in the British as opposed to the American current usage of that term.[7] He is distinguished by wanting only that people be provided with equal or equivalent opportunities, leaving it up to the individual whether or not the opportunities are in fact taken; whereas the egalitarian of outcome, as his label indicates, strives to equalise, in whatever dimensions are under discussion, eventual conditions.

It follows from the basics elucidated in the previous paragraph that to show that certain individuals do not compete, or that if they do they do not in the event win prizes, is not to show that they have not been offered what is ordinarily meant by 'equality of opportunity'. With appropriate alterations, and more to the present point, the same applies to groups. To show, as in a sociologically minded age continually is being shown, that members of some group either do not compete, or that if they do compete they do not succeed in the same proportions to the total population as members of some other group, is not to show that the members of the first group must have enjoyed less favourable opportunities to compete than members of the second group. For to say that Smith and Jones have equal competitive opportunities is not at all to say that the chances of each taking his respective opportunity are also equal. Nor is saying that Smith and Jones are in fact engaged in a fair and open competition at all the same thing as saying that the probabilities of their success in that competition are equal. Indeed, as we shall be arguing in Chapter IV, they necessarily must not be if it truly is a competition and not some sort of lottery.

Once such elementary points have been clearly made they are bound to appear so obvious as not to have been worth making. Yet it is in the main because they have in fact been overlooked or confounded that so many people today – including, indeed most particularly including, professing social scientists – collapse the distinction between equality of opportunity and equality of outcome. They mis-take it that evidence of unequal outcomes, or of big differences between the probabilities of success among several competitors and non-competitors, is sufficient to show that these never had equal opportunities to compete. Very possibly, of course, they in fact did not. But as a conclusion this has to be established, if at all, in some other way.

It is also fairly plain, though scarcely possible to prove, that many are at some level of consciousness or unconsciousness encouraged to muddle the issues by a suspicion that their own Procrustean ideals of an enforced equality of outcome are rather less widely shared than two others mentioned earlier, each of which is of course compatible with the other: first, that of open competition for scarce opportunities; and, second, that of a state-supported welfare floor that is not at the same time the ceiling.

But consider again the case discussed at the end of Section 1. It certainly does look as if this was the motive working there to produce the preposterous misrepresentations of a personal Procrusteanism as being: both the same thing as a concern to relieve poverty; and as something that follows from various widespread aspirations with which it is in fact incompatible. That such Procrustean ideals are, at least in the USA, widely unpopular is something heavily emphasised by Christopher Jencks: 'Income inequality is not yet perceived as a major social problem, much less as a cause of other social ills'; and so, he says, 'We need to establish the idea that the federal government is responsible not only for the total amount of national income, but for its distribution' (Jencks, pp.232 and 264).

It becomes still more plain that this would be a motive for confusing inequalities of outcome with inequalities of opportunity – in the usual idiomatic, not the literal, interpretation of that phrase – if we reflect that for many people who do value such equality of opportunity a large part of the attraction lies in its being opportunity to better the condition of themselves and their families. For such people – human, all too human! – any intrinsic rewards to be found in developing and using talents are as nothing compared with the further and extrinsic rewards which it is hoped by these means to win. Suppose that to them you first offer equality of opportunity; and then explain that, as a devout egalitarian of the third kind, you also propose to ensure that, whatever opportunities they contrive to take, they will be allowed no satisfaction or reward beyond what is freely available to all. You will not be very warmly or widely thanked for your first offer, I think, once your second intention is fully understood. For, as Confucius really did say, without cynical exaggeration and with traditional Chinese realism: 'It is not easy to find a man who has studied for three years without aiming at pay' (*Analects*, VIII, Section 2).

(a) Whatever the truth about concealed motivations, there can be no question but that this confusion is a contemporary common-place, spread by spokespersons of the highest academic distinction. Take as a first example an article under the characteristic and revealing title 'Making Adults more Equal: The Scope and Limitations of Public Educational Policy'. The authoress, Jean Floud, is now Principal of Newnham College, Cambridge. She begins by defining the key expression 'life-chances' in a perfectly straightforward way, 'in terms of people's economic and social opportunities'. She nevertheless proceeds straight off to identify differences in educational opportunity with differences in achieved education, life-chances with actual lives. What she is talking about is correlations, reported by Jencks, between achieved education and achieved income. Yet she insists on calling differences in the former, differences in educational opportunity, while differences in the latter are correspondingly equated with differences in life-chances: ' . . . differences of educational opportunity do not explain much of the variation in individual incomes. Measures of the independent influence of educational opportunity on people's life-chance give different results' (Floud, pp.37 and 41).

A further source of confusion, perhaps even more crucial here, is the so far unnoticed ambiguity which some people have introduced into expressions like 'educational opportunities' or 'career opportunities'. They employ these to refer both to the opportunities arising from already having had an education or having a career, and to the opportunities of getting the one or starting the other. Let us label the first of these two sorts the 'consequence' and the second the 'access' sense. Educational opportunities in this consequence sense are opportunities which someone has as a result of already having had some education – opportunities to pursue a well-paid and otherwise above average agreeable career, and so on. Educational opportunities in the access sense are opportunities which someone has for acquiring education – the chance of attending a grammar school or a private school, of entering a university, or admission to graduate work, or what have you.

However, notwithstanding that it is manifest that Jean Floud and others do sometimes employ the expression 'educational opportunities' in the consequence sense, this usage deserves to be protested as both factitious and misleading. Would anyone – would they? – describe possible alternative purchases from the money in their pockets as their financial opportunities?

Those refusing to make these several distinctions, and to observe them without fail, thereby become equipped to misrepresent what may in truth be nothing but discoveries about relatively poor educational or post-educational performance, as if these were really demonstrations of inequality of educational opportunity. Such late low achievers may well have had, and often in fact have had, more or less equal opportunities to compete for a higher form of education; and may even have been actually exposed to that higher form itself.

(b) The second suitable text-book example is provided by Raymond Boudon, himself the author of Penguin Education's guide to *The Logic of Sociological Explanation.* His own later study of *Education, Opportunity and Social Inequality* is introduced by Seymour Martin Lipset as the work of 'France's leading sociological theoretician and methodologist'; who, fittingly, 'holds the chair at Paris once occupied by Durkheim' (pp.vi and vii).

On the first page of his Preface Boudon defines 'inequality of educational *opportunity* (IEO)' as 'differences in the level of educational *attainment* according to social background'. He draws the immediate consequence that 'a society is characterised by a certain amount of IEO if, for instance, the probability of going to college is smaller for a worker's son than for a lawyer's son' (p.xi: italics supplied). Next 'Inequality of social opportunity (ISO)' is defined similarly. The parallel immediate consequence is that 'a society is characterised by a certain amount of ISO if the probability of reaching a high social status is smaller for the former child than for the latter' (p.xi).

Readers, after first treating themselves to the salutary exercise of applying to Boudon everything said so far in the present subsection, may then reflect upon the reception of Boudon's study in *New Society,* the weekly journal seen by everyone in Britain engaged in either social work or social science. The reviewer, Alan Little, who faithfully quoted both definitions, saw no occasion for remark in either. He ended almost on his knees before such 'originality in approach, a mixture of creative imagination and intellectual vigour, a continual juxtaposition of logic and fact, statistical sophistication, theoretical acumen and wide reading' (23 May 1974). It was still no sociologist, but the psychologist H.J. Eysenck, who two weeks later intervened in the correspondence columns to remark that 'Boudon constructs a whole model of educational and social opportunity . . . very much as if every child . . . were an identical twin to every other child' (6 June 1974: compare Flew 1976a, Chapter 4).

(c) The third illustration, or set of illustrations, came from the discussion of a monumental report on *Equality of Educational Opportunity* prepared for the Office of Education of the US government by James Coleman, a Professor of Sociology in Johns Hopkins University. The Editors of the *Harvard Educational Review* devoted a whole issue to this report, an issue which was later revised and extended for publication as a hardcover book. Their Introduction begins: 'The complacent belief that our public schools provide their students with "equal educational opportunity" has been shattered in the last fifteen years by a combination of social action and social science research . . . black militants have consistently argued that the expression "equal *educational opportunity*" is meaningless for a large number of American schoolchildren. Recent social science research supports this contention, revealing huge gaps in *educational achievement* between racial groups and social classes' (p.1: italics supplied).

From this we may infer that it is not only 'a large number of American schoolchildren', but also some of the teachers of their teachers, who have failed to understand the meaning of a key expression! In his research Coleman himself had been unable to find what he was expecting to find; namely, big differences in the buildings of and the resource input into schools predominantly attended by members of different social and racial groups. What differences there were in these respects bore little or no discernible relationship to the levels of achievement in the several groups distinguished. Most upsetting of all to prejudices which Coleman and his collaborators shared with the whole contemporary enlightenment, the considerable differences in levels of achievement as between these groups did correlate significantly with internal differences both in attitudes to education and in the incidence of delinquency.

Despite these findings – or, more likely, because of them – Coleman insists upon offering and employing definitions which collapse the crucial distinction between opportunity and outcome. Looking back at that work in the Harvard volume, and considering 'where the concept of equality of educational opportunity presently stands', he concludes,falsely: 'The difference in *achievement* at grade 12 between the average Negro and the average white' – and, presumably, between the average members of any other two groups which the sociologist might pick out for comparison – 'is, in effect, the degree of inequality of *opportunity*, and the reduction of that inequality is a responsibility of the school' (p.24: italics supplied).

(ii) The first subsection of this Section 4 has been dealing with the nature of equality of opportunity. It is time to say something about the scope of ideals of this sort, and in particular about limitations imposed upon them by the facts that human beings are organisms with life-cycles, and that we do not have one simul- taneous and uniform beginning. We are not all products of one grand collective cloning. Instead almost everyone is the offspring of a different pair of parents, coming together at a different time. Typically offspring are raised by those same parents as members of a family; for part of that period of upbringing most of us pass parts of most days in educational institutions; at some stage we probably go out to earn our own livings; probably too we become parents ourselves, and grow old; certainly, in the end, we die.

Whether what is wanted is the career open to the talents or literally equal opportunities, the desired provision usually and in practice has to be for people at some particular stage of the life- cycle. Also, and this is a point which should certainly not be overlooked in the theoretical discussion of ideals, in practice the provision can only be for members of one or a few generations.

For the competitions for a grammar school place, or for admission to one of 'les grands écoles', you used to be too old at eleven plus, or are a few years later. If it is a matter of what are intended to be literally equal educational opportunities provided through attendance at a comprehensive school in a completely universal and compulsory system, then these would be oppor- tunities which everyone had – and in some fashion had to take – between two legally prescribed ages. The response of the individual to these various measures will be determined by what, at whatever time they begin to impinge, that individual is; while what in fact any individual is at that or any other time is itself the outcome of his or her whole past. At the other end, what that individual will later become must in its turn be largely determined by the results of that career-open-to-the-talents competition or by the response to what are intended to be literally equal opportunities.

It does not need to be proved that the winners of such competitions, and the most successful respondents to such opportunities, are most likely to come from the offspring of parents who themselves have, by whatever are here the relevant standards, good genes; and also – by no means the same thing – from the children raised in homes which are good at encouraging and supporting whatever it does in fact take to win. So we have no business to be surprised when we find, as indeed we do, that the children of the winners have an above-average chance of becoming winners in their turn. Unless – following an example set for short periods in some newly Leninist countries – we are prepared altogether to abandon the ideal of open competition for scarce opportunities, and either to exclude the children of professional people from the professions or at least to make these peculiarly unattractive to them, then we must expect, however open the competition for places, to see a substantial difference between the proportions of such children entering those professions and the proportions entering from the population as a whole.[8]

Although all these considerations ought to be quite obvious, the statistics of such differences are continually paraded both as if the situation they reveal were self-evidently scandalous, and as if they constituted by themselves sufficient proof of the subsistence of very substantial inequalities of opportunity. We are told, with rasping indignation, for instance, that in 1973 in Britain 59 per cent of the children in grammar schools came from 'white collar' homes, although children from such homes constituted only 38 per cent of the relevant population cohorts; or that in 1968-9 only 28 per cent of university students were sons or daughters of manual workers, whereas 60 per cent of the working population in that year were manually employed.

Confronting us with figures of this kind, and without further reason given, Frank Field's *Unequal Britain* takes it that such findings 'rightly brought into doubt the 11-plus examination and the tripartite education system . . . which results from it' (p.17).

Yet already in a book published first in 1957, and reporting work on years up to 1953 – twenty years before *Unequal Britain* – a research team which certainly could not be accused of wanting to reach this conclusion had reported: 'Virtually the full quota of boys with the requisite minimum IQ from every class was admitted to grammar schools, and the distribution of opportunity stands today in closer relationship to that of ability (as measured by intelligence tests) than ever before' (Floud, Halsey and Martin, p.143).

Just as, even in the most ideally fair and open competition for scarce opportunities, the winners must be those who at the time of the competition do actually have whatever it takes to win, and just as their having this will in fact with every individual be an outcome of that individual's whole past to date; so, even given the most perfectly equal educational opportunities, what any individual makes of those opportunities will depend on what that individual is during the period of education; while that in turn will be an outcome of both that individual's whole past, and his or her ongoing life outside as well as inside the school.

There is one main reason why people, when confronted with tolerably fair and open competition for scarce educational resources or with a system in which educational opportunities are passably equal, are so easily inclined to dismiss them as being in reality nothing of the kind. It is that they refuse to recognise as the actual competitors or the actual pupils the often sadly defective flesh-and-blood creatures who are competing or not competing, getting educated or failing to get educated. Instead they prefer to contemplate those might-have-beens who would now be competing, or getting educated, if only the babies who grew into the present competitors or pupils had been raised in different families and in a different social environment. On occasion they are not thinking even of those babies as they were but of dream babies with different parentages and different genetic constitutions. (See Chapter IV, below.)

What excites such fantasies is evidence of the enormous force of the family, and of its immediate social enviroment. Coleman, in a Review Essay on John Rawls's *A Theory of Justice*, reflecting once again on the revelations of his own monumental report, sums it up: ' . . . those resources under the control of the school were considerably less important than those which were intrinsic to the child's family background. That is, the resources brought to education from the home were considerably more important for achievement than those provided by the schools ... Less important, but still more important than most school resources, were those inputs to a student's educational opportunity provided by the level of background of other students in his classroom.' (Coleman, 1974, p.750).

Let no one minimise any of this. Bookish and scrupulous children forced to share schools with most unbookish and even delinquent peers cannot but become disadvantaged thereby; and, all other things being equal, their school opportunities are bound to be unequal and inferior to those vouchsafed to otherwise similar children attending schools where the rest of the clientele is less unsatisfactory. A concern for such minority children was indeed one of the recurrent themes in the British educational *Black Papers*, the more especially since so many of their abused and dissident authors had their own memories of how much escape from a neighbourhood into a selective school had meant to them (Cox and Dyson 1969, 1970 and 1971, passim).

But what such considerations cannot do is warrant Coleman's own conclusion: ' ... the conventional definition of "equal opportunity" ... accepts the level of motivation it finds in the child and appears to imply that equal opportunity lies merely in provision of equal facilities, with no special responsibility for the child's use of them. But to do that implies, as these results show, that although formal equality of opportunity will exist by definition, little substantive or effective equality of opportunity will exist in fact' (pp.750 and 751: some inverted commas supplied).

There can be no room for doubt but that, if everyone is to have either literally equal educational opportunities or fair and open competition for any opportunities which are scarce, from the moment of birth or even earlier, then the upbringing of children in families has got to be abolished in favour of a universal system of comprehensive crèches – on the lines proposed by Plato in *The Republic* for the children of his élite caste of Guardians. This inevitable opposition between free, various families and the uniform and equalising collective offers as clear an illustration as we could ask of how the drive for ever more equality necessarily calls for an ever more powerful and ever more intrusive state: 'Effective reduction in inequality of opportunity', as Coleman puts it, 'can come about only by increasing the ratio of public to private resource inputs into education, since the public inputs are equalising and the private ones are unequalising' (p.750).

He himself believes that there has to be some limit to the extent of public involvement, and a trade-off between this ideal and the private values of the family. He would certainly not assent to the bold and brutal British statement: 'It is the business of education in our social democracy to eliminate the influence of parents on the life-chances of the young . . . ' (Musgrave, p.135). John Rawls, when the conflict does at last intrude upon his attention, merely mumbles – in the style of a Press Secretary diverting an awkward one: 'Is the family to be abolished then? Taken by itself and given a certain primacy, the ideal of equal opportunity inclines in this direction. But within the context of the theory of justice as a whole there is much less urgency to take this course' (Rawls 1971, p.511).

Of course, some of those who would applaud platform calls for equality of opportunity do not really believe in any imposed and universal equality, but rather in some sort of opportunity floor to serve as the safety net below which no one need fall. (Both these images occurred repeatedly in Sir Winston Churchill's domestic speeches after World War II, and he certainly was not advocating that any ceilings should be screwed down to any floors!)

Those who actually do believe in some way in equality of opportunity for the most part either want to limit it to certain areas (and to somewhat later stages in the life-cycle) or are willing to make fairly large trade-offs against the values of the family. The men of 1789, for instance, were concerned primarily if not exclusively about public appointments; and, of course, competitors for these were to be well past the age of infancy. Nevertheless the inevitability of clashes between ideals of this kind and those of a responsible private parenthood endowed with extensive rights and duties can be illustrated with an example belonging to the stuff of current British and American educational politics.

For many years in Britain the stock response to any appeal for a measure of parental choice in education was to say that in this country real choice is confined to a privileged few able to afford the fat fees of private schools. Although this objection perhaps did too little justice to the differences between the denominational and the more secular schools within the state system, and although by overlooking the number of those who could afford such fees but preferred to spend their money in other ways it certainly underestimated the size of this minority, it was still substantially correct in what it said.

But at last Milton Friedman in America and in Britain various persons associated with the Institute of Economic Affairs, perhaps taking hints from Tom Paine and John Stuart Mill, began to develop and to push the idea of education vouchers. (See Friedman 1955; and compare Harris and Seldon 1963, Peacock and Wiseman 1965, West 1968, Maynard 1975, and Harris and Seldon 1978 and 1979.) This mechanism promises vastly to increase the numbers enjoying a real choice of school; as well as to give these same parents and children some check on, or escape from, the negligence or malpractice of the occasional outrageous teacher or outrageous school – a check far more immediate and effective than any conceivable system of appointed boards or elected governors (Smith, V(i) Part III Article II).

How long, even under the Inner London Education Authority, would Radical deschooling at the now notorious William Tyndale establishment have escaped official notice, had those parents, who were later to display their fury before the television cameras, been from the start able to remove their children to some institution more properly describable as a school? Given such opportunity, as Ed Clark the Libertarian Party candidate was to keep asking in the 1978 California gubernatorial election, how many more desperately concerned poor black parents would transfer their children to the more selective parochial schools; and away from the often violent obstructors who lurk behind Coleman's discreet phrases about peer group handicaps?

But, since choosers will not all choose in the same sense, choice is bound to produce inequalities. So, when an editorial in the London *Daily Telegraph* urged that a prototype voucher scheme be tried out, a spokesperson for the Labour Party at once protested: 'We should worry less about "parental choice" .... The voucher system, which you claim offers freedom of choice to parents, can only operate at the expense of denying children the equality of opportunity they ought to enjoy in a civilised society. Under this system we would very soon have good schools packed with the fortunate children of competent, caring parents with deprived children from disadvantaged homes languishing in sink schools' (25 June 1975: sneer quotes as originally printed).

A second illustration, the more remarkable because it carries no suggestion that the introduction of greater possibilities of choice would leave anyone at all worse off than they are now, is even more indicative of the unavoidable conflict between enforced equality of outcome and liberties for the individual. This one comes from a parliamentary report in the same paper. The Shadow Minister of Health confronts his substantial opposite number, and appeals to the supposedly self-evident scandalousness of any inequality: 'Introducing private insurance will cause people who pay more to expect a better service, and we shall get two standards of health care, one for those who pay privately and one for those who don't' (17 July 1979).

5 *Ideals of equality: outcome*

In their general introduction the Editors of a recent American source-book on *The 'Inequality' Controversy*, write of their country's traditional 'commitment to equality of opportunity and to equality of results' (Levine and Bane, p.5). This in itself should have generated qualms of historical conscience. For, as we have already seen, the first foundation document of the American republic refers only to a third ideal of equality quite different from either of these two. (Compare both Sjöstrand and Pole, passim.) And this third ideal, coming first in the present order of exposition, demands an equality of maximum liberties flat incompatible with the enforcement of a universal equality of outcome. Yet these Editors are content later to claim that one contribution first examines the 'concept of equality of opportunity', and then 'traces the development of the concept to its logically inevitable definition as equality of results' (*Ibid.*, p.198; but compare p.11).

At this stage there is little need further to emphasise the difference between ideals of this third sort and those of our first and second sorts. What does call for some attention is, first, the application to this particular case of points we have already made in general; and second, the significance of a too rarely noticed fact. The fact is that, for almost all its most prominent enthusiasts, equality of outcome is not a personal ideal, to be pursued by individual persuasion, and sometimes sacrificial example, but a political or administrative policy, to be enforced by the full power of an ever more extended state machine.

(i) Under the first of these heads the first points to appreciate are that people may be cherishing equality of outcome as a value, as a good in itself and independent of any further consequences, even though they do not want such equality in every direction; and even though, in those directions in which they do want it, they do not insist on an absolute and perfect equality.

In the first case the problem for such egalitarians is to show why their ideals do not require a completely universal application. Why do the reasons they give for demanding some kinds of equality not apply to other kinds? If, for instance, it is imperative that 'life-chances' be equalised through an equalisation of wealth and income, then we may ask to be told whether the same imperative also requires such measures as are implemented in the nightmare worlds of L.P. Hartley and Kurt Vonnegut; and, if not, why not. (The former, in *Facial Justice*, tells of the pretty undergoing plastic surgery to remove their envy-provoking excesses of appeal. In the story 'Harrison Bergeron', the latter describes those with talents above average being implanted physiologically with anti-pacesetters, curbing them down to the level of the rest.)

In the second case the problem is to appreciate why absolute and perfect equality is relevant. Certainly the playwright Bernard Shaw was very much the exception among socialists in advocating a strict equality of incomes, although he remained altogether representative of his prosperous co-believers in his inflexible refusal to set a costly personal example by surrendering his own very substantial – and, on his own account therefore unjustifiable – surplus above average. But it is wrong to say on this account: 'Extremes are not worth discussing. Perfect equality is not conceivable, let alone workable' (Stretton, p.169). For, if the only reason why you are not advocating the extreme is that you concede, in the words of the leading spokesperson quoted at the very end of Section 1, that some incentives are 'required to keep the economy moving'; then a strict equality here *is* for you a value; albeit one value among two or more. In that event the extremes are not merely important but essential. For it is precisely between the extremes that the trading-off takes place.

The third general point needing to be reiterated – but briefly – in the present particular case is that it is a necessary feature of any egalitarianism to be concerned with relativities. To want everyone to get or to have (at least) this or that, is not essentially egalitarian. To become such the demand has to be that everyone should get or have either the same as, or some equivalent to, whatever it may be that everyone else is getting or having: 'See what the boys in the back room are having, and tell them I'm having the same.'

(ii) 'Can urban, industrial, bureaucratic societies like ours realise the promise of equality and social justice ... without sacrificing the liberties which they have so far attained?' That was the apt penultimate sentence of the second of a recent trio of long articles in *New Society*, a series united by the famous motto of successive French republics. Although the author, David Donnison, seems to have been too embarrassed to offer so much as a single illustration of the possible conflict between equality and liberty, his conclusion was bold and correct: 'That is the central question' (20 November 1975, p.424).

(a) Donnison is an outstandingly suitable spokesman for the *Guardian*-reading, professedly social-democratic, usually social-science trained establishment brand of centrally imposed British egalitarianism. Righthand man to Richard Titmuss at the London School of Economics, and later his successor; eponymous chairman of the Donnison Committee, and formerly member of other bodies working towards a universal state monopoly system of compulsory comprehensive education; appointed to his present plush and powerful Whitehall job by a Labour Minister of Health and Social Security; Donnison has been honoured as one of the four great equalisers. To a generation which read Edgar Wallace such paragons must be the Four Just Men returned: 'Apart from any influence their writings may have had, these four must by now have planned, directed or managed several billion dollars' worth of three or four countries' capital resources, mostly to the purpose . . . of reducing inequalities. They are ambitious men at the top of severely competitive professions . . . . As far as I know each pays his taxes, takes home two or three times the average family income . . . and would work as well for a great deal less if more equal societies required that' (Stretton, p.vi).

Even the unhallowed ranks of Tuscany can scarce forebear to cheer: 'How splendid!' But, after that first burst of spontaneous applause, there is a question which ought to be put, and pressed, much more often than it is. 'And upon what grounds of principle are these four just men proposing *not* to yield up their own remaining unequal, and hence on their own account (socially) unjust, excess – until and unless, that is, they are so compelled by law?

From my own personal acquaintance with one of Stretton's Four Just Men, I am happy to be able to say that he is not at all a person to hang on to stolen property, or make and keep gains by any form of sharp practice. Nor did he, while advocating the passage of a Race Relations Act, and expressing his willingness to abide by its terms, insist on taking advantage of the open possibilities, in the previous state of the law, of racial abuse. I suggest, therefore, in his and many similar cases, that the following is the way to resolve the paradox. In order in their own eyes and in those of others to legitimate the enforcement by an always expanding state machine of their illiberal, bureaucratic and Procrustean ideal they speak always of this imposition as 'the achievement of social justice'. Yet in their hearts they still do not themselves believe that equality of outcome, which they are thus accustomed to represent as the essence of (social) justice, really is an imperative of old-time, without prefix or suffix, justice. About this at least, as will be argued in Chapter III, they are right. Social justice is no more justice than People's Democracy is democracy.

(b) At the end of his original article Donnison asserts that the possible conflict between freedom and equality is 'the central question'. (It was incidentally, an article remarkable for not finding need or space to make even one of the distinctions which I have presented as being fundamental. Donnison did, however, have the grace to begin by conceding that the egalitarianism for which he was speaking is 'muddled', and suggesting, in a usefully provocative way, that it is 'muddled because its academic spokesmen were never challenged by sufficiently tough opposition to compel them to clarify their views'.) Having thus originally concluded that the possible incompatibility between freedom and equality is 'the central question', Donnison went on two weeks later to dismiss all libertarian objectors with mandarin contempt – having perhaps in the meantime been shaken by the unfamiliar experience of meeting tough academic opposition: 'It is nonsense to tell us that nations which have more of the one necessarily have less of the other' (4 December 1975: 'Correspondence').

Suppose that we were talking about freedom and equality in some purely voluntary organisation, such as an Israeli kibbutz. Or suppose more generally that we were being presented with a private moral ideal, which adherents would strive first to reach themselves, and afterwards to recommend to others by example and by argument. Then there would indeed be no necessary conflict. But that is not how it is. This ideal of 'equality and social justice' is in fact one which has been approached (and which it is proposed to continue to approach) primarily, if not quite exclusively, by legal and administrative measures, rather than by individual conversion and self-sacrificing self-discipline. (And to any objection to the emphasis here on force and compulsion, the reply must be:

'Were those "several billion dollars' worth of three or four countries' capital resources" freewill offerings from eager volunteers, all lining up for equalisation?')

The same Procrustean ideal in one of its aspects is, as Robert Nisbet and others have recently been arguing, the uniting and justifying ideology of a rising class of policy advisors and public welfare professionals (Nisbet 1976; compare Moynihan 1972, passim; Hodgson, p.37; also Kristol, pp.15, 175 and 177). Although to say this is of course not, what it is not offered as being, a refutation of the ideal, we should nevertheless notice that these are all people both professionally involved in, and owing their past and future advancement to, the business of enforcing it. Donnison himself, for instance, was Professor of Social Administration at the London School of Economics – training future public welfare officials – before finding his own road to the much better paid and pensioned, and far more powerful, higher reaches of the state bureaucracy. It is tempting to give a fresh application to some famous words from the *Communist Manifesto*. These refer to that section of the intelligentsia which sees fit to throw in its lot with 'the class that holds the future in its hands' (Marx and Engels, 1848, p.91).

In the face of all this the true nonsense is to pretend that there is no sort of inverse connection between publicly imposed equality of outcome and liberties for the private citizen. Consider again, for instance, the way in which both the teachers' unions and the entire educational bureaucracy are solidly opposed to any serious exploration of the mechanism of the education voucher: both on the grounds that they are the official experts appointed to diagnose, and to prescribe for, the needs of pupils (Chapter V), and on the grounds that parental choices, being made in diverse senses, could not but result in – the horror of it! – inequality.

Compare too the forceful comment of David Marquand, sometime holder of an ultra-safe Labour seat, a comment made with the likes of Donnison, and perhaps Donnison himself, particularly in mind. In 'Inquest on a Movement', published in *Encounter* for July 1979, Marquand wrote: ' . . . if the social wage bites into the individual wage . . . the individual wage earner will lose some of the freedom which he would otherwise have enjoyed. . . . A society in which 50 per cent of the gross domestic product is spent by the state may be healthier, better educated, or more equal than a society in which the state spends only 30 per cent of GDP.

But it will also be less free, and it is humbug to deny the fact' (p.10: and, to have it all spelt out in detail, compare Seldon 1977 and Harris and Seldon 1979).

(c) Apart from whatever particular limitations of liberty must be essentially involved in any particular programme for compulsory equalisation – or, for that matter, in any programme of compulsory anything – there are good general reasons to believe that a strenuous, sustained and extensive policy for imposing this ideal, especially in those areas which happen to be of most concern to the subjects, will as a matter of fact require enormous public bureaucracies, and perhaps even some highly authoritarian and repressive form of government.

Earlier, in Section 3, i, b, the suggestion was made that a fully socialist economy is in practice incompatible with democratic political institutions, and hence with the basic civil liberties logically necessary to their working. Notice now that it is precisely such a centralised, socialist, command economy which is necessary in order to make possible – though it alone will certainly not guarantee – the imposition and maintenance of any approved pattern of distribution, egalitarian or other. This socialist pre-supposition of the enforcement of 'equality and social justice' came out very clearly a few years ago in some revealing words of the Chairman of a BBC Radio Three series on 'Whatever happened to equality?', words uttered just a little before his own elevation to a Labour life peerage. He was confronted with 'the idea that the state should determine everyone's rewards according to some system of fairness, and should determine prices accordingly . . . this is the acceptance of the view that there is a rational system of social justice which it is the business of the state to enforce'. The Chairman agreed wholeheartedly: 'That's a view I should embrace very strongly. I believe that that is the way one ought to think about society' (Vaizey, p.566).

His confession may be compared with one of the findings of a much recommended sociological study, *Class Inequality and Political Order*. The author, Frank Parkin, seems to be one of those clear-headed and honest socialists prepared to state quite frankly, with J.K. Galbraith: 'I am not particular about freedom.'[9]

Parkin concludes: 'Egalitarianism seems to require a political system in which the state is able to hold in check those social and occupational groups which, by virtue of their skills or education or personal attributes, might otherwise attempt to stake claims to a disproportionate share of society's rewards. The most effective way of holding such groups in check is by denying them the right to organise politically, or in other ways, to undermine social equality. This presumably is the reasoning underlying the Marxist-Leninist case for a political order based upon the dictatorship of the proletariat' (Parkin, p.183). Which being translated is, as Parkin recognises, the dictatorship of the party over the rest of society; and the dictatorship of the Central Committee over the party. In the Newspeak of established Leninism, the technical expression for these arrangements is 'democratic centralism'.

Their inegalitarian and ultra-élitist character comes out hard and clear in two statements by one of the idols of the allegedly non-Stalinist 'New Left'. Such vanguards, wrote Che Guevara, 'are qualitatively different from the masses who see only by halves and must be subjected to incentives and pressures of some intensity: it is the dictatorship of the proletariat being exercised not only upon the defeated class but also individually upon the victorious class.' Institutions, he continued, are needed to 'permit the natural selection of those who are destined to march in the vanguard and who dispense reward and punishments to those who fulfil their duty or act against the society under construction' (Quoted Lothstein, p.365).

The most remarkable deficiency in Parkin's conclusion, though this is not to say that it is peculiar to him, is that nowhere in the whole book does it ever seem to cross his mind that, even in the enormously unlikely event that such an uncriticisable and irremovable power élite were to subdue all temptations to appropriate massive additional perquisites and privileges for its own members, still its absolute power over, and control of, the rest of the society must in itself constitute the greatest offence to any genuinely universal ideal of equality of outcome. Parkin, who at the time of writing – I am told – still clutched a residual Marxist faith, should have remembered Lenin's favourite question: 'Who, whom?' For there is indeed an irresolvable tension in the whole notion of a universal and compulsory equalisation: 'Who will equalise the equalisers?'

CHAPTER III

Social Justice, or Justice?

> Now, given that unjust conduct and the unjust man are unequal, it is clear there is a mean or average between inequalities; and that this is equality, since whatever action admits of more or less admits of equality too. If therefore, injustice is inequality, justice is equality – a view which commends itself to all without proof; and, since equality is a mean or average, justice must be a kind of mean. Again, equality involves two terms at least. It therefore follows necessarily; both that justice is a mean or average and equal; and that as a mean or average it must be between a more and a less; and that as an equality it must be between [at least] two terms; and that as justice it must involve people. *Aristotle: Nicomachean Ethics (1131A 10-19)*

Aristotle was writing in the fourth century B.C. Yet it seems no less true today that the view that the just is the equal commends itself to all – or almost all – without proof. Section 1 of Chapter II has already provided many citations to show how much it is part of the contemporary climate of opinion to assume both that equality without qualification is a great and manifest good (if not the greatest and most manifest) and that the imposition and maintenance of (social) equality is the supreme imperative of (social) justice. So it should here suffice to add only two further pairs of examples – for the especial benefit of those who, when forced to allow that some opinion has been effectively attacked, at once suggest that no one in his senses has ever maintained anything of the sort.

The first and less weighty pair came from the issues of *New Society* and of *The Times Higher Education Supplement* current when I began work on the present chapter. In the former an article 'Rail Travel is a Middle-Class Game' frequently refers to the fact that the resources available to different people and to different groups of people are unequal. On every occasion it proceeds forthwith, without further reason given, to denounce these inequalities as one and all inequitable. In the latter a main feature on the University of Oxford refers repeatedly to the problem of the inequality of endowments of the various colleges. What is thus picked out as an evil, and what – again without any further reason given – the reader is expected to see as calling for some policy of reform, is not that some colleges are now too poor to do a tolerable job, nor even – though in these days this is, regrettably, not a plausible charge – that others are so rich as to be both able and inclined to squander in riotous living resources which ought to be devoted to the sober business of teaching and learning. No, the evil apparently is the inequality as such.

The second and more academic pair of further examples comes from *Economics and Equality*, edited by the former British Cabinet Minister and perhaps former Conservative Aubrey Jones. This volume consists in the papers to Section F (Economics) at the 1975 Annual Meeting of the British Association for the Advancement of Science. In his own contribution the Editor observes as 'a given fact of life' that 'Inequality of all sorts has lost its legitimacy.' Later C.D. Harbury, Professor of Economics in London's City University, begins by remarking, as if this were the most obvious thing in the world: 'Economic equality, with which the Section is concerned this year, is one aspect of a wider theme of social justice' (A. Jones, pp.2 and 87).

The main aim of the present chapter is to challenge this identification of equality with justice and equity. I shall also be continuing to point out some of the seamier implications of what nowadays is the most popular kind of egalitarianism. But I shall not attempt to develop or to defend an ideal of justice as an alternative to an ideal of equality of outcome. Still less shall I be putting *inequality* forward as a rival value. The first of these two tasks is not for this occasion. The second would be fundamentally misguided. For it is quite wrong (although in the heat of the political kitchen obviously tempting) to represent those who reject an ideal of equality as thereby either always and necessarily – or even usually and in fact – committed to cherishing *inequality* (Crosland 1962, p.22). This, as was argued in the previous chapter, is as absurd as assuming that anyone rejecting classical Utilitarianism must thereby become committed to pursuing as their supreme good the greatest unhappiness of the greatest number. No doubt there would be more and greater inequalities in their ideal societies, but such inequalities do not have to be valued for themselves alone, independent of their causes or consequences, and in fact they rarely are.

In a nutshell, the main moral which I hope to justify is as follows: whereas this third ideal of equality is in an obvious sense forward-looking, and concerned with making and keeping everyone's condition equal; justice is in that sense backward-looking, and concerned that people should obtain and not be deprived of (or, as the case may be, suffer) their several – and presumably often unequal – deserts and entitlements. If this is correct, then our egalitarians of outcome, even if this means sacrificing a powerful propaganda advantage, ought to urge their Procrustean ideal neither as nor as a part of, but rather as a rival to, justice. The pursuit of that they should see as reactionary, backward-looking, unsystematic, irrelevant, antique and gothic. After all, this is exactly how those who pride themselves on being the most forward-looking and science-oriented reformers do present their proposals in the particular sphere of criminal justice.

For example, Dr Karl Menninger, for many years the chief spokesman for American orthopsychiatry, wrote a chilling manifesto of psychiatric imperialism:

> The very word 'justice' irritates scientists. No surgeon expects to be asked whether an operation for cancer is just or not. No doctor will be reproached on the grounds that the dose of penicillin he has prescribed is less or more than justice would stipulate. Behavioural scientists regard it as equally absurd to invoke the question of justice . . . . This sort of behaviour has to be controlled; it has to be discouraged; it has to be stopped. This (to the scientist) is a matter of public safety and amicable coexistence, not of justice (Menninger, p.17; and compare Flew 1973a, passim).

1 Equality: substantial, or formal?

The chapter motto from the *Nicomachean Ethics* is torn out of context. It is the first ten lines of Chapter III of Book V. This book contains Aristotle's treatment of what has to be translated as justice, and he is throughout concerned to fit his account to a cherished theory that both virtue in general and all particular virtues are a sort of average between opposite extremes. In Chapter I he distinguishes one sense in which justice is the whole of virtue from another in which it is one virtue among many. To explain the former he quotes *Melanippe*, a lost play by Euripides: 'In justice is all virtue found in sum.' This sense is not found in English today, though once perhaps it was (Miller, p.17). However, if we may here discount differences between Jew and Greek, it can be said to correspond to the righteousness of the King James' *Bible*.

(i) Chapter II and its successors deal with justice in the particular sense. It is, Aristotle holds, of two kinds: distributive and corrective. The former 'is exercised in distributions of honour or of wealth or of anything else which is to be divided among those who have a share in the constitution; since in these it is possible for one to have an allocation either equal or unequal to that of another' (1130B 30-4).

(a) A generation deafened by the rhetoric of social justice has to work hard to recognise that Aristotle is not taking it that there either has been, or ought to be, an active distribution of all goods of every kind. It is easy to read this modern notion into the words just quoted. But so anachronistic a reading is ruled out when he proceeds, first to entertain the oligarchic suggestion that the relevant criterion of entitlement might be the possession of wealth, and then to conclude that this 'justice in distributing common property . . . when a distribution is made from the common stock . . . will follow the same ratio as that between the amounts which the several persons have contributed to the common stock' (1131A 25-9 and 1131B 28-33). The common stocks from which these distributions are to be made clearly cannot be the only stocks there are. Throughout, therefore, Aristotle is presupposing the subsistence of private holdings, holdings which presumably did not all result from previous public distributions.

It is unfortunate that in this discussion Aristotle ventures no illustrations. One which he might have used is provided by the famous occasion when the citizens of Athens wondered whether to share out unexpectedly large profits from the state silver mines at Laureion as a poll dividend, but were instead persuaded by Themistocles to put defence first. They in fact used the money to build the ships in which they shortly afterwards won the Battle of Salamis. Suppose that we here follow the Athenians in refusing to entertain any claims on behalf of the slave miners. Then this truly was 'manna from heaven', a windfall gain to the achievement of which no one had contributed anything. So the choice between an equal distribution among all the citizens or a use for a public purpose might well appear appropriate.

I do not know whether the Athenian navy had an institution of prize money, such as is familiar to all readers of the Hornblower stories of C.S. Forrester. But if it did this would have provided Aristotle with an illustration of the application of the different principle of allocation according to contribution. The reason why the Captain's share was in those days so spectacularly unequal was that it was thought, whether rightly or wrongly, that his contribution to the taking of the prize would normally amount to roughly that of the whole of the rest of the crew put together.

(b) The upshot of the previous subsection is that Aristotle himself, to whom we owe the very expression 'distributive justice', certainly did not believe that any principles of distributive justice must or could apply to all possession of all goods of every kind. But what puts him even more out of step with most of our contemporaries is his interpretation of 'a view which commends itself to all without proof'. For the motto passage continues immediately: 'So it follows necessarily that justice involves at least four terms: both two persons for whom it is just and two shares which are just. And there will be the same equality between the shares as between the persons, since the ratio between the shares will be equal to the ratio between the persons. *For if the persons are not equal they will not have equal shares. . . .*' (1131A 19-24; italics supplied).

(ii) That final sentence puts an altogether fresh complexion upon the whole affair. It now emerges that everyone accepts without proof: not the substantial practical prescription that distributive justice requires that every person, or every citizen, enjoy an equal share of every kind of good; but instead some more formal principle to the effect that it is an universal and necessary feature of any system of justice that it treat all (relevantly) like cases alike. Such a principle is indeed essential. It is, therefore, important to appreciate that and how it differs from any substantive egalitarian norm. The crux, as Sir Isaiah Berlin put it in a famous essay, is simple: 'All rules, by definition, entail a measure of equality' (Berlin 1956, p.305).

James Fitzjames Stephen was thus able to conclude 'that the only shape in which equality is really connected with justice is this – justice presupposes general rules. . . . If these general rules are to be maintained at all, it is obvious that they must be applied equally to every case which satisfies their terms' (Stephen, p.199; and compare Sidgwick, p.293, also Ross pp.273 and 268). Where rules are not being followed, rules which apply to all who satisfy their terms, there can be no rule of law (Hayek 1960, passim); and hence no question of any established laws being either just or unjust. But although any rules of justice, simply as rules, must apply equally to all those who satisfy their terms, this conceptual truth carries no further implication that everyone subject to a set of rules has to be treated alike. On the contrary: it is, for instance, obvious that every system of criminal justice requires that offenders be treated differently from people who have not offended.

So the great principle of equality before the law cannot and does not mean that a just system of laws will treat everyone exactly alike; much less that it will strive to equalise the conditions of all those subject to it. What it does mean is that the law ought to take account only of what differences are properly relevant; and, of course, what differences are or are not properly relevant may in many cases be reasonably disputed. In Britain today the most explosive example of such a dispute concerns the law's vastly different treatment of companies as opposed to labour unions, and of sellers of labour as opposed to either buyers of labour or buyers or sellers of almost anything else. Do these undeniable differences constitute improper privileges; and are such privileges consistent with an ideal of equality before the law? That is the question.[10] When the men of 1789 proclaimed this ideal they were with reason at some pains to make clear which of the differences recognised by the laws of the Old Regime were no longer to be admitted as properly relevant. Thus Article 3 of the Declaration prefixed to the Constitution of the 5th of Fructidor reads: 'Equality consists in the law being the same for all, whether it is protecting or whether it is punishing. Equality admits of no distinction of birth, no inherited powers.'

2 *The book of Rawls*

In further pursuing the questions put at the beginning of the present chapter I shall from now on be working primarily but not exclusively with Rawls' book *A Theory of Justice*. There are two reasons for this concentration. One is that from the moment of its first appearance it became universally accepted as the work with which anyone hoping to make a contribution in its area had to come to terms. Edmund Burke published his *Philosophical Enquiry into the Origin of Our Ideas of the Sublime and the Beautiful* in 1757, and it has been well said that 'Everyone after Burke either imitates him, or borrows from him, or feels it necessary to refute him.' John Rawls published *A Theory of Justice* in 1971, and that the same applies is one of few points of resemblance between the two authors and the two books. The second reason for this particular concentration is that there is so little alternative, so little literature either expounding and examining the ideal of equality of outcome or trying to explain why it is supposed that it has to be enforced in the name of justice.

On the first count consider the Critical Notice in *The New York Review of Books*. Stuart Hampshire, at that time still Warden of Wadham College, Oxford, wrote: 'I think that this book is the most substantial and interesting contribution to moral philosophy since the war, at least if one thinks only of works written in English. It is a very persuasive book, being very well argued and carefully composed.' It presents, Hampshire continues, 'a noble, coherent, highly abstract picture of the fair society, as social democrats see it. . . . This is certainly the model of social justice that has governed the advocacy of R.H. Tawney and Richard Titmuss and that holds the Labour Party together' (Hampshire 1972a, p.34).

On the second and negative count it is sufficient to offer two notes. First, in his widely circulated, much praised, yet shatteringly criticized book *Unequal Shares: Wealth in Britain* the Essex economist A.B. Atkinson has a chapter on 'The Case for Greater Equality'. He starts with a somewhat incongruous reference to 'the golden section of a line'; which, he seems to have forgotten, is not an equal division. He continues: 'The moral justification of equality is, however, a less straightforward question than its purely aesthetic appeal. Moreover it is a subject which has been much neglected in the past few years, as D. Donnison has recently pointed out' (Atkinson, pp.78-9; compare both Polanyi and Wood, passim, and Joseph and Sumption, Chapters 5-6). Second, hearing in the USA so many urgent demands for 'more equality', though not of course for 'an absolute levelling', Irving Kristol as an Editor of *The Public Interest* has repeatedly invited the demanders to supply 'an article that would describe a proper distribution of American income.' He reports: 'I have never been able to get that article. . . . In two cases, I was promised such an analysis, but it was never written. In the other cases no one was able to find the time to devote to it' (Kristol, p.172).

(i) The book of Rawls opens with a trumpet blast: 'Justice is the first virtue of social institutions, as truth is of systems of thought. A theory however elegant and economical must be rejected if it is untrue; likewise laws and institutions no matter how efficient and well-arranged must be reformed or abolished if they are unjust. Each person possesses an inviolability founded on justice that even the welfare of society as a whole cannot over-ride. For this reason justice denies that the loss of freedom for some is made right by a greater good shared by others. . . . Therefore in a just society the liberties of equal citizenship are taken as settled; the rights secured by justice are not subject to political bargaining or to the calculus of social interests. The only thing that permits us to acquiesce in an erroneous theory is the lack of a better one; analogously, an injustice is tolerable only when it is necessary to avoid an even greater injustice. Being first virtues of human activities, truth and justice are uncompromising' (Rawls 1971, pp. 3-4).

(a) The master concept which Rawls revives is that of a social contract. As in Rousseau and Hobbes, but not in Locke, this contract is strictly hypothetical – a theoretical fiction. And as in all the classical sources, though not in Britain in the early seventies, it is an open contract to which all the members of a society are supposed to be party. (No serious political thinker could ever have applied the expression 'social contract' to a bogus, backstairs, and socially exclusive deal between labour union bosses and the leaders of their own political party!) For Rawls the 'guiding idea is that the principles of justice for the basic structure of society . . . are the principles that free and rational persons concerned to further their own interests would accept in an initial position of equality as defining the fundamental terms of their association. . . . This way of regarding the principles of justice I shall call justice as fairness' (*Ibid.*, p.11).

It is characteristic of these 'mere conditional and hypothetical reasonings', conducted in what Rawls calls 'the original position', that they take place behind 'a veil of ignorance' (*Ibid.*, p.12). Thus he stipulates: 'First of all, no one knows his place in society, his class position or social status; nor does he know his fortune in the distribution of natural assets and abilities, his intelligence and strength, and the like. Nor, again, does anyone know his conception of the good, the particulars of his rational plan of life, or even the special features of his psychology such as his aversion to risk or liability to optimism or pessimism. More than this, I assume that the parties do not know the particular circumstances of their own society. . . . The persons in the original position have no information as to which generation they belong (to). . . . They must choose principles the consequences of which they are prepared to live with whatever generation they turn out to belong to' (*Ibid.*, p.137). Since Rawls was writing in the USA in the late sixties and early seventies, it is remarkable that the book seems never in so many words to rule out knowledge of either sex or race. Virginia Held of the City University of New York has, however, shown me a passage in another article where Rawls says: ' . . . they do not know . . . whether they are . . . man or woman, and so on' (Rawls 1969, p.242).

It is usual to discuss this comprehensive blinkering as being stipulated in order to secure impartiality; which makes the whole exercise nothing but a dramatisation of colourless appeals to the ideally impartial spectator (Hare, pp.150-5). Certainly Rawls does mention this as one purpose: 'We should insure further that particular inclinations and aspirations, and persons' conceptions of their good, do not affect the principles adopted' (Rawls 1971, p.18). But the stated primary aim is wholly different: 'Once we decide to look for a conception of justice that nullifies the accidents of natural endowment and the contingencies of social circumstance as counters in the quest for political and economic advantage, we are led to these principles. They express the result of *leaving aside those aspects of the social world that seem arbitrary from a moral point of view*' (*Ibid.*, p.15: italics supplied).

(b) Having for these two reasons hung up 'The Veil of Ignorance', Rawls now asks his hypothetical contracting parties to choose 'the first principles of a conception of justice which is to regulate all subsequent criticism and reform of institutions' (*Ibid.*, pp.136 and 13). After the captivating frankness of his confession that 'We want to define the original position so that we get the desired solution', it comes as no surprise that they cannot but 'acknowledge as the first principle of justice one requiring an equal distribution. Indeed, this principle is so obvious that we would expect it to occur to anyone immediately' (*Ibid.*, pp.141 and 150-1).

Notice that this 'first principle' is being offered, not as a defeasible methodological presumption, but as a substantive moral commitment; and not as a ruling of prudence, but as a – indeed the – fundamental moral judgement. It is true that Rawls is talking in terms of prudence in the words immediately preceding those quoted already: 'Since it is not reasonable . . . to expect more than an equal share . . . and not rational . . . to agree to less, the sensible thing . . . to do . . . '; and so on. But what they are thus supposed to acknowledge is also a matter of morality; and the two reasons Rawls gives for fixing his epistemological blindfolds both refer to the aim of making the hypothetical contracting parties into sound and reliable moral judges. We must presume, therefore, that this 'first principle' would yield an absolute equality of entitlement to all (social) goods.

However, although Rawls begins with this ultra-radical egalitarianism, that is not where he wants to end. So he asks next: 'If there are inequalities in the basic structure that work to make everyone better off in comparison with the benchmark of initial inequality, why not permit them?' From this question he proceeds, by way of salutary remarks about envy, to his eventual conclusion: 'Inequalities are permissible when they maximise, or at least all contribute to, the long-term expectations of the least fortunate group in society' (*Ibid.*, p.151).

So, Rawls believes, in the last analysis, 'two principles of justice . . . would be chosen in the original position'. In the earliest formulation these run: 'First, each person is to have an equal right to the most extensive basic liberty compatible with a similar liberty for others. Second: social and economic inequalities are to be arranged so that they are both (a) reasonably expected to be to everyone's advantage, and (b) attached to positions and offices open to all' (*Ibid.*, p.60). The principles are arranged in what Rawls calls lexical order: the first, that is to say, has priority over the second; while 2 (a), similarly, has priority over 2 (b).

Of these two final principles the first is elsewhere spoken of as 'the priority of liberty'. It is no doubt this intended priority, inconsistent though it must surely be with some of his other commitments, which has caused Rawls to be ridiculed by Marxists, and by some other consciously socialist critics: he has even been described and dismissed – O most frightful of charges! – as 'an unreconstructed Gladstonian liberal'.

In the second principle the pellucidly unequivocal clause

'reasonably expected to be to everyone's advantage' is at once characterised by Rawls as 'ambiguous' (*Ibid.*, p.61). It is later and laboriously construed as a formulation of what Rawls calls the Difference Principle: 'Inequalities are permissible when they maximise, or at least all contribute to, the long-term expectations of the least fortunate group in society' (*Ibid.*, p.151). To me, I confess, it remains altogether obscure why the advantage of the least fortunate is thus taken to be one of two possible interpretations of the expression 'everyone's advantage'.

(ii) Before proceeding to external objections against the entire enterprise we need to show that the 'two principles of justice' which finally emerge cannot be validly derived, either from the stated conditions of 'the original position' or from the proposed 'first principle of justice'. Showing this will at the same time help to bring out some of the implications both of the later 'two principles' and of 'the first principle'.

(a) Rawls starts, as we have just seen, by maintaining that his hypothetical contracting parties must 'acknowledge as the first principle of justice one requiring an equal distribution.' He is also, as we saw rather earlier, committed to the absolute indefeasibility of the claims of justice: ' . . . an injustice is tolerable only when it is necessary to avoid an even greater injustice. Being first virtues of human activities, truth and justice are uncompromising.' If your egalitarianism is thus not subject to any trade-offs against other values, then for you the heart of the matter should be the end of the affair.

This absolutist position is, it appears, actually taken by the Swedish philosopher Lars Ericsson: ' . . . by conceiving distributive justice as, fundamentally, equal treatment of individuals, I shall reject the idea that inequalities in the distribution of economic goods are justifiable from the standpoint of justice on the ground that they are to the benefit of the least advantaged' (Ericsson, p.121). It is, of course, Rawls who is in Ericsson's sights. For, although starting from his ultra-egalitarian 'first principle of justice', Rawls nevertheless contrives to allow for what must in practice constitute drastic deviations from that norm. He continues: 'Thus the parties start with a principle establishing equal liberty for all, including equality of opportunity, as well as equal distribution of income and wealth. If there are inequalities . . . that work to make everyone better off in comparison with the benchmark of initial equality, why not permit them?' (Rawls 1971, p.151).

'Indeed, why not?' we may want to say. But for Rawls the reason why not is enshrined in the manifesto: since 'truth and justice are uncompromising', trade-offs are not permitted. If justice does entitle everyone to an equal share of all (social) goods, then one can and must immediately infer one universal right and one universal duty: the human right never to be exceeded, and the human duty never to exceed. Suppose that, in the process of everyone's becoming better off, you get more than him. Then in violating his basic right you have failed to do your fundamental duty. Thus the categorical imperative of Rawlsian justice was expressed by Gracchus Babeuf, in his last Defence against charges arising out of the Conspiracy of the Equals: 'Society must be made to operate in such a way that it eradicates once and for all the desire of a man to become richer, or wiser, or more powerful than others.'

The problem for Rawls is, not just to justify the inequalities licensed by the Difference Principle, but to show that they are just: it is not just to justify but – as some would say – to justicise (Frankena, p.16). His only hope of doing this is somehow to introduce a series of willing sales of all rights not to be exceeded. These willing waivers would at the same time nullify the duties of the other hypothetical contracting parties not to exceed. If, given always 'the first principle of justice' and the manifesto commitment, any inequalities are to be shown to be just, then they must result from, or at least be such as would result from, contracts under which I trade some relaxation of my basic human right not to be excelled in return for the largest possible cut of the extra wealth and income to be produced by the consequent unleashing of your skill, effort, and enterprise: *volenti non fit injuria*, that is, it is not a wrong if the subject is willing.

But, since it will not justicise the Difference Principle, this escape route cannot accommodate Rawls. If everyone is entitled to an equal share, then the largest deviations from that norm – both below and above – must be by that token the most obnoxious. But, on that same basic assumption, anyone who wants to be discharged of their obligation not to excel has got to buy off everyone whose right not to be excelled would be violated by that exceller's excelling; and 'everyone' means everyone, not just the least fortunate group. The first thoughts of Rawls were better. Given the supposedly obvious 'first principle of justice', then any inequalities which are not to be unjust have got to be to everyone's advantage –

repeat – everyone's. For if equality is thus to be 'the rest (or rectilinear motion) position of the system' (Nozick, p.223), then the first person to get ahead of the pack necessarily drives all the rest below the average. He must in justice compensate them all for the injuries he is doing to each and every one. And so it must go on for any and every other advance beyond whatever becomes from time to time the present average, the proper compensation due being presumably proportionate to the different degrees of the several parties' deviations both above and below that ever moving norm.

(b) The Difference Principle cannot, therefore, be derived from an absolute and universal equality of entitlement. Unfortunately for Rawls it is equally impossible to derive it from his specifications of 'the original position', directly. Having made some 'remarks' which, he thinks, show 'that the two principles are at least a plausible conception of justice', Rawls undertakes 'to argue for them more systematically'. The nerve of this systematic argument runs: 'There is an analogy between the two principles and the maximin rule for choice under uncertainty. . . . The maximin rule tells us to rank alternatives by their worst possible outcomes: we are to adopt the alternative the worst outcome of which is superior to the worst outcome of the others' (Rawls 1971, pp.152-3).

Suppose that the conditions stipulated do require that the hypothetical contracting parties follow 'the maximin rule'. Then, necessarily, they will strive to maximise the absolute welfare level of the least advantaged. But the Difference Principle is essentially concerned not with absolutes but with relativities. 'The maximin rule' does not demand, as the Difference Principle surely does, that we must never allow any advance above 'the benchmark of equality', save in so far as this advance is 'to the advantage of the least fortunate'. Maximin can tolerate, as the egalitarian Difference Principle cannot, that anyone may advance provided only that others are not thereby disadvantaged.

Note that 'disadvantaging' has here to be construed as actively making worse off, not as making worse off merely relatively, and without any actual alteration of condition. If, in however modest and innocuous a way, you or I improve our own homes, then everyone else whose home lacks that particular improvement must thereby become, relatively to us, disadvantaged. Yet the two of us have not necessarily done anything – and I take it that usually we have in fact done nothing – which actively causes anyone else to be worse off absolutely. It is entirely possible for the rest of the world to remain both ignorant of and altogether unaffected by such private D.I.Y. projects. Furthermore – though it is asking for trouble to utter such an unfashionable truth – quite often it both has been and is in this way, and in this way only, that in the wider world richer people and richer countries have made others relatively, but still not absolutely, worse off. (See, for fuller criticism of the main relevant sophism, Flew 1975, Chapter 3 and Section 6.24. Compare too Bauer 1976 and 1980.)

Nor is it even clear, returning to the Original Position, that the conditions thus stipulated do generate 'The maximin rule'. Rawls has, after all, insisted that 'a person in the original position' is not to know 'his conception of the good, the particulars of his rational plan of life, or even . . . his aversion to risk or liability to optimism or pessimism.' (Can there be, by the way, any legal system in the world which would allow such nescient zombies – we can scarcely rate them persons – to be minimally competent to make a contract?) When and whether someone follows a maximin rule surely says something about their 'aversion to risk' and their 'liability to optimism or pessimism'? Certainly this is not the universally and uniquely rational policy: I for one am not prepared to dismiss as irrational or even as necessarily imprudent all those millions of my fellow countrymen who allocate a weekly investment to a football pool, and then, with their eyes open, choose to bet against the longest odds in order to maximise the maximum.

This leads us to one of the oddest things about both the appeal to maximin in Rawls and the Difference Principle. He wants both these to be applied always, and without inquiry into the level of the minimum. But those solid, ordinary, and not irrational punters suggest by the relative modesty of the pools element in their regular budgets that up to some acceptable minimum standard of living they maximin; and then, but only then, maximax.

Again, *The Guardian* reported Prime Minister Edward Heath as saying: 'Most people would regard it as fair that the imaginative and energetic in our society should have higher rewards – providing always that the resources they created were used to bring effective help to those in real need' (30 March 1972). No doubt most people would. But what the Difference Principle says is different. For that lays it down that no one can justly become better off than others unless in so doing they 'contribute to the long-term expectations of the least fortunate groups in society';

and that quite regardless of the actual welfare levels of the people in those groups. The Rawls principle, unlike Heath's, would apply with the same force whether they are 'in real need' or whether they are in fact well off.

If the explanation of this curiosity which I suggest is correct, then it points to the most important but unstated assumption of the whole programme of what Rawls likes to call 'justice as fairness'. So why then is it that Rawls in his Difference Principle does not specify, with Heath, that those who create extra wealth, and by so doing better themselves, must from that addition make some contribution 'to those in real need'? Why does he instead prescribe that inequalities are licit only in so far as they improve 'the long-term expectations of the least fortunate group in society', whether or not all these people are 'in real need'? The prescription actually given forbids anyone to become better off, even if this is achieved with no help from nor harm to anyone else; save on condition that they transfer a cut of the extra to the least advantaged group – and no one is to ask any Victorian and properly compassionate questions about individual or family need. By what right does the least advantaged class thus become as such entitled to unconditional and permanent flows of tribute?

The answer, surely, has to be that it is because its members are equal sharers in what is all at bottom common property. It is also because – as will come out sharp and clear in later sections – Rawls seems always to be thinking of all (social) goods as actively distributed by some allocating authority. Such a distribution, of what is all at bottom common property, can only be a zero sum operation: if one person lacks something, then the reason is simply and solely that it has been allocated to someone else. So what an outsider might see as one person becoming better off at no one else's expense, looks from inside the world of 'justice as fairness' like that person being gratuitously given what might have been issued instead to another, and perhaps ought to have been. The entire argument in Rawls assumes that all the goods of every kind which have been, are, or will be produced or discovered within their to them unknown national territory, are now available, free of any prior claims, for distribution at the unprejudiced collective discretion of the contractors. These goods are all, as Aristotle said only of certain subclasses of goods, 'to be divided among those who have a share in the constitution'. (See also sections 4, iii and 5, below.)[11]

3 *What Rawls calls justice*

Although his title is *A Theory of Justice*, without prefix or suffix, Rawls from the very beginning indicates, without actually saying, that this is too broad a description of its actual scope: 'Our topic is that of social justice. For us the primary subject of justice is the basic structure of society, or more exactly, the way in which the major social institutions distribute fundamental rights and duties and determine the division of advantages from social cooperation' (*Ibid.*, p.7)

Some of the many ever eager to censure advertisers and advertising might well take note of this gaping discrepancy between what is promised on the package and what it is actually proposed to attempt inside. But for the rest of us there are two more urgent matters of concern. First, 'the primary subject of justice' is certainly not, historically speaking, what Rawls chooses as his own main interest. Second, Rawls neither asks the fundamental Socratic question 'What is justice?' nor tries to show how his social justice relates or fails to relate to those other kinds with which it is by the insertion of the adjective implicitly contrasted. He is, as he puts it later, happy 'to leave questions of meaning and definition aside and to get on with the task of developing a substantive theory of justice' (*Ibid.*, p.579).

(i) It would, nevertheless, clearly not do to maintain that 'the primary subject of justice is the basic structure of society' if this were to be understood as a claim about either the original or the primary applications of the word 'justice'. For any such appraisal of the basic structures of society is a pretty sophisticated activity. Our distant ancestors in closed societies must have spoken of people getting or not getting their just deserts or entitlements, long before anyone brought the basic structure of any society into question. Today too even those who later come to talk of social justice to the almost complete exclusion of any other first learn to apply words like 'just' and 'fair' in theoretically much less elevated contexts (Barry 1973, p.57; but compare and contrast Barry 1965, Chapter V and Barry 1971, p.110). When a parent gives one sister an orange it is, all would allow, only fair that the other sister also should be given an orange. In a good old-fashioned Western, justice is done when the villains are appropriately punished, the displaced farmers repossess their property, and the hero is rewarded by the love of a virtuous and pretty girl. If we think of such homely usages we shall not be surprised by the comment of a distinguished economic journalist: 'the Rawls theory contains very little "justice" in the sense in which the word is normally used' (Brittan 1975, p.24).

(a) It is to be remarked as some sort of feat that in a more than 600 page book, advertised as containing *A Theory of Justice*, Rawls manages never to quote nor to comment on that fine, once widely familiar legal maxim: *Honeste vivere, neminem laedere, suum cuique tribuere*, that is, To live honourably, to harm no one, to allow to each their own. Yet by our reminders of elementary and unsophisticated applications of the word 'just' we have readied ourselves to recognise that this lawyers' tag contains as good a definition as we are likely to get. *Suum cuique tribuere*: to do justice is to see to it that people have what they severally deserve, and what they are entitled to.

This is, substantially, the definition Polemarchus offered Socrates in Book I of *The Republic*; and what Plato's Socrates there, for inept and inadequate reasons, rejected. For, always assuming that our word is sufficiently equivalent to the Greek original, Polemarchus quoted the poet Simonides: 'That it is just . . . to render to each his due' (331E). This is rejected, on the inept ground that it will not provide a clearcut resolution of what should be seen as a puzzle case. (This ground is inept, because a faithful descriptive definition is necessarily equivalent in meaning to the term defined; and hence has to embrace whatever vagueness or confusion is to be found in that term.) In *The Republic* that first Polemarchan definition is soon replaced by an amended version: 'that justice is rendering to each what befits him' (332C). This version in its turn is rejected because, when conjoined with the unquestioned but false assumption that virtues are skills, it is found to generate paradoxes.

If the traditional definition referring to deserts and entitlements is correct, or even on the right lines, and it surely is, then it must be wrong for Robert Nozick, a younger Harvard colleague of Rawls, to present 'The Entitlement Theory' as no more than a rival conception of justice. Since, as we shall be seeing in Chapter IV, Rawls apparently does not believe in desert, and does not hold with any but collective entitlements; and since justice is essentially concerned with deserts and entitlements and at least in the first instance with those of individuals; we have to conclude that, of whatever else his 'justice as fairness' may be a theory, it is not justice (Nozick, p.150; and compare Matson, passim). It is even more preposterous to fault Nozick, as was done in one particularly apoplectic review, for being 'so certain of the relative superiority of entitlement-type justifications over end-state, patterned justifications that he tends to reject other theories of justice merely because they are patterned. Rawls, for instance, is taken to task because his theory is not in the form of an entitlement approach, though, of course, to construct an entitlement theory was never Rawls's intention' (Greenberg, p.60). If Rawls never intended to tell us what severally people deserve and are entitled to, then what he intended to develop was not, despite his own intentions to the contrary, a conception of justice.

(b) Rawls himself would, I think, be inclined to put down all such objections as so much verbalistic nagging: nagging which can only obstruct 'the task of developing a substantive theory of justice'. There must also be many others who, if persuaded that so splendid a thing as they take social justice to be is necessarily very different from justice, would conclude that that is just so much the worse for justice. It was, presumably, with such persons in mind that one contributor to *Economics and Equality* attacked, not the plain injustice but 'the *social* injustice of taxing what are, in reality, negative investment incomes in an inflationary age' (A. Jones, p.97: italics supplied).

Certainly Rawls regards all questions about justice in any other and more particular context as irrelevant:

> I am concerned with a special case of the problem of justice. . . . There is no reason to suppose ahead of time that the principles satisfactory for the basic structure hold for all cases. . . . They may be irrelevant for the various informal conventions and customs of everyday life; they may not elucidate the justice . . . of voluntary cooperative arrangements or procedures for making contractual agreements. . . . I shall be satisfied if it is possible to formulate a reasonable conception of justice for the basic structure of society conceived for the time being as a closed system isolated from other societies (Rawls 1971, pp. 7-8).

This will not do at all. For it is only and precisely in so far as there are strong analogies between justice in this 'special case' and justice in those other and perhaps humbler instances that social justice can genuinely be a kind of justice.

If it is not, then to commend its champions as by that token champions of justice would be as misguided as to accept some Radical apologist for Soviet or People's democracy as an authentic democrat. (Compare, for example, Macpherson 1977 and 1967.) The key words here do matter: these are not among those disputes about words which are, as they say, merely verbal. For the contested word 'justice' like the word 'democracy' carries associations and implications which the various disputants all want to have on their own sides.

Thus, to those who are in any way in the business of enforcing equality of outcome, it is extremely important to be able to see themselves, and be seen by others, as engaged in the hot pursuit of justice. For it is only and precisely in this perspective that their activities are legitimated, both in their own eyes, and in those of the rest of the world. The single key word 'justice' provides at one and the same time the answer to two crucial challenges.

First, why is equality to be received as a social good, perhaps the greatest? Second, however ideally excellent it may be, what right have you and your fellow equalisers to impose this ideal of yours by force upon reluctant equalisees? What right have you to call for, and then to introduce, taxes 'to bite more deeply and more fiercely', purely redistributive taxes designed solely to rob richer Peter in order to treat poorer Paul – sometimes even taxes designed simply to rob richer Peter without intended benefits to any poorer Pauls (Crosland, 1962, p.47)?

But now, given that equality is indeed justice, it just has to be good – perhaps in its area a greatest good: remember the manifesto! Given that equalisation is an imperative of justice, then this must be because those from whom it takes have no right to what is taken, while those to whom it gives have every right to what is given.

Wholly typical of such felt legitimation is a confession by the author of a recent contribution to the still new International Library of Welfare and Philosophy. A Lecturer in Politics at York, he insists that the prime purpose of social policy ought to be the enforcement of equality (rather than, say, the maintenance of a minimum). To warrant this commitment he sketches a Rawlsian account of (social) justice as (a qualified) equality. He then announces that one 'reason for linking equality and justice is that within the theory of justice one can provide the necessary moral premises for adopting the principle of equal welfare as a prescriptive recommendation' (Weale, p.32)!

Rawls himself, as has been shown already, has an almost contemptuous insensitivity to the need to show that 'justice as fairness' is genuinely a kind of justice. This makes him instructively different from the Plato of *The Republic*; a work which must surely be rated the first philosophical treatise on social justice, as presently understood. For, however unsatisfactory his efforts may be, Plato does realise that he has to try to show that justice 'writ large' in the institutions of his ideal Kallipolis is the same as justice 'writ small' in the individual (441Cff; and compare 368D-369A. On the question of Plato's success or failure in this attempt see, for instance, Sachs and also Popper 1965, Vol. I Chapter 6).

Certainly the author of *The Republic* was the first precursor of Rawls. For there – admittedly after some preliminary skirmishings around 'questions of meaning and definition' in Book I – Plato gets down to 'the task of developing a substantive theory of justice.' This he too construes as a matter of telling us how 'major social institutions' ought to 'distribute fundamental rights and duties and determine the division of advantages from social cooperation.' Of course Plato's doctrine is no sort of egalitarianism, however qualified. On the other hand he not only does in fact articulate, he is also fully conscious and proud of articulating, the legitimating ideology of a new class; or, in actual effect though not in his intention, a new caste. After long and rigorous training in the hard science of dialectics the Guardian élite, endowed now with absolute power, are to make and maintain a new order, forgetting and falsifying its past: 'They will take the city and characters of men, as they might take a tablet, and first wipe it clean – no easy task . . . this would be their first point of difference from ordinary reformers, that they would refuse to take in hand either individual or state or to legislate before they either received a clean slate or themselves made it clean' (501A).

4 Plenipotentiaries with a clean slate

Wiping it clean would indeed be, at least for the socially engineered, 'no easy task'. For it appears that Plato's Guardian party was to consist of spiritual ancestors of Pol Pot and the Khmer Rouge: '"All the people in the city who are more than ten years old", Socrates said, "they will send out into the fields; and, getting hold of the children outside the set ways maintained by their parents, they will bring them up in their own customs and laws – which will be as we have already described"' (540E-541A). Of course Rawls would be horrified by such monstrous Radicalism in practice. But he does insist upon a clean slate in his theorising; and, although he seems not to realise this, his own ideal of 'justice as fairness' could not be realised except through the working of an enormously powerful and extensive state machine. His Difference Principle, or indeed any other principle determining an imposed pattern of distribution, must be in practice incompatible with the Priority of Liberty.

(i) The slate has to be clean as regards both the persons who are to be recipients in the ideal distribution and the goods which are to be distributed. I have already quoted the statement which Rawls provides of his primary reason for insisting upon this in the case of the beneficiaries. It is one which will bear repetition: 'Once we decide to look for a conception of justice that nullifies the accidents of natural endowment and the contingencies of social circumstance as counters in the quest for political and economic advantage, we are led to these principles. They express the result of leaving aside those aspects of the social world that seem arbitrary from a moral point of view.'

This statement ought to take the reader's breath away. It constitutes decisive reason for saying that whatever Rawls was producing, and whatever the merits of his product, it cannot be a theory of justice. For deserts and entitlements, which are what justice is about, have to be grounded in some sort of fact or facts about the persons who deserve and are entitled. That this is true of deserts is too obvious to require support, while that it holds also of rights has been explained and argued in the previous Chapter II (2, ii, c). Any and all deserts and entitlements not general and common to the whole human race must be grounded in precisely those particular accidents and contingencies which Rawls is so quick to discount as morally irrelevant.

Consider again the distribution of treats to daughters, and the justice very satisfactorily done to all at the end of the old-fashioned Western. If I choose to give a treat to one daughter, then – save in special countervailing circumstances – fairness if not justice requires that I give the same or some equivalent to the other. But neither fairness nor justice demands, supposing always that I want to provide treats, that I must provide these for everyone else as well: these two have claims on me because they are my daughters, claims which no one else has. Then in the Western: the unjustly dispossessed farmers must get their land back, for they have claims on those lots which no one else has – claims which presumably they acquired in some just way, most likely by fair exchange for something else which was in turn justly theirs. It cannot be just to seize all their lands without compensation in order to make a new distribution, even if it would perhaps be in some way fairer or better. The various good or ill deserts of the other several characters must all be similarly grounded upon accidents and contingencies; namely, the contingent facts about what they did or failed to do. All such particular and essentially backward-looking claims about entitlement and desert are in the broadest sense moral and as such, perhaps inherently, disputatious. Yet anyone who proposes systematically and at a stroke to devalue the lot, in the interests of a new strictly forward-looking distribution, is by this move abandoning the whole notion of justice in favour of another, alternative ideal.

The Rawls slate also has to be clean in the case of the goods which are to be distributed. Notwithstanding that he makes no explicit stipulation to this effect, the entire contractual project tacitly presupposes that all goods, whether tangible or intangible, whether produced or discovered already or whether to be produced or discovered in the future, are the common collective property of the hypothetical contracting parties. Unless this is the case, by what right are they undertaking to decide how best to distribute or redistribute these goods; and exclusively among themselves, at that?

With characteristic gaiety Nozick has made much, and rightly: both of the observation that the conditions of his thought-experiment commit Rawls to treating all goods as if they 'fell from heaven like manna'; and of the objection that in the real world most goods have in some way to be produced, and are for this or other reasons subject to antecedent claims. 'Things,' he says, 'come into the world already attached to people having entitlements over them' (Nozick, pp.198 and 160). The force of these criticisms is felt still more strongly when we recall that the goods to be distributed or redistributed at the unfettered discretion of our social contractors apparently include not only cash and consumer durables, but also services of every kind. Yet services, typically, are in the most intimate way linked with the people who provide them: they are most often actions which those people perform.

Too little has been made so far of the fact that Rawls limits himself to social justice within a single society: 'I shall be satisfied if it is possible to formulate a reasonable conception of justice for the basic structure of society conceived for the time being as a closed system isolated from other societies' (Rawls 1971, p.8). At first blush this restriction seems sensible. If it is going to take 600 or more pages 'to formulate a reasonable conception of justice for the basic structure' of one isolated society, then what chance could there be of ever completing the corresponding job assignment for a whole United Nations?

Such humility is, nevertheless, unfortunate. For this confinement – 'Social justice in one country!' – tends to conceal a vital assumption. Rawls from the start takes it that the unknown country which the contractors are to inhabit is theirs, and that whatever natural and artificial resources it may contain are theirs to exploit rent free. Some warrant is required for this: ' . . . it is not only persons favouring *private* property who need a theory of how property rights legitimately originate. . . . Those believing in collective property, for example those believing that a group of persons living in an area jointly own the territory, or its mineral resources, also must provide a theory of how such property rights arise. . . . ' (Nozick, p.178: italics original).

(ii) Similar 'clean slate' assumptions are demanded by, yet must at the same time vitiate, other attempts to support the ideal of (qualified) equality of outcome. Many appeal, for example, to Berlin's argument for a rational presumption in favour of equal distribution: 'If I have a cake, and there are ten persons among whom I wish to divide it, then if I give exactly one tenth to each, this will not, at any rate automatically, call for justification; whereas if I depart from this principle of equal division I am expected to produce a special reason' (Berlin 1956, p.305). This pronouncement is the foundation stone of 'The Case For Greater Equality' in Atkinson. This case is in fact more extensive than Joseph and Sumption allow; yet not, as will emerge, much better. (Compare their p.48 with his pp.79 ff.)

Atkinson, after the excursus into aesthetics mentioned earlier, quotes this pronouncement by Berlin. Atkinson then infers immediately: 'If this basic principle be accepted, the case *against* measures to bring about greater equality in the distribution of wealth must be made on the grounds that existing inequalities can be justified according to what are considered relevant principles'

(Atkinson, p.80). This move turns the tables on the opposition very smartly, insisting that the whole burden of proof must rest on anyone having the effrontery to obstruct Atkinson and his fellow Procrusteans. Yet why do people have to submit reasons satisfactory to Atkinson before they can be permitted to continue holding whatever they happen not unjustly to have acquired? 'Why is equality the rest (or rectilinear motion) position of the system, deviation from which may only be caused by moral forces?' (Nozick, p.223).

Berlin's pronouncement, so often quoted or mentioned, does not even begin to constitute an answer. Certainly it expresses a principle which 'might be important if some benefactor of the human race were to wake up one morning with his pockets stuffed full of money which he wished to distribute so as to produce a maximum of enjoyment, but it has very little relation to the state of the world as we know it' (Stephen, p.191).

By all means let us allow that, in default of any reasons for giving any one of his chosen recipients more than he gives to any other, it is indeed wholly reasonable for Berlin to portion out his gift cake equally among all the ten; just as, in default of any reason for thinking one of a series of alternatives more probable than any other, it is reasonable to assume them all to be equiprobable. But this is worlds away from what Atkinson wants, and believes that he has got. For he is not seeking guidance on how to divide up and distribute cakes which he is proposing himself first to bake and then to give away. Instead he wants, no doubt with a little help from his friends, to institute or extend a general and compulsory shareout of all cakes – cakes nearly if not quite all of which were of other people's baking.

Or rather – and here 'the dirty little secret' has to be uttered – what it is to be presumed that Atkinson himself wants, and what his political associates are most eager to do, is to impose and maintain confiscatory capital taxes through which what they see as offensive excesses in personal fortunes are transferred not to other less prosperous individuals, but to the state (Kristol, p.224). For, except where an improvident Chancellor spends the proceeds as income, this is precisely what is achieved by Estate Duties, Capital Transfer, and Capital Gains Taxes; which last, of course, unless indexed for inflation tend to become egregiously arbitrary and erratic Wealth Taxes. If genuine redistribution among individuals is what you want, then you have to go for a Lifetime

Capital Receipts (or Accessions) Tax; a proposal which has always, understandably, been turned down flat by British socialists (A. Jones, p.109; and indeed compare Atkinson himself, pp.184-91). The same significant hostility to any increase in private holdings, even among those at present innocent of any stock of capital, is seen in the unrelenting opposition of the socialists to sales both of council houses even to their sitting tenants and of shares in nationalised industries even to those employed in those industries.

To obtain the desired presumptions, whether in favour of an equal redistribution of present holdings or of their transfer to the state, Atkinson would need to strengthen Berlin's example by introducing something like those clean slate assumptions for which already Rawls has been taken to task. Yet whatever arguments anyone might excogitate for saying, both that all goods of every kind produced or to be produced or discovered within the national territories must be in the last analysis parts of the collectively owned national cake, and that there is nothing that anyone could do or suffer or be which could justicise their possession of holdings substantially above the average; there is, surely, no hope of putting forward either these claims themselves, or anything immediately inferred from them, as self-evident and inescapable principles of reason.

(iii) The suggestion, if not the assumption, that the distribution of all (social) goods is, or ought to be, an activity consciously executed by one or several public or semi-public organisations is found in Rawls from the very beginning. This has, of course, been one reason for the instant strong appeal of his book to so many of those who believe that 'there is a rational system of social justice which it is the business of the state to enforce' and that 'the state should determine everyone's rewards according to some system of fairness, and should determine prices accordingly' (Vaizey, p.566 – quoted already in Chapter II, 5, ii, b, above).[12] Nevertheless Rawls himself has been slow and reluctant to recognise the socialist presuppositions and implications of his own project of social justice: he appears genuinely to be dedicated to 'the priority of liberty'.

The suggestion of an active central distribution of goods is there in Chapter I, in his own definition of 'social justice'. This is, Rawls says, concerned with 'the basic structure of society, or more exactly, the way in which *the major social institutions distribute fundamental rights and duties and determine the division of advantages from social cooperation.* .... The justice of a social scheme depends on how fundamental rights and duties are *assigned*' (Rawls 1971, p.7: italics supplied). As he begins, so he continues: 'For simplicity, assume that the chief primary goods *at the disposition of society* are rights and liberties, powers and opportunities, income and wealth. .... All social values – liberty and opportunity, income and wealth, and the bases of self-respect *– are to be distributed equally* unless an unequal distribution ... is to everyone's advantage (*Ibid.*, p.62: italics supplied).

Rawls is thus talking as if people always and everywhere are or ought to be the passive creatures of active social institutions, with all goods of whatever kind doled out as unearned benefits to inert recipients. The same unfortunate sociological mode of speech reinforces his tendency to assume that all the goods which are or might be achieved by the individuals or the groups in any society must be products of everyone's cooperation in that society. (I suspect that that is a large part of what he has in mind when he characterises goods as social – 'social' being here exclusively opposed to 'natural'.) But this ignores the anti-collectivist objection that individuals and groups often achieve for themselves advantages upon which other members of their societies have no proper claims at all.

Certainly, to the extent that any society is in the ideal condition which Adam Smith called 'the natural system of perfect liberty and justice' or 'the obvious and simple system of natural liberty' (Smith, IV (vii) Part 3, and IV (ix)), we have to say that its members 'are not in the position of children who have been given portions of pie by someone who now makes last minute adjustments to rectify careless cutting. There is no *central* distribution, no person or group entitled to control all the resources, jointly deciding how they are to be doled out. .... There is no more a distributing or distribution of shares than there is a distributing of mates in a society in which persons choose whom they shall marry' (Nozick, pp.149-50: italics original). By contrast the whole project of social justice, requiring and determining a proposed ideal pattern of relativities, leads necessarily to some central control of distribution. For who or what other than the state – advised no doubt by innumerable quangos of wage-and-price-controlling Galbraiths – is to decide which and how great are the inequalities satisfying the Difference Principle; and to enforce, or try to enforce, their decisions?[13]

It is true – notwithstanding the fact that his original position tacitly assumes total collective ownership – that Rawls believes his 'justice as fairness' can be neutral on the issue of socialism: 'the means of production may or may not be privately owned' (Rawls 1971, p.66). In his discussion of the four branches of government, 'the transfer branch' reallocates only a part of privately held income in order to provide a prescribed minimum for all, while 'the distributive branch' does specifically permit private property (*Ibid.*, pp.274-84). Nevertheless, the overall conception Rawls has – and which, as a spokesman for social justice, he has to have – is that of a central agency with unlimited power to allocate and reallocate, constrained only by that agency's interpretation of his principles of what he calls justice.

Plato the precursor anticipated and, however inadequately, tried to answer the question of how an élite of omnipotent Guardians is to be kept from exploiting those subjected to it (412B-417B). He would, I think, have been neither surprised nor shocked to hear Aaron Director's Law of Public Income Redistribution: 'Any government will redistribute resources to benefit whatever group can take command of its machinery.' But Rawls seems not to feel any anxieties about maintaining 'the priority of liberty' under the proposed redistributive state of social justice. More than a century before the Difference Principle was first formulated, John Stuart Mill in his *Political Economy* left a rod in pickle for it: 'A fixed rule, like that of equality, might be acquiesced in, and so might chance, or an external necessity; but that a handful of human beings should weigh everybody in the balance, and give more to one and less to another at their sole pleasure and judgement, would not be borne unless from persons believed to be more than men, and backed by supernatural terrors' (I (ii) 4).

5 *Further considerations on what Rawls calls justice*

Early in his book Rawls provides a too hasty sketch of a distinction between 'the concept of justice', which should be comparatively undisputatious, and rival 'conceptions of justice', which most emphatically are not (Rawls 1971, p.5). This useful and needed distinction can be made a little more precise by contemplating, as an example, chastity. The concept of chastity is in effect the meaning of the word, as this might be defined in an impartial dictionary: chastity, it might say, is sexual purity. Yet among

people who all give the word this same meaning there might still be
several different conceptions of what true chastity is. Some might
say that it consists in abstention from illicit sexual activity (maybe
with some internal disagreements as to which activities are licit
and which illicit); others might insist that only complete sexual
abstinence scores as the real thing; while still others, yet more
rigorous, could hold that perfect chastity demands also the
absence of any private lustful thoughts.

Suppose that someone were to publish a book with the
ambitious title *A Theory of Chastity*, in which he explained that he
was going to confine himself to social chastity, and that his
conception of this lay in two principles: first, that in the chaste
society no one owns more goods than are necessary to support life;
and, second, that all subordinates yield unquestioning obedience
to their superiors. Then we should have to say that, admirable
though this scheme might be, it does not articulate a conception of
chastity. There are simply no logically necessary connections
between poverty and obedience on the one hand and chastity on
the other (Matson, pp.45-50).

Section 3, above, has already argued that the concept of justice
refers to people getting and having whatever is their due, what they
severally deserve or to which they are otherwise entitled. Yet
Rawls does not really want to say that people either deserve or are
entitled to those goods which would be assigned to them in
accordance with his two principles of justice. Admittedly he does
in his statement of the first of these lapse by saying that 'each
person is to have an equal *right* to the most extensive basic liberty
compatible with a similar liberty for others' (Rawls 1971, p.60:
italics supplied). But, as we shall be discovering in Chapter IV, his
official view is that no individual deserves anything; while the
possibility of unearned and undeserved entitlement is not even
entertained. So what Rawls offers can scarcely rate as a conception
of justice.

To this someone might respond that Rawls undertook to treat
social justice, rather than justice to individuals: and 'institutions
are just when no arbitrary distinctions are made between persons
in the assigning of basic rights and duties and when the rules
determine a proper balance between competing claims to the
advantages of social life' (*Ibid.*, p.5). But, if that is what social
justice is, or what by prescription it is to be for Rawls, then it just is
not justice in the ordinary and primary sense of the word. In that

ordinary sense social institutions are just, or unjust, to the extent that they make for, or make against, people getting and keeping their individually just deserts and entitlements. To label a book about social justice, as construed by Rawls, *A Theory of Justice*, is like calling a treatise on Bombay duck simply *Ducks*.

This sounds a somewhat bold contention; though a Nobel Laureate recently recorded that, after ten years of trying 'to discover the meaning of what is called "social justice"', he had concluded that, 'with reference to a society of free men, the phrase has no meaning whatsoever' (Hayek 1978, p.57). Perhaps the most persuasive way of providing further support for this audacity will be to deploy a miscellany of instances in which *aficionados* of 'equality and social justice' suggest that they are not themselves securely and constantly convinced that this really is a kind of justice.

First, it cannot be too often emphasised that these enthusiasts are rarely, if ever, willing to unload their own individual excesses until so compelled by law. As W.C. Runciman – one of them – said in his review of *Unequal Shares* in *The Listener*: 'there is no more reason to expect the lucky inheritors of fortunes to give them away than to expect left-wing intellectuals voluntarily to reduce their standard of living to that of Upper Volta or Bangladesh' (14 December 1972, p.835). Yet, if these inheritances really were unjust, then this is precisely what we ought to expect – at least in the prescriptive if not the descriptive sense of 'expect' (Flew 1975, Sections 5.9 and 6.11). Are such people, as has been nastily suggested, really unwilling to act on their own moral principles until others have been legally prevented from acting on theirs (Acton, p.72)? My own more charitable explanation, suggested first in Chapter II (5, ii, a), is that they have at least half realised that, since those excesses were honestly acquired and are in no sense stolen goods, the prescriptions of their egalitarian ideals are, whatever else they may be, not the dictates of justice.

Second, in Britain one of the two parties of government is forever issuing pamphlets with titles like *Equality: Labour's Policy for Social Justice*. Yet typically the opponents of these policies are abused for lacking, not justice, but compassion. So what such terrible hard persons are refusing to support would, after all, appear to be a kind of compulsory public charity, not justice. Nor, of course, are the great majority of those so accused in fact opposed to the maintenance of a welfare safety net to sustain the unfortunates who would otherwise be in real need. The true position of the accused is regularly misrepresented, for what is the usual reason: the misrepresenters, being at a loss to refute the truth, prefer what is for them the easier alternative of misrepresentation.

A third, and slightly more philosophical point is suggested by the slogan 'justice as fairness'. The two terms are close relatives and there is a tendency for 'fair' to replace 'just' in much colloquial speech. But fairness and justice are not exactly the same thing. 'A lottery is fair', for instance, 'if honestly run, but a lottery which distributed prizes *justly*, i.e. according to desert or need, would no longer be fair' (Barry 1967, p.193: italics original). The writer, himself a socialist, here sails dangerously near to the truth, being saved only by the insertion of the word 'need' in place of 'entitlement'.

The crucial difference is that fairness, but not justice, applies to distributions where there are no various antecedent claims. If none of the children at a party had done anything in particular to deserve any cake at all, and none has any other special prior claim, it would be a solecism to complain of injustice if one is given a larger piece than another; although this distribution certainly would be unfair. It is significant that this is the case which Rawls treats as the paradigm of 'pure procedural justice' (Rawls 1971, p.85); for in truth it is precisely not the paradigm but the degenerate case. Fairness is the moral principle which takes over when considerations of desert and entitlement either do not or cannot arise. 'And fairness, unlike justice, does (in general) demand equality' (Matson, p.54). It is again significant that those who want equality do most often demand not just but fair shares.[14]

Fourth, last, and surely most impressive, is the fact that Rawls himself offers *A Theory of Justice* as an alternative, not to a utilitarian account of justice in particular, but to utilitarianism as a whole. 'During much of modern moral philosophy,' he says, 'the predominant systematic theory has been some form of utilitarianism.' What previous anti-utilitarians have all failed to do is 'to construct a workable and systematic moral conception to oppose it' (Rawls 1971, pp.vii and viii).

Suppose that we refer to our cherished copies of J.S. Mill's classic statement of classical *Utilitarianism*. We find that he makes it clear from his very first paragraph that he is concerned with the whole of morality: 'the question concerning the *summum bonum*, or what is the same thing, concerning the foundation of morality' (Mill, p.1). The more particular subject of justice is reached only in the final Chapter V 'Of the Connection between Justice and Utility'. The great problem here for Mill, as for any would-be utilitarian, is how to square a general doctrine concerned only about maximisation of a total with a kind of claim which essentially refers to allocation to particular sorts of individuals and groups.

As a contribution to the resolution of that problem the chapter is unremarkable. But there are at least three points for us to notice. First, as Roland Hall tells me, it contains the earliest application of the adjective 'social' to the noun 'justice' so far recorded by the compilers of the *Oxford English Dictionary*: the 'duty to do to each according to his deserts', treating 'all equally well (when no higher duty forbids) who have deserved equally well . . . is the highest abstract standard of social and distributive justice. . . . ' (*Ibid.*, pp.57-8). Second, it contains a lot of that logical geographising which Rawls eschews in favour of the more splendid 'task of developing a substantive theory of justice'. Third, Mill repeatedly presses the claims of utility as a standard by reference to which otherwise intractable disputes about justice might be resolved. Such greater ease and decisiveness of resolution may or may not be a good reason for pursuing utility rather than justice. But it certainly is not, what Mill at one point actually urges that it is, either a reason for saying that the two ideals are really the same, or a reason for saying that the one is an interpretation of the other. Having contended that justice in fact promotes, and is to be justified by reference to, 'general utility', Mill proceeds to argue that 'if justice be totally independent of utility, and be a standard *per se* . . . it is hard to understand why that internal oracle is so ambiguous . . . ' (*Ibid.*, pp.50-1). It would be equally wrong to argue from the confused and contested character of everyday notions of justice to the conclusion that the supposedly clearer and more decisive conceptions either of equality of outcome or of 'justice as fairness' must be identified with justice as ordinarily understood.

Rawls, however, does not engage with this or any other utilitarian treatment of justice. By instead offering his 'justice as fairness' as an alternative to utilitarian accounts of all morality he in effect confesses that what he calls justice is something quite other than traditional, old-time, without-prefix-or-suffix, justice.

Also, although this is not an issue for us to pursue here, he thereby presents an understanding of what essentially morality is about which to the wise and good of former times would surely have seemed bizarre: 'it is the relative goodness or badness of people's lives that forms the kernel of moral or ethical thinking in general' (Ericsson, p.11; and contrast Brittan 1975, pp.28-9).

CHAPTER IV

Who are the Equals?

I'm just average, common too
I'm just like him, the same as you,
I'm everybody's brother and son,
I ain't no different from anyone.
Ain't no use to talk to me,
It's just the same as talking to you.
Bob Dylan: 'I shall be free No. 10'

The chief aim of the previous Chapter III was to challenge a now common identification of justice with equality, albeit sometimes a more or less drastically qualified equality. We stressed the point that, in any traditional understanding, justice is essentially backward-looking. It is, that is to say, concerned with securing those deserts and those entitlements with which people are held to be antecedently endowed. It thus becomes a matter of what is due to them in virtue of what they are or are not, and of what they have done or not done.

The present Chapter IV aims to discover what is, whether logically or in other weaker ways, presupposed about the nature of man by the comparatively new ideal of equality of outcome or equality of condition. Or, rather, the main concern will be significantly more particular. For, more precisely, this main concern is to try to discover assumptions about the nature of man presupposed by this ideal, or by these ideals, when it, or they, are presented – as nowadays they almost always in fact are presented – as imperatives of justice; or, at any rate, of social justice.

Equality of condition may of course be pursued as a limited ideal, with scant pretensions to moral universality. As we noted in Chapter II it may be in reality, whether more or less frankly, a matter of equality for those who are to be equalised but not for those who hope to do the equalising. This must be true of the very unequal egalitarians who nowadays flourish in the plush pastures both of Whitehall and of Washington, as well as of those who in other countries control ruling Marxist-Leninist parties. And certainly it is far too rarely recognised that all those whose living lies in the public sector, and in particular the public welfare sector, are in their demands for the equality of universal, compulsory and monopolistic state services pursuing their own particular sectional interest.

In a recent article on 'Equalizing Education: In Whose Benefit?' the future US Senator D.P. Moynihan did well to insist: 'We don't presume disinterestedness on the part of persons whose interests reside in the growth and prosperity of the private sector of the economy. Why should those whose interests reside in the public sector be treated differently?' (Moynihan, p.76). Even as I was writing this paragraph I happened to hear a radio report on the attempt by COHSE (The Confederation of Health Service Employees) to persuade the 1978 Trades Union Congress in Blackpool to censure the electricians' and plumbers' union EETPU for negotiating private medical services for some of its members. COHSE, like the Union of Postal Workers and others, has and clearly recognises its interest in state monopoly provision. This is what makes possible the extortion of a high monopoly price for a poor monopoly service. It is, as the most formidable of our political thinkers once said, easy to recognise 'the benefit that proceedeth from such darkness, and to whom it accrueth' (Hobbes, IV, xlvii).

Such limited and non-moral ideas and ideals of equality of outcome appear to lack any interesting or formally deducible presuppositions. Perhaps the most to be said is that they would lose much if not all of their point if it were not the case that inequalities would in fact emerge wherever the equalisers relaxed their efforts. This is the same kind of presupposition as supports the first of the three ideals distinguished in Chapter II: 'If individual diversity were not the universal rule, then the argument for liberty would be weak indeed. For if individuals were as interchangeable as ants, why should anyone worry about maximising the opportunity for every person to develop . . . to the fullest extent possible?' (Rothbard, pp.x-xi).

Things begin to hot up only when the claim is made that an universal (even if qualified) equality of condition is, in a Kantian sense, categorically imperative; and, in particular, that this is the mandate of justice. Traditionally – the point has already been laboured in Chapter III – justice demands that everyone should have their own, their due; *suum cuique tribuere.* This very definition suggests (though it does not by itself entail) that what is due to different people must be different. However, whereas the definition of the word 'justice' is a scarcely controversial derivative of the correct usage and established meaning of that term, what any particular person does or does not deserve (or is or is not entitled to) remains a substantive moral issue, and perhaps as such inherently disputatious.

Again, what facts about a person we ought to recognise as giving rise to his own particular deserts and entitlements must, by the same token, be a controversial moral question. But that all deserts and entitlements have to be grounded in some facts about the people so endowed is a truth which follows logically from the conceptions of 'deserts' and 'entitlements' themselves. (This point, also, was made in Chapter III.) The consequence is that, if people are indeed equal in their deserts and entitlements, then they must also be, in whatever are allowed to be the relevant respects, equal in fact.

But now, the characteristics in respect of which we can be quite sure that all human beings are equal must be precisely and only those characteristics that define us as human beings. So anyone who wants to derive a fundamental equality of desert and entitlement from the moral notion of justice must be committed to dismissing all our individual and differentiating characteristics as morally irrelevant. That this revolutionary move both has to be made and is made, and what it involves, will become clearer as we engage with two leading spokesmen.

1 *'As interchangeable as ants': John Rawls*

There is in Rawls, as was noticed in the final section of Chapter III, at least a reluctance to state outright that people deserve or are entitled to all and only those (social) goods which would be assigned to them under 'the two principles of justice'. This is, as was also hinted in the same section, a consequence of construing 'justice as fairness', rather than as justice. Although consciously perhaps they were not, these principles might well have been designed for the guidance of anonymous collectives of assigners – assigners owing nothing to the equally faceless assignees. *A*

Theory of Justice 'will be for a long time to come the central work in moral philsophy for those belonging to the clerisy of power. It is tailor-made for the needs of those for whom egalitarianism and central power are but two sides of the same coin' (Nisbet 1975, p.215).

Be all this as it may, to the extent that Rawls really does want to hold that equal assignments are just, he becomes committed to maintaining that the grounds for these equal entitlements lie somewhere in the defining characteristics necessarily shared by all people simply as people; or perhaps, and at most, in these plus whatever else those who happen to be members of the single society of his thought-experiment do as a matter of fact have in common. (A corollary is that, if the Difference Principle is to be indeed a principle of pure justice, then there also have to be appropriate grounds in the natures and histories of all the people concerned for all the licensed inequalities.)

Given the main theorem, therefore (and neglecting the corollary), it is no accident that – in already twice-quoted words – Rawls maintains: 'Once we decide to look for a conception of justice that nullifies the accidents of natural endowment and the contingencies of social circumstance as counters in the quest for political and economic advantage, we are led to these principles. They express the result of leaving aside those aspects of the social world that seem arbitrary from a moral point of view' (Rawls 1971, p.15).

That they are in truth 'arbitrary from a moral point of view' Rawls argues on two grounds: first, that these natural endowments are not themselves deserved; and, second, that, in consequence, what they make possible cannot be either itself deserved or a proper basis of desert. The more fundamental notion that anyone might be entitled, or have a moral right, to anything which they had neither earned nor deserved is not entertained at all. As Rawls sees it, the crux is that 'the natural distribution of abilities and talents' is the (morally arbitrary) outcome of a 'natural lottery'. And, furthermore: 'Even the willingness to make an effort, to try, and so to be deserving in the ordinary sense is itself dependent upon happy family and social circumstances' (*Ibid.*, p.74).

Notice that he is not saying, what no one should dispute, that natural endowments are neither deserved nor undeserved; that the notion of desert does not apply. His is a much stronger claim, carrying an important practical implication: it is a matter of 'principle that undeserved inequalities call for redress; and since inequalities of birth and natural endowment are undeserved, these inequalities are to be somehow compensated for' (*Ibid.*, p.100).[15] So he takes it from there: 'We see then that the difference principle represents, in effect, an agreement to regard the distribution of natural talents as a common asset and to share in the benefits of this distribution whatever it turns out to be. Those who have been favored by nature, whoever they are, may gain from their good fortune only on terms that improve the situation of those who have lost out' (*Ibid.*, p.101). Or, in other words, 'The two principles are equivalent... to an undertaking to regard the distribution of natural abilities as a collective asset, so that the more fortunate are to benefit only in ways that help those who have lost out' (*Ibid.*, p.179: a comma supplied).

(i) Before examining arguments offered to support this conclusion, let us spell out two disturbing wider consequences.

(a) Early in Chapter II Christopher Jencks was quoted as saying: 'Most educators and laymen evidently feel that an individual's genes are his, and that they entitle him to whatever advantages he can get from them.... For a thoroughgoing egalitarian, however, inequality that derives from biology ought to be as repulsive as inequality that derives from early socialisation' (1, i, a). Presumably any such 'thoroughgoing egalitarian' would urge that all the members of future generations ought ideally to be genetically identical offspring of single, big-batch clonings. Rawls is much less radical: 'No one deserves his greater natural capacity nor merits a more favorable starting place in society. But it does not follow that one should eliminate these distinctions. There is another way to deal with them. The basic structure can be so arranged so that these contingencies work for the good of the least fortunate' (Rawls 1971, p.102).

Although his is a much less revolutionary proposal than that of the 'thoroughgoing egalitarian', it does nevertheless have more drastic implications than any drawn out by Rawls himself. Since both his arguments and his conclusion refer without discrimination to all natural differentiating characteristics, he has no business to limit the application of the Difference Principle to some of these and not others. For example: consider for a moment those natural characteristics – whatever they may be – which constitute sex-appeal, or which make it possible. No one could deny either that these are distributed very unequally indeed or that they can have a great impact upon the quality of life. Both this inequality of distribution and one of its indirect effects can be seen in the phenomenon of the often spectacular upward social mobility of the pretty (Rothbard, p.104): a cue, this, for our ancients to retell tales of the glamour girls of the old Gaiety Theatre! The same massive inequality is seen in the all too familiar fact that some lucky lads can, and do, bed almost every woman they want; whereas others less fortunate cannot, and do not. It is, therefore, perfectly clear that it behoves Rawls, and everyone else accepting the same principles, to develop policies for – to interpret the words in a fresh way – sex equality: ' . . . since inequalities of birth and natural endowment are undeserved, these inequalities are to be somehow compensated for.'

What these policies might be I hesitate to suggest. For I fear, even if I say no more, that I shall be accused of frivolous carping; a shameful display perhaps of that reactionary 'malevolence' which, notoriously, characterises opponents of the most fashionable egalitarianism (Halsey 1977, p.8). But Rawls could – indeed should – consult some Classical sources here. Herodotus, for instance, tells of one custom – 'the wisest in my judgement' – shared by the Babylonians and the Illyrian tribe of the Eneti. Each year in every village all the girls of marriageable age were auctioned off to the peer-group males, the high prices paid for the pretty being employed to furnish compensatory marriage-portions for the plain (*History*, I 196). Again, Aristophanes puts into the mouth of the Woman Power militant Praxagora a very comprehensive egalitarian scheme. This sister starts by urging a radical redistribution of wealth and income, conventionally construed; but she soon swings into a new sexual politics, legislating parallel arrangements for both male and female: 'The drabber and scruffier girls will sit down beside the stunners, so that if a man wants a bit of that he will have first to knock up one of the other lot'; while – ensuring equality between the sexes as well as among the sex – 'Poorer male specimens will escort handsome men as they go out to dinner, and keep them under surveillance in public areas so that it is impossible for the women to go to bed with the handsome before they have first granted their favours to the weedy little fellows' (*Ecclesiazusae*, 611-12 and 626-9).

I must insist that the questions which I am raising, even though light-heartedly expressed, are wholly serious. If Rawls does not want such Herodotean or Aristophanic conclusions to be drawn from his prescription of 'justice as fairness', then it is up to him to

show why they do not follow. Certainly nothing in what he has at
such great length told us about his principles justifies a prim
reluctance to investigate their proper application in this most
important area.

(b) Rawls from the beginning wants 'justice as fairness' to be
assessed as an alternative to utilitarianism. He urges that the fatal
weakness of any utilitarianism is that it must concentrate on the
maximisation of the total of whatever it takes to be good, attending
to questions of who gets what only in so far as they happen to bear
on that maximisation. Rawls complains, and it is fair comment:
'Utilitarianism does not take seriously the distinction between
persons' (Rawls 1971, p.27). He is also much concerned with the
importance of self-respect: 'On several occasions I have mentioned
that perhaps the most important primary good is self-respect'
(*Ibid,.* p.440). Again, I am myself not merely content but eager to
concur.

But then it has at once to be objected that it is grotesque for this
criticism to be put, and for this stand to be taken, by someone who
is at the same time summoning us both 'to regard the distribution
of natural abilities as a collective asset' and to dismiss 'the
accidents of natural endowment and the contingencies of social
circumstance' as irrelevant and arbitrary 'from a moral point of
view'. For these two summonses carry, surely, two implications.
First, we are indeed 'from a moral point of view' and in the present
context 'as interchangeable as ants'. Second, and consequently,
nothing which could distinguish any one individual from any other
– including even their own conduct – is truly either part of them or
theirs. So where is anyone to find any true and relevant basis for
self-respect?

In one vital way this last concept resembles those of deserts,
rights, and entitlements: self-respect, deserts, rights, and entitlements all have to be grounded in facts about the persons who
possess them. (Or perhaps, in the case of self-respect one should
say 'facts or imagined facts'?) But the atoms of a Rawlsian society
seeking grounds for self-respect could be allowed to refer only to
those characteristics which all persons – or, at most, all persons in
their particular society – have in common. In a sense doubtless
different from that of the young Marx, they would thus be, at least
'from a moral point of view', species-beings; and nothing else
(Feuerbach, and Marx 1844).

(ii) It is perhaps just worthwhile to take note in passing that the extreme collectivism of *A Theory of Justice*, published in 1971, is not to be found in the original sketch 'Justice as Fairness', which first appeared in *The Philosophical Review* for 1958. There are several other differences too. For instance: Rawls there was careful not to confront classical Utilitarianism as a whole; and equally careful to insist that justice is 'but *one* of the many virtues of social institutions', his own account being 'not to be confused with an all-embracing vision of a good society' (Rawls 1958, p.165: italics original). Again, in the earlier essay, if the inequalities of a practice are to be tolerable, they must 'work for the advantage of *every* party engaging in it'; and we read not one word about '*every* party' being an ambiguous expression which has to be interpreted as referring only to the least advantaged group (*Ibid.*, p.167: italics original). But in the book the collectivism has become extreme: the indefeasible imperative of justice now rules that we treat all 'natural abilities as a collective asset so that the more fortunate are to benefit *only* in ways that help those who have lost out' (italics supplied).

(a) The first objection is that there neither has been nor could have been any active distribution of genes: neither God nor Nature doled out prepared packets to each and every pre-existing person. So there can be no question of the contents of these putative packets constituting anyone's pay, whether deserved or undeserved. It is, nevertheless, as common as it is misleading to talk of genetic 'inheritances' – as if these were on all fours with the estates we may hope to receive under someone's last will and testament. For instance, the article 'Making Adults More Equal: The Scope and Limitations of Public Educational Policy', mentioned in Section 4, i, a of Chapter II, gives a sharp warning to all who share the Procrustean zeal of the authoress: 'To obtain the maximum equalising effect from a given amount of public educational resources, the distribution must be not only independent of, but negatively related to, the distribution of inherited inequalities of fortune, *including genetic make-up*' (Floud, p.50: italics supplied).

Hold it now! Just who is it who is supposed to have inherited their genetic make-up? Certainly my genetic constitution is not something which I have earned or deserved. But then neither is it an inheritance; nor yet a windfall which I have been so fortunate or unfortunate as to pick up. It is, rather, something at least the greater part of which must be essential to what I am. Of course, I can significantly suppose that my genes had been in some comparatively modest way different; just as I can suppose that I had been born on a different date, or raised in a slightly different way. But any drastic supposition in either direction ceases by that token to be a supposition, *about me*. For I just am the person who was born to such and such parents, with such and such a constitution, and so on. Although I can know what it is like to be a very different person, very differently circumstanced, I cannot by that token understand a suggestion that I might either be or become a person born at a different time, in another country, and to different parents. It is rather like the case, which I have argued elsewhere, in which, although I can imagine what it will be like (for someone else) to witness my funeral, I cannot without contradiction speak of *my* witnessing *my own funeral* (Flew 1976b, Chapter 9).

(b) The second objection is that it will not do to argue, with Rawls and with so many others, from the premise that our natural characteristics are not themselves deserved, to the conclusion that what they make possible cannot be either itself deserved or a proper basis of desert. The desired conclusion simply does not follow. That Rawls is indeed resting his case upon this invalid argument becomes still clearer when we attend to another passage. It also happens to be quoted by Hampshire, and endorsed enthusiastically, in what the trade must have relished as a 'rave review'.

Rawls is talking about the earnings and attainments of 'those who, with the prospect of improving their condition, have done what the system announces that it will reward'. Maybe in some contexts we are allowed to allow that they are 'entitled to their advantages'; which here means the earnings which their various natural advantages alone made possible. But then, what about those natural advantages themselves? The answer to that question, Rawls believes, will show that in the last analysis no one truly deserves anything: 'Perhaps some will think that the person with greater natural endowments deserves those assets and the superior character that made their development possible. Because he is more worthy in this sense, he deserves the greater advantages that he could achieve with them. This view, however, is surely incorrect. It seems to be one of the fixed points of our considered judgements that no one deserves his place in the distribution of native endowments, any more than one deserves one's initial starting place in society' (Rawls 1971, pp. 103 and 103-4).

Hampshire does not protest that Rawls is erecting and demolishing a straw man. Instead he welcomes an occasion to renew his own long-running war against desert. But those of us who do still wish to conserve this endangered concept refer, as bases of good or ill desert, not to anyone's native talents or temperament, but to what they have actually done or abstained from doing. Rawls himself appears to be at least half aware that that is the proper habitat of the concept. For, in the sentence immediately following the one with which Hampshire ends his quotation, Rawls concedes: 'The notion of desert seems not to apply to these cases' (*Ibid.*, p.104). Yet he still assumes that, by showing that natural endowments cannot be said to have been deserved, he has shown that we cannot acquire deserts by using those endowments.

What Hampshire does is to set off in the steps of another Harvard figure, the psychologist B.F. Skinner: 'But, one may ask: "Is there anything whatever that, strictly speaking, a man can claim credit for, or he can properly be said to deserve, with the implication that it can be attributed to him, the ultimate subject, as contrasted with the natural forces that formed him? In the last analysis, are not all advantages distributed by natural causes, even when they are the effects of human agency? And if we are not strict theists, we will surely not suppose that there is cosmic justice in these distributions?" ' (Hampshire, p.34).

I shall say little here about the denial of man as 'the ultimate subject, as contrasted with the natural forces that formed him'; partly because Rawls does not himself proceed either very far or very explicitly on such Skinnerian lines, and partly because I have recently had a full say elsewhere against these depreciations of the nature of man (Flew 1978a, Chapter 7). Yet it is very much to the point to challenge those professing moralists, like Hampshire and Ericsson, who do wittingly accompany Skinner *Beyond Freedom and Dignity*. What is the nature, relevance, and authority of their urgent and allegedly moral commitment to universal, compulsory equalisation? How can imperatives of morality in general, or of justice in particular, arise from or apply to creatures who – it is said – do not ultimately make choices, and who in consequence surely cannot be the bearers of either deserts or rights?

(c) The third objection concerns entitlements. This is a broader notion than that of desert: an entitlement, or a right, may be neither earned nor deserved; whereas a desert, of course, can not. Suppose that you want to present an absolute equality of entitlement as the mandate of justice: 'Any and every human being has as much right as anyone else to what gives value to human life. If anyone questions this judgement one can reply: on what grounds should it not be so? Why should I have more right to happiness than you?' (Jay, p.4).

Since people in fact do, and fail to do, such very different things there would seem to be no way of admitting deserts while concluding that everyone is in truth equally deserving – no way, that is, short of insisting that thanks to our damnable heritage of Original Sin we are all equally and abominably undeserving. In this predicament the preferred strategy is first to try to discredit the very idea of desert, and then to assume or assert that no one has any entitlements other than whatever may be the universal and hence equal rights of man. Rawls, followed by Hampshire, makes much of the first move, while apparently ignoring other entitlements altogether. Even Matson, perhaps the most punishing critic of Rawls, always construes justice as referring only to deserts.

Both Rawls and Hampshire thus assume, both that no one can be entitled to anything which they have not deserved, and hence that nothing can be either earned or deserved unless everything which makes the earning or the desert possible was itself earned or deserved. The first of these two assumptions is made in a fairly obvious way by Rawls when he takes it that he can dispose of any claim that someone might be entitled to 'the greater advantages' achieved by the employment of 'greater natural endowments' simply by showing that these latter were not themselves earned or deserved. The same first assumption is perhaps also, but less obviously, involved in the making of the second. Hampshire's 'ultimate subject' is presumably impossible because, on the second assumption, if he were genuinely to deserve anything he would have to have earned or deserved all those characteristics which made his earning or deserving that thing possible: he would have to be the inconceivable ultimate in self-made men!

Both assumptions are catastrophically wrong. Since an examination of the second will yield conclusions needed in a critique of the first, I begin with the second. The crux is that, whereas entitlement does not entail desert, desert itself does logically presuppose entitlement. So if it really were true that nothing could be either earned or deserved unless everything which made the earning or the desert possible was itself earned or deserved, then the moral would be, not that we are not, as it happens, 'deserving ultimate subjects', but that this complex notion is itself ultimately incoherent. It is illuminating here to be reminded of the Incompatibilist contention that I cannot properly be accountable for actions springing from desires which I never chose to have. Now, certainly, I can choose to acquire or to lose some tastes; and, given time and persistence, succeed. I can decide to acquire a taste for beer, or to lose my craving for tobacco. It is nevertheless incoherent to suggest that I might have chosen all my desires, from the beginning. With no desires and no inclinations no one could ever act or choose at all (Flew 1978, pp.77-8 and 193).

The case of earning or deserving is very similar. To act in any of the various ways which can on occasion constitute earning or deserving, I have to have some talents, some temperament; as well indeed as some desires and some inclinations. I have, in a word, to be a person. So, while some of my personal characteristics may be products of my own earlier endeavours, I cannot possibly have earned or deserved everything that I am and ever was, from the beginning. None of this, however, has any tendency to show that actual flesh-and-blood individual people, who cannot have earned or deserved everything they are, cannot be entitled to their own natural talents and other characteristics; and entitled also to what they may succeed in earning or deserving by their employment of these talents, and of all the rest of what they have, and are. If anyone is to succeed in showing this, then they will have to deploy arguments other and better than those offered by Hampshire.

In a nutshell: Hampshire simply takes for granted that there can be no entitlements which are not deserved; and then, in order to dispose of entitlements that *are* deserved, argues that there can be no deserts at all. The conceptual truth here seems to be: not, as he assumes, that entitlement presupposes desert; but rather, as I have been suggesting, that desert presupposes entitlement – entitlement, that is, to whatever attributes people may exercise or fail to exercise in the acquisition of good or ill desert.

It will help here to compare the notions of honest trade and contract; emphasising that it is these, and not those of either desert or merit, which are fundamental to 'the obvious and simple system of natural liberty'. Notwithstanding that this is nowadays frequently done by academic and other persons paid to know better, it is muddled and misinformed to maintain the contrary: 'Under the market, let us recall, the principle of desert reigned supreme – a man's deserts being estimated by the quantity of goods and services he brought to the market' (Miller, p.308).

The truth is that markets are for and about trade. Now the one universal and essential presupposition of (honest) trade is, not that everyone has earned or deserved what they either surrender or acquire, but that the sellers are entitled to the goods or services which they offer for sale while the buyers by buying them become in turn entitled to whatever it is that they have bought.

Nor is the notion of reward in place here: typically people are rewarded for some service which they have *not* contracted to perform – returning valued lost property, supplying information leading to the conviction of terrorists, or what have you. Trade and contract, which are the key notions, ultimately presuppose rights or entitlements which could not have been themselves obtained in any market. For the parties to a contract, like the intending acquirers of desert, have to be already entitled to whatever they propose to trade, or to employ in this acquisition.

Turning now to the first assumption, the first and killing blow is that no one can afford to deny entitlements which are not deserved if they propose to stay in the business of deploying conceptions of justice. This is an immediate consequence of the two necessary truths: first, that justice is essentially concerned with deserts and entitlements, and, second, that all desert and entitlement ultimately presupposes some entitlement which is neither deserved nor earned nor in any other way acquired through trade.

Second, and more particularly, Rawls himself cannot consistently deny entitlements which are not deserved so long as he requires his hypothetical contractors to act on the assumption that all the present and future wealth produced or discovered in the unknown territory which they are to inhabit is unconditionally available for distribution to themselves at their own absolute discretion: in so doing each one 'regards himself as justified in performing his actions . . . and implicitly makes a corresponding right-claim' (Gewirth 1974, p.52).

Someone might try to support the claim to collective ownership by appealing to some version of the Labour Theory of Value: Gracchus Babeuf, for instance, the leader of the original Conspiracy of the Equals, used to contend that all the wealth of France was by rights the common property of its sole producers, the French workers (Cranston 1967a, p.98; and compare Talmon Part III, passim). Waiving all other objections, this sort of move cannot serve the present purpose. For the whole notion of earning by work presupposes entitlements which are not themselves deserved or earned, entitlements both to our constitutive bodily parts and to their laborious and fruitful exercise.[16]

Nor is it so easy to dispose either of inheritance or of the investment income so excoriated by socialists: 'The existence of unearned income is wrong in itself no matter how it is distributed' (Gaitskell, p.6). For, provided that the parties to the Rawls contract belong to some generation other than the first, a large proportion of their collective national property is bound to be a collective inheritance passed on from previous generations. It will be this inherited capital – capital of every kind – which alone makes possible higher individual and social wages than could be paid were the present generation starting from scratch. (Why, after all, are living standards so much better in Soviet Germany than in Soviet Bulgaria?) It appears, therefore, that the objection must be, not either to investment income or to inheritance as such, but to both inheritance and investment income when these are individual as opposed to collective; a conclusion revealing a face of socialism unacceptable to some, but to others doubtless a main part of its attraction.

The third objection to the first assumption was first put, with an unnecessary apology, by Nozick (Nozick, pp.207-8). Suppose that in the country of the contract half the population is born with two normal eyes, and half with empty sockets. Suppose too that eye-transplant operations have become possible, safe, and not uncomfortable. Now, is it a matter of traditional justice that all the two-eyed must yield up one eye each to the transplant surgeons; or even of social justice that the state should compel them so to do? Or would any volunteering be a deed of supererogatory charity; and any compelling an act of tyranny and oppression?

Rawls himself seems not to have thought of people's claims to their constitutive bodily parts, though if he did he could say that any compulsion here would be a violation of 'the priority of liberty'. This, however, does nothing to contain the force of the objection. For it would take a very far-gone collectivist – more far-gone, I think, than Rawls – simply to deny all such rights claims. Yet, if once they are conceded, then it has to be goodbye to that first assumption that there are no entitlements which are neither earned nor deserved. And, furthermore, it becomes excessively difficult to maintain that the 'natural abilities' manifested in the employment of these parts are properly a 'collective asset' to be exploited '*only* in ways that help those who have lost out'.

2 'As interchangeable as ants': Bernard Williams

The author of the much discussed article 'The Idea of Equality' has been a Professor of Philosophy in the University of Cambridge, and is now Provost of King's College in that same university. His initial concern here is with ideals of the first and second sorts distinguished in our Chapter II. For us, however, the main interest lies in an explosive yet perhaps slightly embarrassed development of the latter in the direction of our third category, equality of outcome.

(i) It is common today, especially perhaps among educational sociologists, to collapse this distinction; and common too to pass from one ideal to the other through various sophisms. Some of the most popular of the fallacies were exposed in Section 4,i of Chapter II. Now consider the angry treatment of an imaginary track event by another egalitarian: 'Three of the competitors are forty years old, five are overweight, one has weak ankles, and the tenth is Roger Bannister. What sense does it make to say that all ten have an equal opportunity to win the race? The outcome is predetermined by nature, and nine of the competitors will call it a mockery when they are told that all have the same opportunity to win' (Schaar, p.233).

Maybe they will. But, if so, then they will show that they are not sufficiently apprised of the ordinary meaning of 'equality of opportunity'; which would, in that sense, be better expressed by 'open competition for scarce opportunities' (Lloyd-Thomas 1977). It will not do to argue that, because the chances (probabilities) of success for one competitor or class of competitors are different from those for another competitor or class of competitors, therefore these competitors cannot have had equal chances in an open competition. For the equal chance offered by what is usually called equality of opportunity is – as we saw in Chapter II – an equal chance in a fair and open competition. Equal chances in this sense not merely are not necessarily, they necessarily cannot be, equiprobabilities of success. A 'competition' in which the success of all contestants is equally probable is a game of chance or a lottery, not a genuine competition. (When I read a first draft of the present chapter in Ramat-Gan, several Israeli colleagues were misled by the fact that the controlling authorities in many sports take trouble to ensure that contestants are evenly matched, heavyweights boxing only heavyweights and so on. But the aim there is close and exciting contests, not fair and open competition. Those other aims are secured, if at all, in other ways.)

(ii) Williams starts from a similar example. His first conclusion is 'that a system of allocation will fall short of equality of opportunity if the allocation of the good in question in fact works out unequally or disproportionately between different sections of society, if the unsuccessful sections are under a disadvantage which could be removed by further reform or social action' (Williams, p.245). About the first part of this conclusion, before the proviso, it is enough at this stage to say only that outcome and opportunity are sometimes confused in a way even more scandalous: 'Surely,' it has been suggested, 'we could always define "real chance" in such a way that it becomes analytically true that if two members of a society have the same real chance to achieve equality of economic welfare, then their actual economic welfare level will be the same' (Ericsson, p.130: inverted commas supplied). Yes indeed, nothing easier; nor more arbitrary; nor more obscurantist.

(a) The fresh interest lies in the proviso: 'if the unsuccessful sections are under a disadvantage which could be removed by further reform or social action.' For without exception every feature which differentiates one human being from another must in principle be alterable (if not yet – or ever – alterable in practice). Whatever is in fact determined by the environment could theoretically have been altered by changing that. The same applies to genetic constitutions. Science fiction can easily imagine a society in which all the babies become identical, as products of cloning – too many professing social scientists and practising social engineers assume that we do already (Flew 1976a, Chapter 4). From this it might seem a short step, though one which Williams himself visibly hesitates to take, to the conclusion that there can be no essential difference between Robert and Lucinda, or any other two persons. As the *Encyclopaedia of the Social Sciences* had it, in the days of the Model T: ' . . . at birth human infants, regardless of heredity, are as equal as Fords' (Quoted Hayek 1978, p.290).

The move which Williams does make is to say: 'In these circumstances, where everything about a person is controllable, equality of opportunity and absolute equality seem to coincide; and this itself illustrates something about the notion of equality of opportunity' (Williams, p.247). The something which he sees it as illustrating is a tension between ideals of our second and first sorts:

' . . . the feeling that a thoroughgoing emphasis on equality of opportunity must destroy a certain sense of common humanity which is itself an ideal of equality' (*Ibid.*, p.247). What Williams does not recognise is that on his assumptions the notion of equality of opportunity must self-destruct, leaving the field clear for his 'absolute equality'; which belongs, presumably, to our third category, equality of outcome. Since he has effectively collapsed the distinction between opportunity and outcome, he naturally finds no occasion to remark that in any case ideals of these last two sorts are ultimately incompatible.

They must ultimately be incompatible, because, in so far as the outcomes are to be made the same for all, there can not only be no incentive to compete for scarce opportunities but no scarce opportunities for which to compete. The hypothesis requires that the attractions of anything which is inherently and incorrigibly scarce must be artificially offset by compensating disadvantages; otherwise there must remain or emerge that most infamous thing, inequality. Nor again, on the present Williams assumptions, can there be those fair and open competitions presupposed by the ideal of equality of opportunity. For if, following Williams, all the competitive advantages of all the competitors have to be removed, then there can, as we saw in the preceding subsection, be no competition at all; only a game of chance or a kind of lottery – a Lewis Carroll caucus lottery in which all participants have to win equivalent prizes.[17]

(b) Another comment which Williams makes, proceeding from the first passage quoted in the present subsection, is 'that one is not really offering equality of opportunity to Smith and Jones if one contents oneself with applying the same criteria to Smith and Jones at, say, the age of 11; what one is doing there is to apply the same criteria to Smith as affected by favourable conditions and to Jones as affected by unfavourable but curable conditions' (*Ibid.*, pp.245-6).

This too is instructively wrong. For that there should be open competitions for scarce opportunities, with the same criteria applied to all candidates, is precisely what the ideal of equality of opportunity does demand. So if you offer this to Smith and Jones you really are 'offering equality of opportunity'. The genuineness of this proposition is in no way prejudiced by the maybe lamentable truths: first, that in any competition held some time after the birth of the contestants, and where there have been

differences between their several environments, some are likely to
have become advantaged and some disadvantaged; second, that in
any competition held at any time, and embracing more than a field
of monozygotic single-sex siblings, genetic differences are almost
bound to advantage some and disadvantage others; and, third, that
if things are so set up that the success of every contestant is equally
probable, then we no longer have a competition at all. The
protagonist of equality of opportunity, therefore, has no choice but
to accept that some competitive advantages must be compatible
'with applying the same criteria' to all candidates; or, in other
words, if there is to be any competition at all then competitive
advantages cannot all be disqualified as unfair. And, furthermore,
unless this protagonist is ready to abolish the family, his tolerance
will in practice have to embrace at least come competitive assets
which are environmentally conditioned.

(iii) It is essential to grasp exactly how it is that Williams
contrives thus to reject equality of opportunity as not really being
what it is. The trick is done by refusing to admit to the competition
the actual competitors; or, at any rate, by refusing to admit those of
them whose prospects are poor. According to Williams the truly
legitimate and qualified competitors are not those actual but
sometimes rather wretched specimens seen now trooping up to the
start line. Instead they are the hypothetical people who might have
been competing if only the entire Williams programme for total
social transformation had been effectively and successfully implemented. So, referring still to Smith and Jones, he gives his
Olympian ruling: 'Their identity, for these purposes, does not
include their curable environment, which is itself unequal and a
contributor of inequality.' Next, referring to his own stunningly
high-handed proceedings, he comments: 'This abstraction of
persons in themselves from unequal environments is a way if not of
regarding them as equal, at least of moving recognisably in that
direction.' It was a pity to offset the impact of this restrained truth
by adding the false gloss: 'and is itself involved in equality of
opportunity' (*Ibid.*, p.246).

Only after he has extended his approach to cover alterable
genetic constitutions also does Williams begin to display a little
anxiety, even if not nearly enough, about the presuppositions now
revealed: 'Here we might think that our notion of personal identity
itself was beginning to give way; we might well wonder *who were*
the people whose advantages were being discussed in this way . . .

if one reached this state of affairs, the individuals would be regarded as in all respects equal in themselves – for in themselves they would be, as it were, pure subjects or bearers of predicates, everything about them, including their genetic inheritance, being regarded as a fortuitous and changeable characteristic' (*Ibid.*, pp.246-7: italics original).

There is no call now to labour the earlier objection to talk about genetic inheritances: 'Who is the fortunate, or unfortunate, legatee?' The important thing is to recognise that the Williams treatment of equality of opportunity, in effect reducing this to equality of outcome, is leading him towards a conception of the human individual thinner and more etiolated even than that of Rawls. For whereas Rawlsian man is allowed straightforwardly to possess all, but only, the characteristics common to the whole body of his fellow contractors, it looks as if the Williams campaign for equalisation is going to be launched for – or should it be against? – 'pure subjects ... everything about them ... being regarded as a fortuitous and changeable characteristic'. Both conceptions are very different from those which are, perhaps in a weaker sense, presupposed by ideals of the first or second sorts. In the second case, there surely could be no point in, or possibility of, competition for scarce opportunities where in fact everyone was in all relevant respects equal. And the first ideal, of respecting all persons equally, inasmuch as we are equally entitled to choose our own ends and to do our own things, would lose much of its charm if the only important characteristics of any individual human being were those necessarily common to all mankind.

(iv) Although Williams is by his egalitarian commitments led towards this view of the human individual, he does pull back a short way from the brink: 'Here we might think that our notion of personal identity was beginning to give way; we might well wonder *who were* the people whose advantages and disadvantages were being discussed in this way.' Wait though: 'But . . . in the end, we could still pick out the individuals by spatio-temporal criteria, if no more' (*Ibid.*, p.246).

Williams, I suspect, believes that this concession disposes of the difficulty at no cost. Let it be conceded that it does dispose of that difficulty. Yet it still carries costs which must be serious for anyone wanting to present equality of entitlement as 'the first principle of justice'. For those who are going to be picked out as individuals 'by spatio-temporal criteria' are going thereby to be picked out as creatures to whose several individualities various different particular relationships to other individuals of the same kind must be essential. To anyone so reactionary as to be prepared to countenance such infamous diversity, these essential differences will be quite enough to serve as bases for considerable inequalities of entitlement.

The crux arises from the fact that personal identity just *is* the identity of persons. But persons are very complicated and peculiar creatures, having their distinctive way of coming into existence; and with from the very beginning a deal of consequent difference one from another. If they are to be identified and individuated by spatio-temporal criteria, then these criteria cannot but refer to the time and place of each one's origin; and hence to the mating of the particular man and the particular woman of which that birth was a product. Like all human beings all parents have their places within networks of blood relationships. All have their places also within networks of social relationships. So all the children of such parents are born into particular networks of both kinds, which are more or less different from each other. Then again, (almost) every human child is in its genetic constitution different from every other, with all that follows from that. Most important of all, we are all creatures who make and cannot but make choices; conducting our own lives under the guidance of our memories of the past and of our hopes and fears for the future. By that conduct we also to some extent make ourselves. As Aristotle used to insist, dispositions are formed by acting in the ways which become habitual.

If, therefore, we are going to identify individuals by spatio-temporal criteria, then at least some elements of these connections are bound to appear in accounts of what is essential to any particular individual; and, as we have already observed in passing, so in fact they do (Chapter IV, 1, ii, a). This at once yields plenty of essential differences between individuals, offering purchase for differences of entitlement; and that too before we even begin to take account of the contingent differences brought about by what they later do or do not do. Nor should we overlook the fact that, whereas equal entitlements have to be grounded in necessary or at any rate universal human characteristics, unequal entitlements do not have to be grounded in either these or the essential peculiarities of unequal individuals. The grounds of difference do not have to be common at all; indeed they must not be.

CHAPTER V

Wants or Needs: Choice or Command?

'Now, if to be filled with what is naturally right is
pleasant, then that which is more really filled with real
things must more really and truly cause us to enjoy a
real pleasure; while that which partakes of the less truly
real must be less truly and surely filled, and will partake
of a less reliable and less true pleasure.'

'That is altogether necessary,' he said.

'Then those who have no experience of sound
judgement and excellence, but are forever engaged in
feasting and the like . . . have never really been filled
with what is real nor even tasted stable and pure
pleasure. . . . The fact is that they have been trying to
fill with what is not real what is not the real and
continent part of themselves.'

'You describe the life of the masses, Socrates,' said
Glaucon, 'in a quite oracular style.' *Plato: The Republic
(585E-586B)*

This chapter considers the logical relations and the necessary
differences between the notions of want and need. The main
concern will be to bring out the truth that an emphasis upon needs,
as opposed to wants, cannot but appeal to those who would like to
see themselves as experts, qualified both to determine what the
needs of others are, and to prescribe and enforce the means
appropriate to the satisfaction of those needs. Needs are in this
respect, though not in all others, like interests. Just as someone
may want what it is not in his interests to have, or have some
interest in securing what he nevertheless does not actually want to
obtain, so we may want what we do not need, and need what we do
not want. The possibility of this lack of congruence, and its
importance, can be illustrated at once in the case of interests by

quoting two revealing expressions of what is often described, from a parochial Old World standpoint, as an Eastern as opposed to a Western conception of democracy. That the same applies in the case of needs, and how this matters, will become progressively more obvious as the chapter develops.

The first statement was made by Janos Kadar, addressing the Hungarian National Assembly on 11 May 1957, the year after the ever-ready tanks of imperial normalisation had first installed him in office. *East Europe* for July 1957 reported him as saying: 'The task of the leaders is not to put into effect the wishes and will of the masses. . . . The task of the leaders is to accomplish the interests of the masses. Why do I differentiate between the will and the interests of the masses? In the recent past we have encountered the phenomenon of certain categories of workers acting against their interests.'

The second statement was made on 7 July 1967 by Abdul Kharume, First Vice-President of Tanzania, addressing the annual foundation celebrations of the ruling and – of course – sole legal party on the Tanzanian mainland. This one I copied myself from the report the following morning in the official English-language newspaper for Dar-es-Salaam: 'Our government is democratic, because it makes its decisions in the interests of and for the benefit of the people. I wonder why men who are unemployed are surprised and resentful at the government . . . sending them back to the land for their own advantage.'[18]

These two statements suggest that we can usefully distinguish for the word 'democracy' in political discourse two fundamentally different areas of meaning. In one – the Western or 'by the people' sense – the crux is what people themselves want, or at any rate decide. If some group takes decisions by majority vote, then that is, as far as it goes, democratic. So too are institutions under which decisions are made by representatives or delegates who have not only been voted in but may in due course also be voted out. It is today more than ever necessary to underline that final clause. For leaders or groupings to be democratic in this authentic sense it is essential, not that they have already been popularly elected, or hope in the future to be elected, but that, if and when they are voted in, they will maintain and promote arrangements to ensure that they can also be voted out. By this criterion the government against which Lenin launched his successful October coup was democratic, since it was at that time in process of conducting such elections; whereas the Bolsheviks themselves were not, since they proceeded to dissolve the resulting Constituent Assembly by armed force (Carr, I pp.115-29).

In the second of the two areas of political meaning the crucial reference is quite different. In this Eastern or 'for the people' understanding, arrangements may be said to be democratic inasmuch as they are supposed to be in the interests of, or to further the good of, or to meet the needs of, whoever is here allowed to constitute the true and relevant people. As before, some stress has to be put on the last clause. Thus Noam Chomsky – not only famous for his linguistics but notorious also for his Leninism – does not scruple to write 'the people of Vietnam (the Communists, that is) . . . ' (Chomsky, p.14). Again, during the rule of President Allende, the pro-government daily *Puro Chile* announced what it found the disappointing results of some inadequately rigged legislative elections under a memorable headline: 'The People: 43%. The Reactionaries: 55%' (Moss, p.23).

Among the classical political philosophers this second tradition finds its inspiration in Rousseau. His General Will, often deceived but never corrupted, is by definition always upright and necessarily directed to the collective good. Yet it is notorious that it is not to be reliably discovered, either in the hurly-burly of contested elections, or through the deliberations of representative assemblies. Precisely this is what gives such doctrines of the true people's real but often hidden will their powerful and perennial appeal to all who like to think of themselves as members of a new Platonic élite of Guardians, as adhering to 'a party of the Vanguard' (Talmon, passim). So Hugh Macdiarmid, poet of modern Scottish nationalism and ultra-hardline Muscovite Communist, in his 'First Hymn to Lenin' wrote:

> Here lies your secret O Lenin, – yours and ours
> No' in the majority will that accepts the result
> But in the real will that bides its time and kens
> The benmaist [= inmost] resolve, is the poo'er in which we
> exult
> Since nobody's willingly deprived o' the good;
> And, least o' a', the crood!

1 The logic of wants and needs
So far one analytical point has been made: we may want what we

do not need and need what we do not want. Like the point that
rights are necessarily grounded in facts about the bearers of those
rights, it is in itself formal. But, as in that first case, such
conceptual points can, when combined with other more substantial
premises, carry substantial implications (Chapter II, 2, ii, c).

(i) A second and third point of the same kind are suggested by
the earlier observation 'that an emphasis upon needs, as opposed
to wants, gives purchase to those who see themselves as experts,
qualified both to determine what the needs of others are, and to
prescribe and enforce the means appropriate to the satisfaction of
those needs.'

(a) The second is that the satisfaction of people's needs must be
in their interests, or in some other way good for them. If you need
medical attention, for instance, then getting this must be in itself,
and all other things being equal, good for you; even if your likely
conduct on your return to health is such as to make the whole
business anything but good for others. Again, if I prescribe
something which you definitely do not want, as what is required to
meet some need of yours, then I must in consistency at least
pretend that my prescription is to your ultimate advantage: 'What
you need is a thorough thrashing, which will do you a power of
good'; or 'What you need is a few months in an infantry training
depot, which will make a man of you.'

(b) The third such point is that what is needed is supposed to be
needed not for its own sake but as a means to the fulfilment of some
further function, purpose, or end. If I want to climb this particular
route, then there may be no further answer to the question 'Why?'
Suggestions that I could get to the top more easily and more
quickly by train or by helicopter may simply miss the point – that
what I *want* is to climb, and to climb this particular route. Yet if I
say that I need something it is never inept to ask: 'What for?' I need
food and drink in order to maintain life and health; I need a lift in
order to get me to Manchester in the morning; and so on. But if I
claim just to need something, but not for the sake of anything
further, then what I really have is not a need at all, but only a wish
or a craving.

None of this is falsified – shown to be false, that is – by citing the
fact that these further purposes may not be in the minds of the
persons while they are engaged in satisfying their supposed or
actual needs. President Kennedy, for instance, is said to have told
Prime Minister Macmillan and others that he himself needed very

frequent sexual intercourse. In saying this the President was implying that, when he had not had plenty, he did or would get into a bad state. Sex was for him a 'behaviour tendency whose denial or frustration leads to pathological responses' (Bay, p.242). Without it there would be 'apathy or such impairment of intelligence, initiative and skills' as would gravely prejudice the interests of the republic (Fromm, p.18). He was not saying, what nobody would have believed, that these things and these alone were on his mind while he was engaged in the strenuous exercise of satisfying this need.

(c) A fourth analytical point is suggested by the conclusion: 'A need, therefore, is a legitimate or morally sanctioned demand' (Minogue, p.46). The writer later quotes Simone Weil: 'Where there is a need, there is also an obligation.' But then he makes in his own person the much more cautious assertion: 'Desire may be capricious; need always claims to be taken seriously' (*Ibid.*, p.103).

The truth, surely, is significantly different. Certainly there is always something hypothetically imperative about any need. For to say that this or that is needed is to say that it is a necessity for the fulfilment of some function, or purpose, or end: if I want any of those fulfilments then I must have those necessities. But this is by no means to say either that that function, purpose or end is 'legitimate or morally sanctioned' or that this necessary means to it is also licit. Much less is it to say positively that 'there is an obligation' upon everyone to assist all others to secure their every genuine need. It is not incoherent to assert that people need to do things, which ought not to be done, if they are to achieve objectives, which in any case they ought not to be pursuing: 'They needed to employ every instrument of terror if they were to secure their firm control over the countries which their armies had conquered.' Nor is it improper to speak of needing to do or to have this or that in order successfully to pursue what is admittedly only a pastime: 'We shall need to do much better in the scrum if we are to have any chance of winning on Saturday week.'

On the other hand we do often contrast basic human need – what is needed simply to sustain life, or to maintain whatever is taken to be the minimum tolerable standard of living – with luxuries and frivolities. No doubt Simone Weil had this contrast in mind when she said what she said. But it is only some needs that are thus distinguished – those essential to certain minimum or otherwise approved ends. That fact is the decisive reason why all needs cannot – as such and necessarily – be, as both she and Minogue maintain, 'legitimate or morally sanctioned'.

(ii) The various essentials picked out in the previous subsection conspire together to endow the notion of needs with much charm for all those longing to belong to an authoritarian and powerful paternalistic élite. First: because people's needs may not match their wants, it happens that whereas each individual is usually his or her own best judge of wants, needs may be far more satisfactorily determined by someone else. Second: because to meet my needs is necessarily in some way good for me, the person who directs or secures the satisfaction of these must be my benefactor; even though I may still, in my ignorance, resent or reject their surely well-intentioned services. Third: because needs are necessarily means to ends, there must be room for expertise in determining what in fact is needed as the means to this or that end. Fourth: because needs are of their very nature imperative, and typically fundamental and serious, those who are by profession engaged with such necessary matters must seem on that account important people, whose prescriptions are to be accepted without question.

In the percipient essay containing the two sentences already quoted, Kenneth Minogue mentions some later substitutes for that esoteric vision of the Platonic Forms or Ideas, which was what was supposed to qualify his Guardians – the Philosopher Kings – for absolute power. Two such substitutes are: 'The notion of the General Will, or that of the class-consciousness of the proletariat . . . in each case a small set of people may establish themselves as experts in the pronouncements of those oracles. Actual popular support is unnecessary; it can be rigged up after the event. . . . ' Minogue then goes on: 'The concept of need is a less dramatic example. . . . Most of its practitioners are mild social scientists, or benevolent welfarists, rather than wild-eyed fanatics like Robespierre or Lenin' (*Ibid.*, p.109).

One might question whether this statement about 'most of its practitioners' was ever true. Certainly if his complacent confidence that in Britain socialism is a dead issue was ever justified it was in the fifties and sixties rather than the seventies and eighties. For perhaps in those earlier decades you did not have to be purblind or wilful to dismiss 'some people for whom socialism is itself a dogma' as an insignificant remnant, and to be sure that everyone who mattered would 'support a more experimental attitude to social reform' (*Ibid.*, p.14). But Minogue can still point, for instance, to the fact that in a period in which so much is being heard from the British teachers' unions about the achievement of full professional status, we also find that 'The concept of need is being increasingly widely used in educational discussions . . . ' (Dearden, p.50; and compare Langford passim).

This raises, as it is intended to raise, the general question of the relations between professional or other people offering skilled services and the public who may from time to time wish to make use of these services. A consideration of these relations will bring out: first, that although our needs cannot be identified with our wants, it is nevertheless impossible completely to separate the two; and, second, that although some expert may be qualified to tell me what I need for this or that end, there is no room for an expertise referring not to means only but to ends.

Suppose that I visit, as I often do, my friendly neighbourhood DIY storeowner. I tell him about a job I want to do. He from his expert knowledge can, and does, help me. He explains what I need, and then sells me whatever it is I need for the job but do not have. But no expert knowledge would enable him to discern what I need if I did not tell him what I want. It is just the same with a visit to a solicitor, or a surveyor, or an architect. They have to discover what I want before they can begin to bring their expert knowledge to bear in order to advise me on my needs. The reason why a doctor is, generally, able to prescribe for the needs of his patients without first asking them what they want, is that he can take it for granted that they want to be as fit and as free from pain as they can be.

These are all simple cases of employment of experts to determine needs, as means to the achievement of the actual and present ends of the employer. But there are, of course, also cases where the need or the supposed need relates to some want which cannot be expressed immediately, or which would or will be felt only on certain hypothetical conditions, or even one which it is thought ideally ought to be, rather than actually is or will be, felt by the person to whom that need is attributed. The first thing to stress about all such complicated and off-centre cases is that they do still manifest, in the various ways just indicated, the same logical link between a person's needs and that same person's wants.

A second point to be emphasised, most strongly, is that the further we get from actual and present desires, the more dubious becomes the status of the expert, and the more questionable his putative expertise. The first harmless step is when the need corresponds to a want which, although not in fact felt at the moment of prescription, will be felt as soon as the expert communicates some relevant item of his own knowledge: 'You need to have that treated at once; or the infection will spread, and you will lose the whole arm.' But at the end of the road there is the Platonic Guardian, whose absolute power is warranted by nothing else but a putative expertise consisting precisely and only in alleged privileged access to the objectives that everyone ought to have (*The Republic* 484A-485C and 487C-489C; and compare Bambrough). Deviation or defection from these ideal – indeed Ideal – objectives is in Plato's book necessarily an expression of psychological disease. Such disease must, of course, tend to discredit any conduct or conviction to which it gives rise, as well as being – like all disease – bad for the subjects themselves; inevitably it is for the Guardians to decide who is diseased and which diseased desires are, by reprogramming, to be inhibited or eliminated (Flew 1973, Part I).

Consider now in the light of the previous paragraphs two more or less off-centre examples. In the first a woman is lying injured and unconscious after a car smash. The doctor who steps forward to treat this victim both discerns and meets her need for such attention. For he can, and indeed must, assume that, were she able to ask for help, she would. In the second a man wants to kill himself. Choosing a time when he may reasonably expect not to be disturbed he goes to his garage, locks the door, shuts the window, seals as best he can any cracks or crevices which catch his eye, starts the engine of his car, and lies down comfortably with his head by the car's exhaust. A doctor chances by, breaks into the garage, and rushes the now unconscious victim off for emergency hospital treatment.

No doubt this doctor behaved exactly as both our laws and our conventional morality require. Yet it would be quite wrong for him to claim, as the doctor in the other case properly might, that he was acting simply as a professional man, rendering services to his patient or client. Our second doctor was certainly not, on this occasion, acting on the instructions of the would-be suicide. For that one made it as clear as he could that he wanted no interference. If, therefore, the patient's needs are to provide justification for the drastic intervention in this case too, then those needs will have to be specified by reference to hypothetical and ideal wants rather than to actual desires.

These two examples bring out the crucial differences between, on the one hand, the independent professional expert as servant, determining needs by reference to the wants of the individual client, and, on the other hand, Platonic experts as masters, paternalistically prescribing needs by reference to their own judgment of what their subjects ideally ought to want.

It is today common to excoriate élitism, without making clear whether the objection extends to every form of selection for quality; and, if not, why not. If it really does then those who employ the word as a term of abuse betray not only education, but also every other form of striving after excellence. Suppose however that the epithet has to remain dyslogistic, and so needs to be found some suitably obnoxious reference. Then it would surely be much better to specify the obnoxiousness as being that of pretending to enjoy privileged Guardian access to ultimately authoritative values, and of claiming as a consequence to possess the right by all available means to impose these uniquely authentic ends. In this understanding, of course, by far the most numerous and menacing of contemporary élitists are the Leninists.

(iii) Back in Chapter III Brian Barry was quoted as saying: 'A lottery is fair if honestly run, but a lottery which distributed prizes *justly*, i.e. according to desert or need, would no longer be fair.' The assumption that justice is concerned with deserts or needs rather than with deserts and entitlements appears here only as it were between parentheses. Elsewhere it is nearer to the main text.

(a) Thus in writing about *Social Justice* David Miller, a Lecturer in Politics at Lancaster, says: 'An influential minority view in political philosophy is that, conceptually speaking, needs have nothing to do with the concept of justice' (Miller, p.311). But he himself is one of what he holds to be the solid majority: 'One could say that the principle of need represents the most urgent part of the principle of equality. The urgency finds its expression in our undoubted willingness to regard the satisfaction of needs as a matter of justice' (*Ibid.*, p.149). He also objects against the 'minority view' that it commits its supposedly influential supporters to contending that: 'although we can say that an individual living in a country with a welfare state who does not receive the expected benefits has been unjustly treated, we cannot say that a country *with* a welfare state is more just than a country without one. .... But this contradicts 'welfare state philosophy', which surely regards the establishment of the welfare state itself as a matter of justice' (*Ibid.*, pp.122-3: italics original).

The contention of these unnamed welfare state philosophers – who are not to be contradicted – is, presumably, that all the health, education and welfare benefits either provided already or in the future to be provided are, will be and always have been due to the beneficiaries as a matter of moral right; that these vast and various welfare rights are all grounded in their needs; and that (social) justice just is the legal enforcement of these moral rights. Even if all this were true it would still not prove that needs are, as both he and the supposed majority claim, connected with justice conceptually. To prove that Miller would have to make out that it would be contradictory to assert, that, although someone had some need, nevertheless they had no right to the satisfaction of that need. It would not. (Whose particular duty was it to satisfy Kennedy's extravagant sexual needs?)

(b) In 'The Idea of Equality' Williams maintains: 'It is a matter of logic that particular sorts of needs constitute a reason for receiving particular sorts of good' (Williams, pp.241-2). Had this been a claim that any desire constitutes a reason in favour of its own satisfaction, then we might well have concurred – perhaps with some hesitation still over this being 'a matter of logic'. For that claim would have been, for instance, part of what is involved in rejecting the illiberal and authoritarian contention that the fact that people want to do or to have something is no reason at all why they should be allowed to do or to have it; not even a defeasible reason – a reason, that is, which may well have to be overridden by other and stronger reasons.

But in fact Williams is maintaining something different. Realising perhaps that it will in practice often be impossible to satisfy all the different desires and needs of one person, much less those of every person, Williams qualifies. He restricts the claim to 'particular sorts of needs'. Unfortunately he makes no attempt to specify what 'particular sorts' are and are not privileged; or, consequently, why. What he does volunteer is treatments of two examples, medicine and education; a pair chosen presumably because he wants to justify state monopoly 'free' services in these areas but not, or not yet, in the supply of – say – food, drink or shelter.

The case of medicine is the simpler of his two, because 'it can be presumed for practical purposes that the persons who have the need actually desire the goods in question', and because it is not complicated by considerations of merit (*Ibid.*, p.240). About this simpler case he says: 'Leaving aside preventive medicine, *the* proper ground of distribution of medical care is ill health: *this is a necessary truth*' (*Ibid.*, p.240: italics supplied). The intended significance of the words here italicised is then spelt out: 'When we have the situation in which, for instance, wealth is a further necessary condition of the receipt of medical treatment . . . this is an irrational state of affairs. . . . What is meant is that it is a situation in which reasons are insufficiently *operative*; it is a situation insufficiently controlled by reasons – and hence by reason itself' (*Ibid.*, pp.240 and 241: italics original).

So it now appears that these unspecified 'particular sorts of need' constitute not merely good nor even essential reasons, but also the only possible good reasons, justifying their own fulfilment. Yet Williams, aside from dismissing one factitious objection, is unwilling or unable to offer any warrant for this crucial further claim. It is hard to come to grips with such extraordinary pronouncements, made with an equally extraordinary curt confidence. Certainly, however, the first thing to stress is that Williams throughout treats medical and educational benefits as if these were 'manna from heaven'; and as if it were up to him, as Reason's mouthpiece, to decide where this manna should fall.

This is wrong; because, as was argued in Chapter III, since such benefits have to be in some way discovered or produced, they come into being with claims attached. Because medical and educational benefits consist so largely of services rather than of stuff, the earlier point applies here with peculiar force: such services are actions of their providers. Would Williams, would anyone, really be willing to live with the implication that it must be irrational for a doctor or a nurse or a teacher to provide their services to these patients or pupils rather than to those because and only because these had made payments for such services, or had payments made on their behalf? Would Williams, would anyone, really be prepared to defend the further consequence that it is 'an irrational state of affairs' when a parent, or a spouse, or a son or daughter, is prepared to nurse a sick person because, and only because, that sick person is also their child, or their spouse, or their parent?

2 *Guardians for our every need*

The previous section picked out some features of the logic of wants
and needs. This will try to show 'that an emphasis upon needs, as
opposed to wants, gives purchase to those who see themselves as
experts, qualified both to determine what the needs of others are,
and to prescribe and enforce the means appropriate to the
satisfaction of those needs.'

(i) The first exemplar is a Professor in the University of
Calgary, possibly the ablest and certainly the most productive
English-speaking philosopher to identify with Marxist-Leninist
Radicalism and the professedly New Left. Two sufficiently
representative papers are, 'Is Empiricism an Ideology?' and 'In
Defence of Radicalism' (Nielsen 1972 and 1974).

(a) The first begins with the conciliatory statement that
empiricism in the sense of an insistence 'that all our knowledge . . .
of matters of fact . . . is and must be . . . based upon or derived
from experience' not only is compatible with his own new-found
secular religion but also 'implies a constraint on theorising that
any scientifically oriented realist, materialist or indeed any tough-
minded man ought to welcome' (pp.266-7). In making this
concession to intractable and stubborn fact Nielsen falls out of
step with most of the Radicals operating under the code-word
'critical'. They prefer to maintain 'that the assumption that there
exists a realm of facts independent of theories which establish
their meaning is fundamentally unscientific' (Blackburn, p.10; and
compare Flew 1976a, Chapters 1-3).

But Nielsen gets back into line by explaining that logical
empiricism, which he rejects, contends: 'For fundamental normative
judgments . . . there can be no truth-conditions' (*Ibid.*, p.267).
This darkly technical proposition is tantamount to Hume's Law;
which in turn, being interpreted, is the thesis that no neutral
description, stating purely and simply what *is* the case, entails any
sort of prescription of what ideally *ought* to be. For Nielsen it is a
stone of stumbling: ' . . . such an account . . . indirectly supports
and reinforces pluralism and bourgeois individualism. . . . If
someone . . . takes this conception of valuation to heart, he is very
likely to accept democratic pluralism as the most adequate
political model and to be sceptical of . . . what he is likely to
characterise as "total ideologies". . . . On such a model . . . it is
very difficult to talk about . . . a truly human society, alienated
labour and the like' (*Ibid.*, pp.270-1).

So – as a dedicated enemy of (Western) democracy, of pluralism, of individualism, and of everything else soundly to be damned as bourgeois – what Nielsen wants is some suitably materialist analogue to that privileged access to the ideal Ideas or Forms enjoyed by the Platonic 'philosopher Kings'. Only such objects can provide the true and authoritative values through which experts are enabled to identify the ideally human needs; and hence those favoured desires every one of which, under total socialism, alone may and will be satisfied. Plato, as can be seen from the motto of the present chapter, laboured to prove that the pleasures to be gained by satisfying disfavoured desires could not be, by that token, real pleasures, nor the satisfactions genuine satisfactions. Nielsen now proposes to discount and discredit both all actual or possible but unapproved wants, and the needs or satisfactions arising from those wants, not as unreal or non-existent, but as artificial, and hence not truly human. Thus he complains that the defender of 'bourgeois individualism', that terrible fellow, 'conveniently ignores considerations . . . concerning the way wants are artificially created and sustained by the ruling classes to enhance and protect capitalism' (*Ibid.*, p.271).

It is tempting to respond to such paranoiac protestations by labouring a luminous truth: all that is ever done by anyone to preserve the present political economy of those remaining countries called capitalist is as nothing compared with the unsleeping oppressiveness of the measures maintained for parallel purposes by the ruling classes in the socialist world. Certainly no one who is still permitted to vote not only for but also against should neglect to ponder the fact that in most – probably all – socialist countries it is a criminal offence to try to organise an anti-socialist movement, or even simply to propagandise against socialism. But here and now the task is to reveal the absurdity of dismissing, as either unreal or not truly human, desires which may in some sense be artificial.

Nielsen appeals for support to Marx and Engels, Marcuse and Gorz. It is curious that he makes no mention of Galbraith; but perhaps less curious that he is, apparently, not able to think of any suitable citation from either of the Founding Fathers of Communism. They seem in fact never to have spelt out in any discussable degree of detail and precision the principles on which they proposed to select some of our myriad present and possible desires as alone properly and truly human. Certainly it is never

revealed upon what grounds, if any, they are asking us to believe
that a godless universe is in fact ordered so providentially that we
all are or will be by nature adapted to a complementary and
conflict-free social life: ' . . . an association in which the free
development of each is the condition of the free development of all'
(Marx and Engels 1848, p.105).

So we have to turn to Marcuse. His contribution here is even
more than usually confused and confusing. Maybe because he is
still thinking in a language which provides no exact equivalents for
our terms 'want' and 'need', the crux for him is the 'divergence
between the objective and the subjective need' (Marcuse 1968,
p.182). The former is those wants and needs which he believes
that people ought to have, while the latter is the felt wants that they
actually and so deplorably do have. His article 'Liberation from
the Affluent Society' opens with a categorical affirmation: 'For
without an objectively justifiable goal of a better, a free, human
existence all liberation must remain meaningless. . . . I believe
that . . . socialism *ought* to be' (*Ibid.*, p.175: italics original). The
problem as he sees it is that far too few of those people who have
any choice in the matter actually want his brand of 'objective
liberation'. The rotten shame is that the existing order, in defiance
of the Marxist prophecies, 'delivers the goods to an ever larger part
of the population' (*Ibid.*, p.176). So, following Chernyshevsky
and Lenin, he has to ask himself: 'What is to be done?'

For answer we have, relishing its appropriate Orwellian title, to
turn to another essay. In 'Repressive Tolerance' Marcuse makes it
about as plain as he ever makes anything that his revolution
requires 'the dictatorship of an élite over the people'. It is indeed
for him and his followers a main grievance against the 'late
capitalist' order that the silent majority does not want, and has no
interest in, the revolution proposed: 'By the same token, those
minorities which strive for a change in the whole . . . will . . . be left
free to deliberate and discuss . . . and will be left harmless and
helpless in the face of the overwhelming majority, which militates
against qualitative social change. The majority is firmly grounded
in the increasing satisfaction of needs' (Marcuse 1969, pp.107-8
and 134).

The justification offered for the imposition of 'the dictatorship
of an élite over the people' is in sum this: 'Radical social change is
objectively necessary. . . . But, while this objective need is demon-
strably there, the subjective need for such a change does not

prevail.' Worse still, 'It does not prevail precisely among those parts of the population that are traditionally considered the agents of historical change' (Marcuse 1969, p.182). So, whereas in *1984* the slave Winston Smith rested his fleeting hopes upon the proles, the master Marcuse now hails 'the intelligentsia as the catalyst of historical change' (*Ibid.*, p.188). What is wrong with the vulgar, he thinks, is that their felt wants do not correspond to their objective needs, as he and his associates have determined these: 'The subjective need is repressed . . . firstly by virtue of the actual satisfaction of needs, and secondly by a massive scientific manipulation and administration of needs . . . ' (Marcuse 1968, p.182).[19]

It is remarkable, though maybe not surprising, that Marcuse finds it either unnecessary or impossible to deploy so much as one single illustration of this allegedly massive manipulation; notwithstanding that it constitutes his sole excuse for putting down, as merely subjective and altogether inconsiderable, wants which he allows to be actual. So let us try Galbraith. After warning that 'Nothing in economics so quickly marks an individual as incompletely trained as a disposition to remark on the legitimacy of the desire for more food and the frivolity of the desire for a more elaborate automobile', he attempts to find some difference between fundamental and less fundamental wants and urgent needs (Galbraith 1958, p.147). No doubt there are purposes for which such distinctions can and should be made. But the basis which Galbraith proposes will not do: 'If the individual's wants are to be urgent they must be original with himself. They cannot be urgent if they must be contrived for him. The fact that wants can be synthesised by advertising, catalysed by salesmanship, and shaped by the discreet manipulations of the persuaders shows that they are not very urgent' (*Ibid.*, pp.152 and 158).

This purple passage takes no tricks, for two reasons. First, commercial advertisers – those monster bogeypersons of the New Left – are not in fact secret and irresistible manipulators. They operate in the open, sometimes effectively and sometimes ineffectively, attempting to inform and to persuade. In this they are entirely at one with the author of *The Affluent Society*; who, as has often been remarked, would have been equally successful on Madison Avenue. We must not, and need not, allow ourselves to be misled by Galbraith's hardsell eloquence. Desires are not being implanted by compulsory brain surgery or surreptitiously conditioned by subliminal reinforcers. And, furthermore, by comparison with the amounts directed to establishing and maintaining brand loyalty or to telling possible buyers about what is available where and for how much, precious little advertising is designed to arouse desires for products which people have heard about but not previously wanted.

The second, more philosophical objection is that only a man's most elemental and least differentiated desires can be 'original with himself' if this means, as it must, uninfluenced by the environment: 'The innate wants are probably confined to food, shelter and sex. All the rest we learn to desire because we see others enjoying various things. To say that a desire is not important because it is not innate is to say that the whole cultural achievement of man is not important' (Hayek 1967, p.314). Indeed even this is still too weak. For the particular directions of our tastes in food, housing and sex are not, surely, genetically determined.

Nor may we overlook that Galbraith himself has not always been a jet-setter, wintering there, summering here, living high off book royalties and television fees. At the time of writing *The Affluent Society* he was, like Nielsen and Marcuse and the present writer, a university teacher. I hope that we were all labouring then, and not without success, to arouse interest in our subjects, even enthusiasm, among students who most surely were not all born economists or born philosophers. So what price now Galbraith's final, supposedly damning reproach: 'If the individual's wants are to be urgent they must be original with himself. They cannot be urgent if they must be contrived for him. *And above all they must not be contrived by the process of production by which they are satisfied*' (Galbraith 1958, pp.152-3: italics supplied)?

(b) The second Nielsen paper, 'A Defence of Radicalism', displays the author as a paradigm case of Popper's wholesale utopian social engineer (Popper 1965, Chapter 9). But for us now the interest lies in its further revelation of the self-image of a Leninist would-be Guardian. He is not, he assures us, 'suggesting that a small tightly-knit group of intelligentsia [and] class-conscious workers' should try 'to impose socialism from above' (Nielsen 1974, p.65). He could have had us all fooled! For he has already insisted: 'radical workers and intelligentsia should not be afraid to regard themselves as a vanguard, and should not lack the courage to insist on a vision of society – a positive conception of a truly human life – which does not correspond to the only one prevailing in our intellectually and emotionally drugged capitalist mass culture. And if the situation ever becomes ripe for this vanguard to translate such a vision of society into a social reality, they must not hold back from such a translation because they fear imparting or inculcating, through structural means, a set of values that some plain, but manipulated men, would not in their ideologically drugged state choose . . . ' (*Ibid.*, pp.62-3).

Nielsen continues: 'This may sound – brought up as we have been in a liberal ethos – like an invitation to tyranny, but if it is done with integrity and with a full commitment to socialist and indeed egalitarian values, this must not and indeed will not be so' (*Ibid.*, p.63). Yes, this does sound like a prescription for absolutism. But – to parody a later and funnier Marx – do not be misled. It is.

When Plato was dreaming dreams of his own ideal city, stately as a Dorian temple, he did wonder for one uneasy moment how his guard dogs were to be inhibited from themselves preying upon the sheep. Plato then saw 'the chief safeguard' in their 'being really well educated' (416A-B). He never got around to suggesting any other. Nielsen, who claims to be no dreamer bringing news from nowhere but a 'scientifically oriented realist', a 'tough-minded man' possessing Marxist clues to history, can do no better than simply to assert that 'this must not and indeed will not' happen. For him the sole but sufficient guarantee is not strict Platonic education but 'a full commitment to socialist and indeed egalitarian values'. Nielsen, therefore, never gives a moment's thought to constitutional checks and balances, the institutional separation of powers, accountability to an electorate. All such worldly wise and Whiggish concerns are, no doubt, expressions of an 'ideologically drugged state' – product of masterful manipulations by the unspeakable bourgeois. Yet the only guarantee which he either asks or offers surely has been and is, in his view, provided by all actual Leninist parties – including the first, the party of *The Gulag Archipelago*. We, by contrast, should not fail to challenge the authenticity of an 'egalitarianism' which can marry with a commitment to absolute power for Guardian élites.

(ii) The second exemplar is British, and can at this stage be dealt with in very short order. Benjamin Gibbs is a Lecturer in the University of Sussex. His book *Freedom and Liberation* is one of the first members of a series of essays in Radical Philosophy, published by the Sussex University Press. The statement with which the author's Preface concludes is the exact opposite of the truth: 'It will be sufficiently obvious that this is not a tract *against* freedom' (Gibbs, p.8: italics original). On the contrary: it has become perfectly obvious what this author is about by (at latest) the moment in Chapter 1 when, with an explosion against what he calls 'heartless laissez-faire policies', he rejects Berlin's epitome: 'Political liberty . . . is simply the area in which a man can act unobstructed by others' (Quoted *Ibid.*, p.24 from Berlin 1969, p.122).[20]

What, in a word, Gibbs is about is this. He is persuasively so redefining 'liberty' that the favourable sentiments now attaching to that good old cause shall in future sanctify the activities of 'a few enlightened groups and persons of influence who understand what is involved in a truly liberating reformation of society, and who are endeavouring to bring it about' (*Ibid.*, p.141). Such 'true liberation' and 'true liberty' has, of course, no truck with anything so negative and so bourgeois as the absence of coercion: 'For freedom', as this élite understands and would impose it, 'is a very different thing from being allowed to do what one desires'; and, therefore, 'A free society is not simply one that *makes* its people do what is right and good. It is a society that respects the human nature of its members, and that *makes* them do what is right and good by *making* them do it understanding that it is right and good' (*Ibid.*, pp.93 and 109: italics supplied).

What is right and good, and thus what the rest of us are to be *made* to do and *made* to want to do and *made* to understand to be right and good, is, presumably, for the élite to decide. Certainly the suggested rationale for these decisions is, as usual, going to make much of contrasts between truly human needs and real interests, on the one hand, and, on the other hand, merely actual wishes and desires: 'If perfect freedom encompasses the whole spectrum of human goods . . . Natural freedom involves harmonious develop-ment of all one's human powers . . . '; while the proposition 'that grown persons are always the best judges of what is in their own interest' is ridiculed as 'this fatuous and fantastic claim' (*Ibid.*, pp.129, 130 and 90).

Strictly speaking, by the way, what Gibbs so ridicules is a different and truer statement, which Gibbs falsely asserts to be equivalent to the proposition pilloried above. What Mill actually said was that ' . . . with respect to his own feelings and circum-stances, the most ordinary man or woman has means of knowledge immeasurably surpassing those that can be possessed by anyone else' (Mill, p.133). Is there anything wrong with that?

3 Necessities and luxuries, profit or command

The previous section looked at two examples of the Guardian mentality, illustrating the appeal to such minds of the notions of need or interest as opposed to want or desire. Both these exemplars happen to be socialist Radicals. Others could have been summoned who are or were neither Radicals nor socialists. Plato himself, while proposing in *The Republic* that his élite should constitute a commune, tax-supported as a fully salaried Guardian service, never suggested that any such arrangements should be extended to the vulgar, engaged in the banausic business of production. Plato was – like General de Gaulle – perhaps too little interested in 'the baggage train' either to require or to forbid the public ownership of all the means of production, distribution and exchange. Nevertheless, in today's world most actual or would be Guardians in fact are socialists. Indeed most of the most powerful and least inhibited are – in the words of an old song – Lenin's lads.

It is in a brief final section worth suggesting that this is more than an ephemeral contingency. That concentration of economic control, and that synthesis of the economic with the political, which are both of the essence of socialism, must by their very nature both attract and foster the Guardian mentality. From the very beginning this has been clear both to the acutest socialists and to their acutest critics. Saint Simon, for instance, foresaw that those who did not obey his proposed planning boards would be 'treated as cattle' (Quoted Hayek 1944, p.18). Ruskin was equally frank: 'My principles of political economy . . . in a single phrase . . . "Soldiers of the ploughshare as well as soldiers of the sword"' (p.102). Mosca warned: ' . . . state control of the means of production would leave the administrators of the state – who are sure to be a minority – in a position where they should be able to combine all economic and political power in their hands . . . ' (Quoted Andreski, p.158). As one of the makers of the first triumphant socialist revolution was able to reflect, before his murder in exile: 'In a country where the sole employer is the State, opposition means death by slow starvation. The old principle, who does not work shall not eat, has been replaced by a new one: who does not obey shall not eat' (Trotsky, p.76).

In a less strident, less dramatic vein – more in tune with the temper of Minogue's 'mild social scientists, or benevolent welfarists' – consider the evergreen false antithesis between production for profit and production for use. It is, as we shall see in Chapter VI, at least as old as Aristotle's *Politics*. Although antique, it is nevertheless false, for what ought to be the very obvious reason that there can be no profit in producing what no one has any wish to buy and, presumably, to use. Of course, what plain or not so plain folk choose to buy may not be what the superior and right-minded – or, as the case might be, the left-minded – staunchly believe that they ought to want. It may be conspicuous waste or, to borrow a favourite word of the Mark I 1964 Harold Wilson, candyfloss.

Again, much may be said – and at appropriate times and in appropriate places most certainly should be said – about people who cannot earn enough to buy even the most minimal necessities of life and health. But none of this justifies any general opposition between, on the one hand, the profit system or production for profit, and, on the other hand, production for use or production to satisfy human needs.

The true antithesis here is quite different. A market confronts a command economy: in the former what is produced is ultimately determined by what people with money to buy are prepared to buy; in the latter the crux is what people in a position to enforce their commands choose to command. This comes out as clearly as could be wished from a section on 'Profit or Planning' in John Strachey's *Why You Should Be A Socialist*, a work which made or guided a whole generation of converts in the decade after its first appearance as a massively circulated Left Book Club pamphlet: 'Well, we all know what production for profit means . . . Under Socialism . . . you have got to arrange some other principles on which to decide what to produce. This alternative principle of regulation we call planning. There must exist in every socialist society . . . a planning commission, which will decide year by year what kinds of things, and in what proportions, shall be produced. It has . . . to make an estimate of the total needs of the population, and then another estimate of the country's total productive resources. Then it must see how best to fit one to another' (Strachey 1944, p.68).

In another, longer work Strachey was even more succinct: 'As Mr and Mrs Webb write, "Once private ownership, with its profit-seeking motive of production for the competitive market is abandoned, specific directions must be given as to what each establishment has to produce" ' (Strachey 1936, p.57: the Webb quotation comes from Chapter XIII of their *Soviet Communism: A New Civilization*). Strachey continues in the pamphlet: ' "Is not this a very difficult job?" you may say. Yes, indeed it is' (p.68).

Never fear. We do not and never shall lack for Guardians eager to pronounce upon our needs; and, with a minimum of reference to any actual wants which might be expressed in the market place, to issue what they consider to be the appropriate commands. There is in the *Critique of the Gotha Programme* what sounds a generous, romantic slogan. Yet already implicit in that slogan we can hear both thin overtones of wartime austerity and the strong threat of a centralised, collective, total absolutism: 'From each according to his abilities, to each according to his needs' (Marx 1891, p23).

CHAPTER VI

Competition and the Profit Motive

> Besides, there is nothing so plain boring as the constant repetition of assertions that are not true, and sometimes not even faintly sensible; if we can reduce this a bit, it will be all to the good. *J.L. Austin: Sense and Sensibilia (p.5)*

At the head of *Labour's Programme 1973* stands the statement: 'We aim to bring about a society based on cooperation instead of competition, where production is for people's needs, not for private profit.' These two antitheses are entrenched deep in the British public mind. Certainly they have strong claim to be parts of what, in Hampshire's phrase 'has governed the advocacy of R.H. Tawney and Richard Titmuss and that holds the Labour Party together'. Some of the most eloquent of that advocacy is in Tawney's own earliest prophetic work, *The Acquisitive Society*. He there assailed what he was always to view as a 'system in which industry is carried on, not as a profession serving the public, but for the advantage of shareholders'. He therefore wanted 'to release those who do constructive work ... to apply their energies to the true purpose of industry, which is the provision of service....' And he reflected with satisfaction: 'Over a considerable field of industry the Cooperative Movement has already substituted the motive of communal service for that of profit...' (Tawney 1921, pp.140, 150 and 152).

A few years later these thoughts were echoed by the then once and future Prime Minister Ramsay MacDonald: to transform 'capitalism into socialism ... industry must be converted from a sordid struggle for gain into a cooperative undertaking, carried on for the service of the community and amenable to its control' (Quoted Beer, p.136). Much later still, a few months before his death, Albert Einstein was quoted in *Socialist International Review* as saying: 'The economic anarchy of capitalist society ...

the main cause of our evils. Production is carried on for profit, not for use.' And so it goes on, it seems without end.

1 Competition, cooperation and monopoly

So let us begin by taking a short, straight look at the concept of competition. That will make us better able to see with what competition is and is not compatible.

(i) Three features of this concept are relevant here.

(a) The first is that competition essentialy involves relationships between two or more competitors. In this it resembles both cooperation and equality: it takes at least two to compete, or to cooperate, or to be equal. You could say that this first conceptual fact makes competition, in the very weak sense just indicated, an essentially social notion: Robinson Crusoe cannot engage in any competition on his desert island until and unless he meets Man Friday.

(b) The second point follows from the first. It is that competition essentially involves comparisons; and comparisons with another person or persons. Thus it is one thing to say that someone in some direction put up a better performance than his own previous best, or that he in some way bettered or worsened his own former condition. But we cannot begin to talk of competition until it is a question of making such a comparison between different persons. Any competitive bettering or worsening is always a bettering or worsening relative to at least one other competitor. You could say again that this second fact makes competition, in what now becomes a slightly stronger sense, an essentially social notion: it not merely requires at least two people, it also requires comparisons between at least two people.

This second point applies to equality also but not to cooperation. There is, too, a further resemblance here between the ideas of equality and of competition. It lies in the truth that neither of these notions has any necessary links with an absolute position on any scale of achievement. It is in principle possible to get and to stay ahead of all the competition, even though your position on some absolute scale is steadily declining; and equally possible in principle to fall and to remain behind all the competition while your absolute situation is actually improving. The second of these wry possibilities has for many recent years been actualised in the British economy: the gross national product (GNP) has risen even in real terms; but in the competitions of international comparisons we have been almost always at or near the bottom.

It is this essential indifference to absolute position which those of us for whom equality of outcome is not a value find most alien in those for whom it is. If for you such equality is a value then, it follows necessarily, there must be at least some possible cases in which you will prefer a more equal distribution, even where this is bought at the cost of a lower average level, or even a lower minimum level, in the absolute.

Having spoken of the essential indifference to absolute position which characterises both the idea of competition and the ideal of equality of outcome, it is necessary to insist once more that this point is purely conceptual – that is to say, it is inherent in the concepts of equality and competition themselves. Success or failure in competition does not in itself guarantee that you will achieve or fail to achieve any particular position upon some absolute scale; and the ideal of equality is achieved as perfectly in an equality of magnificence as in an equality of misery.

Suppose, however, that we turn from questions of the logical relations and non-relations between concepts to what David Hume called 'matters of fact and real existence' (Hume 1748, IV,i). Then we find an altogether different story. For it would be easy – and on some less philosophical occasion appropriate – to argue that it is in fact impossible to attain and maintain the highest levels of achievement without a deal of competition, and that this applies as much in the economy and in education as it does in sport.

(c) The third conceptual point about competition is that it essentially involves a striving by every competitor in some way to do better than the rest of the competition. Thus, if someone takes part in a race without trying to win – or, at any rate, without trying to do better than at least one of the other competitors – then we say, truly, that he is not really competing in that race. Once again you could say that this fact makes competition an essentially social notion, in what is now a pretty strong sense of the word 'social'. For it is social in the sense that it requires at least two people; that it involves comparisons between them; and that for each it is an activity presupposing and conditioned by a reciprocal awareness of the other.

A corollary of this is that competition, like equality, is essentially concerned with relativities rather than absolutes. This is a slightly different way of putting a point already made in commenting on the second main conceptual fact. But the difference here makes it easier to see what is often an unlovely aspect of both things. A recent, profound and disturbing essay on 'The Economic Contradictions of Democracy' reaches the conclusion: 'It could yet be saved if contemporary egalitarianism were to lose its hold over the intelligentsia.' Mentioning 'concepts such as "relative deprivation" in sociology, inequality (a loaded way of describing differences)' and ' "interdependent utilities" in economics', he deplores 'the contribution of the so-called intelligentsia', which is 'to focus all attention on relativities to the exclusion of absolutes' (Brittan 1975, pp.21, 27 and 28).

But, if we accept this, then both consistency and integrity require us to notice that competition too is essentially concerned with relativities; even as we go on to insist, as we surely must, on two things which are frequently neglected or even denied by supporters of the 'contemporary egalitarianism'. First, competition, though conceptually concerned only with relativities, is often the practically necessary condition for promoting and securing the absolutely better. Second, it is perfectly possible for people engaging in competition to be aware of this first truth, and to be in fact themselves as much directed at absolute as at relative bettering.

But again, having insisted upon these two 'matters of fact and real existence', we still have to go on to allow that conceptually there is a world of difference between trying to improve on one's own previous performance and trying to do or be better than someone else; between striving to improve the condition of oneself and one's family, and trying to ensure that that condition is better than that of other people and their families. Aims of the second of these two kinds may indeed be unlovely, socially disruptive, and essentially insatiable. They are then, to adapt another phrase from Edward Heath, part of the unacceptable face of competition.

It is a face which many will have seen in the world of education, though nowadays perhaps, even there, it is less familiar in Britain than in some other countries. I have, for example, heard tell of a Japanese mother, ambitious for her children, who forced them to concentrate on their homework while she watched exciting TV programmes. She then gave them vivid accounts of these programmes in the hopes that these accounts – retailed at school with adornments – would tempt other children to neglect their own homework. Competitive desires are also, in the nature of the case, peculiarly liable to frustration; and in a way in which the desire to do better than one was doing before is not. For suppose we have a group every member of which wants to do better than all the others. Then, if we discount the tiresome possibility of dead heats, we can be sure that all but one are bound to be disappointed.

(ii) Having by now become a little clearer about the essentials of the concept of competition, we are ready to challenge the antithesis between competition and cooperation. Despite its hardy perennial popularity, especially perhaps among educationists, this is as false as its even more popular companion – that between production for profit and production for use, or to meet human needs.

Certainly there are occasions when a choice has to be made between alternatives of cooperation or competition. Two firms, for instance, may have to decide whether to compete against each other for a big contract, each of the two submitting its own rival tender, or whether to form a consortium, submitting one joint tender in competition with the rest of the field. But this does not mean that cooperation and competition cannot coexist within the same universe.

In the first place, competition can be, and in commerce and industry usually is, between two teams; and no team is going to do well in any competition if its members refuse to cooperate with one another. (In the education world there is, surely, room for an explosive growth of such cooperative competition, with schools and forms competing to reach higher average levels of scholastic achievement; their different performances being honestly and realistically assessed, of course, by independent, objective, and external examinations.)

In the second place, in some cases – most strikingly and most familiarly in competitive games – a modicum of cooperation is a condition of the competition itself. I cannot play tennis unless someone is willing to cooperate with me so far as to have a game. (Here I find myself thinking of two personal illustrations. First, there was my father's attempt to explain the game of tennis to his Indian batman in World War I. The immediate response was, that, if the point of the game was to get the ball to bounce unreturnably in the opposite court, then he would get up to play alone and unopposed in the middle of the night! Second, there was my own experience as a young don of the pressures to sacrifice whole evenings 'to make up a four' – if once one had been so unwise as to learn, and to admit to knowing, how to play bridge. It was in the eyes of my seniors, I fear, one of my many unclubbable faults to refuse to be so cooperative as to join in this highly competitive activity.)

In such sporting cases the cooperation among those who are at the same time competitors can scarcely fail to be a part of the intentions of all those who are cooperating. But it is also possible for people to be cooperating in practice to achieve ends which are no part of their intentions – ends of which they may even be wholly unaware.

This is precisely what happens in competition in trade and industry. It is easy, yet too rare, to understand why competition is so often uncongenial to those who may be pressed to compete. How much more comfortable for us it would be, they reflect, to stabilise the whole trade or the whole industry by sharing out the business between all the established suppliers. Maybe then – whether with or without suitably hypocritical and sanctimonious talk of being released 'to do constructive work', and of how all can now 'apply their energies to the true purpose of industry . . . the provision of service' – those established suppliers can somehow contrive their own ways of warding off the upsetting threat of intruders offering either goods and services which 'their' customers might find more attractive, or the same goods and services at a keener price. It is, nevertheless, through competition – abused perhaps as 'cut-throat', 'dog-eat-dog', or 'rat-race' – that competitors, whether willing or unwilling, whether with or without this intent, cooperate to serve customers by providing what those customers themselves find most acceptable.

It was one of the great Scottish founding fathers of social science, ever alert to the unintended consequences of intended action, who epitomised such cooperation through competition. He made, with particular reference to middlemen grocers, a completely general point: 'Their competition might perhaps ruin some of themselves; but to take care of this is the business of the parties concerned, and it may safely be left to their discretion . . . . It can never hurt either the consumer or the producer; on the contrary, it must tend to make the retailers both sell cheaper and buy dearer than if the whole trade was monopolised by one or two persons' (Smith, II,v).[21]

(iii) It must by now be obvious, even if it was not before, that in an economic context the true antithesis of competition is not cooperation but monopoly. Those, therefore, whose declared aim is 'to bring about a society based on cooperation instead of competition' are at least half right in wanting to proceed by setting up more and more monopolies – whether these take the form of nationalised industries or of labour union closed shops. That there is a certain reluctance to stress this aspect of their policies is also easy to understand: the rest of us could scarcely fail to see that all producers' monopolies are against everyone's interests as consumers.

This reluctance takes a mildly amusing form in those speeches, without which no Labour Party conference is complete, where the speaker begins by asserting that some trade or industry is dominated by three or four big 'monopolies'; (perhaps adding, as the internationalists' ultimate condemnation, that some or all of these are multi-national), and failing to notice that if there are three or four firms in competition they are not monopolies. From this premise it is forthwith inferred that the private firms involved should 'all be taken into public ownership'; and so reconstituted into yet another nationalised industry. It is, of course, not said that this is a proposal to establish there, what on the speaker's own incoherent account we at present both do and do not have, a monopoly.

More common, and not amusing at all, is the reluctance to recognise that labour monopolies too are monopolies. Yet is not the whole point and purpose of closed shops to gain for the union concerned, and to maintain, an impregnable position as sole seller of its particular sort or sorts of labour, with all the consequent possibilities of both extorting a high monopoly price and providing poor monopoly quality? In this perspective it becomes less surprising that, as was remarked in Section 2 of Chapter I, most of the main British labour unions, along with the general Trades Union Congress (TUC) itself, are by their constitutions committed to the advancement of socialism; to setting up, that is, state or other public monopolies in 'all the means of production, distribution, and exchange.' Equally unsurprising is the fact that it is officials of public sector and closed shop unions who are loudest and most unanimous in hostility to any suggestion of competition in the areas in which their members are employed.

Take, for example, the Union of Post Office Workers (UPW). Its Secretary recently boasted that he had alerted his members to spot, and to report for prosecution, British firms having their circulars to Britain posted in Holland; where, it appears, better paid but far more productive workers provide faster and cheaper service. You could scarcely ask for a sharper or clearer example of a labour monopoly in cahoots with a monopoly employer to exploit the captive consumer.

Although the truth of the two previous paragraphs can scarcely be denied, it still does not do to say such things in Britain. If said, they will be put down as right-wing extremism, or union-bashing. (The second charge is truly quaint. Who or what in this country and at this time has the power to bash the unions?) Often this unwillingness to hear or to face the most manifest facts springs from a syndrome for which it may be salutary to have a name. Something suitably offensive should prepare us to pick out and to pillory the offending condition. So I hereby christen it the Tolpuddle Fixation; defined as stubborn insistence upon seeing all trades unions and trades unionists, at all times and in all places whatsoever, on the shining model of the flawless George Loveless and his companions, men who stood up bravely against over-whelming and intolerable oppression.

2 Two first thoughts about the profit motive

It is, as we have seen, constantly asserted or assumed that, inasmuch as (private) profit is an essential characteristic of anything approaching 'the obvious and simple system of natural liberty', such economic arrangements have to be more selfish and hard-nosed than their actual or possible rivals. Thus, in the summer of 1972, under the headline 'Waiting for a Sign from the Egoists', *The Times* of London reported that Archbishop Camara of Brazil had asked a meeting of members of both Houses of Parliament: 'Why do you not help to lay bare the serious distortions of socialism such as they exist in Russia and China? And why do you not denounce, once and for all, the intrinsic selfishness and callousness of capitalism?' (27 June 1972).

Later in the same week the *Catholic Herald* reported other meetings at which the Archbishop – described as 'one of the great voices of our time' by Cardinal de Roy, President of the Pontifical Commission for Justice and Peace – called on British Catholics to fight the forces of capitalist imperialism (30 June 1972). It appears that no one was sufficiently curious about the insertion of the adjective 'capitalist' to ask why imperialism apparently becomes venial, or even ceases to be a sin at all, once 'all the means of production, distribution, and exchange' have been soundly nationalised.

(i) To the Archbishop's question the best first response is another: 'Why is it that we never hear of the rent motive or the wages motive?' Perhaps the classical distinction between profit and rent is obsolete. But, if it is proper to speak of a profit motive, it should surely be equally proper to speak of a wages motive. By parity of reasoning we shall then have to admit into our new economic psychology the fixed interest motive, the top price motive, and the best buy motive. And, of course, if it is proper to argue that those who are paid wages must be stirred by the wages motive; then it has to be not merely proper but positively refined to say that those whose wages are paid at longer intervals, and called a salary or even compensation, are inspired by, respectively, the salary motive and the compensation motive:

> And, when folks understood their cant
> They changed that for 'emolument';
> Unwilling to be short or plain,
> In any thing concerning gain . . . .
>
> (Mandeville, p.66)

A first general suggestion is that it is misguided to insist on applying to psychology (one element from) a system of categories originally developed in, and appropriate to, economics. To insist on doing this is rather like postulating a set of chess motives, distinguished one from another by reference to those similarities and differences which have been found relevant to the interests and purposes of chess theoreticians; and then labelling these factitious postulations with expressions drawn from the technical vocabulary of chess – the knight's move motive, the Fool's Mate motive, the queening motive, or what have you.

Consider as another example of such a misapplying of economic or financial categories to psychology, and savour as a mischievous intellectual treat, one of the most bizarre and delightful of those high theoretical fantasies which adorn *A Treatise of Human Nature*. For there, in the section 'Of the Probability of Causes', Hume concludes that, upon his then principles, 'a man, who desires a thousand pound, has in reality a thousand or more desires, which uniting together, seem to make only one passion; tho' the composition evidently betrays itself upon every alteration of the object, by the preference he gives to the larger number, if superior only by an unit' (Hume 1739-40, I(iii) 12).

Noticing that suggestive 'or more', one is tempted to go on to urge: that before decimalisation the desire for a thousand pounds was – 'in reality' – two hundred and forty thousand old penny desires; that now it has diminished to a mere hundred thousand new pence hankerings; and that a desire for a thousand piastre pounds must, by parity of reasoning, simultaneously constitute one million indiscernible atomic yens. The mind boggles at the unfolding vista of possible implications of other currency differences and equivalences for the psychology of the notorious gnomes of Zurich and the infamous moneychangers of Beirut! But enough is enough to indicate the nature of the first general objection to the economic psychology implicit in all this loose talk about the profit motive.

(ii) The second general suggestion is that no one – not even an Archbishop – has any business simply to assume that the desire to make a profit is always and necessarily selfish and discreditable, while the corresponding desires to obtain a wage, or a salary, or a retirement income, are – apparently – not. No doubt all these various desires are interested, in the sense that those who are guided by any of them are – in the immortal words of Damon Runyon, the Balzac of Broadway – 'doing the best they can'. But, precisely because this does apply equally to all, we can find no ground here for condemning one and not the others.

This neglected fact is awkward for the denouncers. For no one, surely, is so starry-eyed as to believe that any kind of economic organisation can dispense with all such interested motives: 'Every economic system devised for ordinary human beings', we may read even in a Fabian Tract, 'must have self-interest as its driving force' (Lewis, p.7). If, therefore, one such system is upon this particular ground to be condemned as 'intrinsically selfish and heartless', then, by the same token, all must be. Yet that, of course, is precisely not what is wanted by those who thus denounce capitalism root and branch, and as such, while tolerantly dis-counting, as more or less 'serious distortions', whatever faults they can bring themselves to recognise in the already fully socialist countries.

A further fundamental mistake here is to identify the interested with the selfish. This is wrong. For, though selfish actions are perhaps always interested, only some interested actions are also selfish. To say that a piece of conduct was selfish is to say more

than that it was interested. The point is that selfishness is always
and necessarily out of order. Interestedness is not, and scarcely
could be.

For example: when two healthy children eagerly eat their
dinners it would, presumably, be correct to say that they are
pursuing each their own interest; and, if there were any choices
involved, no doubt the economist would describe them as thereby
maximising their utilities. Yet this is no reason to start reproaching
them. Time for that after brother has grabbed and eaten sister's
dinner too, or perhaps in some less flagrant way refused to
consider others and to respect their proper claims. Again, even
when my success can be won only at the price of someone else's
failure, it would be inordinately austere to insist that it is always
and necessarily selfish for me to pursue my own interests. Is
anyone prepared to say that rival candidates competing for some
coveted position are culpably selfish in not all withdrawing in
order to clear the way for the others?

The upshot, therefore, is that it will not wash to dismiss any one
economic system as 'intrinsically selfish and heartless' simply
because that system depends upon and engages interested motives,
or even simply because it allows or encourages people to pursue
their own interests in certain situations of zero sum conflict. If
there is something peculiarly obnoxious about wanting to make a
(private) profit, it will have to be something about making a
(private) profit, rather than something about just wanting to
acquire some economic good, or even about competing to acquire
scarce economic goods in any zero sum conflict situation, as such.

3 Three Aristotelian misconceptions

That it is indeed essentially scandalous to make a profit – and
hence, presumably, correspondingly scandalous to wish to do so –
is an idea both as old as the Classical Greek philosophers and as
topical as tomorrow's party political broadcasts. Consider what
was said by the one who has had (and, mainly through Aquinas
and Hegel, continues to have), by far the greatest influence.

Paradoxically, the economic thought of Aristotle is found
mainly in the *Politics*. One characteristic is that he accepts as
normative whatever he believes to be, as it were, the intention of
nature. For those inclined to follow this lead it should be salutary
to discover where it took Aristotle: 'Now if Nature makes nothing
purposeless or in vain, all animals must have been made by nature

for the sake of men. It also follows that the art of war is in some sense a natural mode of acquisition. Hunting is a part of that art; and hunting ought to be practised, not only against wild animals, but also against those human beings who are intended by nature to be ruled by others and refuse to obey that intention. War of this kind is naturally just' (1256 B 20-6).

No one after reading this will be surprised to find that, when Aristotle thinks of an ideal universal provider, this is Nature, and not, as it would be today, the state. His pronouncement is oddly reminiscent of 'the original position' as stipulated by Rawls: 'On a general view, as we have already noticed, a supply of property should be ready to hand. It is the business of nature to furnish subsistence for each being brought into the world; and this is shown by the fact that the offspring of animals always gets nourishment from the residuum of the matter that gives it its birth' (1258 A 33-6).

(i) It is significant that, after this high-minded Classical formulation of the shabby familiar doctrine that the world owes us a living, Aristotle, like Rawls, emphasises acquisition rather than production: 'The natural form, therefore, of the art of acquisition is always, and in all cases, acquisition from fruits and animals. That art . . . has two forms: one which is connected with . . . trade, and another which is connected with the management of the household. Of these two forms, the latter is necessary and laudable; the former is a method of exchange which is justly censured, because the gain in which it results is not naturally made, but is made at the expense of other men' (1258 A 37 – 1258 B 2).

(a) Aristotle's point is that trade is in essence exploitation. The acquisitions of the trader must, Aristotle thinks, be made at the expense of that trader's trading partner; whereas the only creditable acquisitions are those achieved from non-human nature direct. Shorn of these notions of what is and is not in accord with the intentions of Nature, Aristotle's is the same thesis – and the same misconception – as we find in *Unto this Last*: 'Whenever material gain follows exchange, for every plus there is a precisely equal minus' (Ruskin, p.131).

It has for centuries been, and still remains, a most popular misconception; perhaps now especially in a form referring particularly to all trade in labour (power). For instance: the author of a recent book on *Social Justice*, who reveals no other Marxist cloven hoof, tosses off, as if this were the most uncontentious of truisms, the remark that 'the mystique of capitalism . . . disguises the transfer of benefits from worker to employer under the form of an equal exchange of values, through the device of a free contract of employment' (Miller, p.204). This first Aristotelian misconception nevertheless provides a happy occasion to quote from A. E. Housman's *Juvenal* a blistering rebuke to a rival scholar's lapse: 'Three minutes' thought would suffice to find this out; but thought is irksome and three minutes is a long time' (Housman, p.xi).

(b) The crux is that trade is a reciprocal relationship. If I am trading with you it follows necessarily that you are trading with me. Trade is also, for both parties, necessarily voluntary. If you succeed in seizing something from me by force, it is not being either acquired or relinquished in trade. So, if any possible advantage of trade to the trader could be gained only at the expense of some corresponding disadvantage to his trading partner, it would appear that in any commercial exchange at least one party must be either a fool, or a masochist, or a gambler.

But, of course, as all must recognise when not either by theory or by passion distracted, the truth is that the seller sells because, in his actual situation, he would rather receive the price than retain the goods, while the buyer buys because, in his actual situation, he would rather pay the price than be without the goods. Ruskin was, therefore, diametrically wrong. It is of the essence of trade, not that any advantage for one party can be achieved only at the expense of the other, but that no deal is made at all unless, whether rightly or wrongly, both parties believe that they stand to gain thereby – or at least both prefer the deal actually made to any available alternative deal, and to no deal at all.

Certainly one of the trading partners, or even both, may be mistaken or in some other way misguided in his decision to deal. Certainly too the actual situation of either party, the situation in which it seems better to him to make the deal than not, may be in many ways unfair or unfortunate. But all this is contingent, and hence to the present question irrelevant. This question is: 'What is and is not essential to the very idea of trade?' Mutually satisfactory sex is a better model here than poker played for money. For in the former the satisfactions of each depend reciprocally upon those of the other; whereas the latter really is a zero sum game in which your winnings precisely equal, because they are, my losses.

One temptation to conclude that trade necessarily involves a zero sum confrontation lies in the fact that both buyers and sellers would often, if they had to, pay more or accept less than they do. Obviously it is in such a situation possible to regard either the more which might have been got or the less which might have been given as an advantage forfeited by one trading partner to the other. But this, which is perhaps often the case, certainly is not so always. And both buyer and seller may be, and I imagine typically are, simultaneously in similar situations with regard to such forfeited possible advantages. So it cannot be correct to infer, as a general conclusion, that all the gains of trade must always be achieved by one trading partner at the expense of the other.

Another less intellectual but in practice more powerful temptation lies in the unappealing human inclination rather to attend with eager jealousy to the gains of others than to find a modest contentment in one's own; to forget that the deal was to your advantage in order to resent that it was to his also. Surely he would not – as you so ungraciously insist – 'have made his profits out of you', had it not also been the case that you saw some advantage to yourself in your dealings with him? Yet how true it is that 'Few men can be persuaded that they get too much by those they sell to, how extraordinary soever their gains are; when at the same time there is hardly a profit so inconsiderable, but they'll grudge it to those they buy from' (Mandeville, p.113).

(c) In general – and it is a reflection which has a wide relevance – economic arrangements are best judged by results. Concentrate on the price and quality of the product. Do not officiously probe the producer's purity of heart. If, nevertheless, we are to consider motives, then this jealousy which resents that others too should gain, and maybe more than us, must be accounted much nastier than any supposed intrinsic selfishness of straight self-interest. Some might even discern the hand of Providence at work when it appears that, for thus putting the resentment-of-profit motive first, 'the envious society' of the United Kingdom pays a heavy price in forfeited economic growth (Schoeck, passim).

The second such reflection is that the most minimally prudent persons must always hope, and try to ensure, that their suppliers have some interest in supplying them to their satisfaction; and this quite irrespective of whether or not these interests provide the main or sole motives of the suppliers. You do not need to be the total cynic to feel anxious about the quality and reliability of supply where the suppliers have no interest in giving satisfaction, and their clients have to depend on the universal presence and strength of 'the motives of community service'. The author of *The Wealth of Nations* was, as usual, both dignified and realistic when he wrote: 'It is not from the benevolence of the butcher, the brewer, or the baker that we expect our dinner, but from their regard for their own interest. We address ourselves, not to their humanity but to their self-love, and never talk to them of our own necessities but of their advantages. Nobody but a beggar chooses to depend chiefly upon the benevolence of his fellow citizens' (Smith, I,ii).

(ii) Aristotle's next contribution is equally unfortunate, and has been equally important. Immediately after the last passage quoted earlier he continues: 'The trade of the usurer is hated most, and with most reason . . . . Currency came into existence merely as a means of exchange; usury tries to make it increase. This is the reason why interest is called by the word we commonly use [the word 'tokos', which in Greek also means offspring]; for as the offspring resembles its parent, so the interest bred by money is like the principal which breeds it, and it may be called "currency the son of currency". Hence we can understand why, of all modes of acquisition, usury is the most unnatural' (1258 B 2-8).

(a) 'Usury' is now, thanks first to Aristotle and still more to his medieval successors, such a bad word that we may at first fail to realise to what he is objecting. It is not only to those very high rates of fixed interest which would nowadays be condemned as usurious. Nor even is it only to all fixed interest as such; which, as we shall soon see, was the prime target of those medieval successors. No, Aristotle's objection here is to any money return upon any money investment. It is, he thinks, against nature for money to breed money.

The moment Aristotle's point is appreciated, it becomes quite clear that both his objection and his supporting reason are superstitious and muddled. For a sum of money is the convertible equivalent of any of the goods or collections of goods which it might buy. There can, therefore, be nothing obnoxiously unnatural about receiving a money return upon an investment in money, unless it would be equally obnoxious and unnatural to ask for some return either in money or in kind for the use of the goods themselves.

There are three corollaries to draw from this explication of the essence of money. First, it must be psychologically unilluminating to speak of any money motive; and, by the same token, still more unilluminating to try to develop a complete economic psychology upon a basis of a series of economic distinctions between various mercenary motives. For that someone wants to make a profit or to earn a wage tells us nothing of what he wants the money for. Almost any desire can take the form of a desire for money. It is obvious that this is a necessary consequence of the essential nature of money as a conventional instrument of exchange. Aristotle himself elsewhere makes this point about the nature of money, but he misses its application to the point now under discussion.

Second, it must be wrong to hope that the abolition of money, or a reduction of the range of goods which money can buy, might by itself reduce greed and competition. Certainly it is tautologically true that the profit motive, the fixed interest motive, the wages motive, and all the other factitious motives listed or suggested in the previous Section 2, are mercenary. All, that is, may be defined in terms of the acquisition of money. So it might seem that totally to abolish money, or to reduce its importance as a means of acquisition, must be to abolish, or at least to weaken, all mercenary motives.

In an empty sense this no doubt is true. Yet, unless these changes happened to be accompanied by something quite different, an enormous transformation of present human nature, people would continue to pursue, and to compete for, whatever it was which they had always wanted, but which money could not now buy. In a word: if cars are not on sale for money, but are available as a perquisite of public office, then this will by itself tend only to increase the competition for such privileged official places. It is of course true – only too true – that the abolition of money must make us less mercenary. But it could not so much as begin to make us less materialistic or less competitive.

Third, money, and the extension of the range of goods and services which money can buy, are sovereign instruments of choice: 'If all rewards, instead of being offered in money, were offered in the form of public distinctions or privileges, positions of power over other men, or better housing, or better food, opportunities for travel or education, this would ... mean that the recipient would no longer be allowed to choose, and that, whoever fixed the reward, determined not only its size but also the particular form in which it should be enjoyed' (Hayek 1944, p.67; and compare Seldon 1977, and Harris and Seldon 1979, passim).

(b) It is within parenthesis worth noticing that the medieval condemnation of usury proscribed all and only loans at fixed rates of interest. In his study of *Religion and the Rise of Capitalism*, the prophet of *Equality* had said: 'Medieval opinion, which has no objection to rent or profits, provided that they are reasonable – for is not everyone in a small way a profit-maker? – has no mercy for the debenture-holder. His crime is that he takes a payment for money which is fixed and certain, and such a payment is usury' (Tawney 1938, p.55).

But Tawney also shares responsibility for spreading the notion that the leading Scholastics believed the just price for any good or service to be one to be determined by some committee of official wise men. It now appears that this is as wrong as that other great popular misconception about the Scholastics – that they were devoted to a full-time flat-out debate about the possible angelic population of a pinhead. From Albertus Magnus onwards, with the exception of a handful of Scotist holdouts, all the leading figures seem to have defined the just as the normal free market price. They were very hot, too, on the point that an authentic free market must exclude both all fraud and all coercive monopolies; which latter specifically included – what are today by far the most powerful and least tractable – labour monopolies (de Roover; and compare Viner, a reference supplied by Brian Barry).

(iii) Aristotle's third unfortunate contribution is a tricky and precarious distinction between two forms of the art of acquisition, acquisition for household use and acquisition for financial gain. This must surely be an ancestor – perhaps *the* ancestor – of what we have already seen (in Section 3 of Chapter V) to be the false though evergreen antithesis between production for profit and production for use.

4 Interests and operative motives

Section 2 queried the propriety of a direct transfer of concepts from economic theory to individual psychology. It is time to consider some related but different topics, namely, relevant aspects of the connections and lack of connections between actual individual interest and operative individual motivation.

(i) The first and most general point is that we cannot draw valid inferences from the premise that someone has some interest in something, or even that this is their only interest in it, to the conclusion that their conduct will in fact be motivated by the pursuit of that interest, much less that that must be their only operative motivation. At some stage in most traditional British detective stories, for example there is a review of possible suspects, characters who had both a motive and an opportunity to commit the murder. But it still remains to discover whether this possible motive, which usually if not always rates as an interest, was in fact operative; whether, that is, he or she did in fact attempt or commit the murder, and for that reason. Nor is it ever precluded that the action might have been overdetermined, in the sense that the agent had two or more operative motives any one of which alone could have been sufficient to secure their acting as they did.

These abstract logical points carry morals for those who really are concerned about purity of heart here – about the true motivation of economic agents, whether interested or disinterested. For it follows that these new economic puritans have no business to infer either (from the fact that the sole interest of equity investors as such is profit maximisation) that all the investment decisions of actual flesh-and-blood investors will be directed solely to that end, with no other operative motivation, or (from the fact that the sole interest of employees as such is correspondingly their pay) that they will work only to secure that pay, with no other operative motivation. Not only are such arguments invalid. Their conclusions are also false. Maybe most people most of the time do act to further what they believe to be their own interests; although, unless it is construed as a made-to-measure tautology, this is certainly not true of everyone always. But the more general and substantial objection is that Dostoievsky, second to none as an expert on human nature, was not exaggerating much when he said: 'No one ever acts from a single motive.'

There is, therefore, nothing in the nature of either the profit motive or the wages motive which must exclude the operation of any others. A man may invest his capital in a bassoon factory, both because he wants the highest possible return on his investment, and because he wants to popularise bassoon playing, and because he wants to infuriate his unmusical ex-wife. Less light-heartedly, and more to the present point, there is nothing at all to stop either the profit-maker or the wage-earner from being partly or wholly motivated by concerns to serve whatever customers present themselves at the receiving end of the whole operation.

To the angry shouts that there is not much reason to expect that capitalists will be so benevolent, the most apt although perhaps pessimistic response is that there is exactly as much reason, or as little, to expect this of them – made as they are of our common human clay – as there is to expect the same of employees of state-owned and other non-profit organisations. (No one who lived through the British public sector strikes of the winter of 1978-9, or is prepared to face the facts of union enforced overmanning and unproductivity in British Steel or British Leyland or the British Ports Authority or the British Post Office, could now easily write with Tawney's optimism of releasing 'those who do constructive work from the control of those whose sole interest is pecuniary gain, in order that they may be free to apply their energies to the true purpose of industry, which is the provision of service . . . .')

(ii) The important points about profits, however, refer to interests rather than to motives; while the relevant kind of overdetermination is that in which the interests of one may coincide, instead of conflicting, with those of another. What matters to me directly is what people do, and what effects their actions actually have; not their reasons for so doing, nor the effects which they may have had it in mind to produce. About these things there is more to be said in the next chapter. Let us in the meantime conclude with two examples of how hatred of (private) profit and the pursuit thereof can, and all too often does, produce moral blindness and intellectual paralysis.

(a) The first is borrowed from Max Beloff's Critical Notice, in *Encounter* for February 1972, of Margaret Cole on *The Life of G.D.H. Cole*. In this biography Cole's widow confesses: 'Douglas, like so many more of us, saw in Soviet Russia the negation of the immoralities of industrial capitalism and the system of private profit . . . ' (Quoted, p.64); and later, 'It cost him a good deal of mental suffering towards the end of his life to admit that "democratic centralism" and Stalinism in Russia had produced horrors which outweighed the advantages of their having abolished private profit. Even then he was apt to maintain that the Americans, who had retained private profit, were much worse' (Quoted, p.66).

Some might have wished to find in both partners a little more concern for the victims of their pet nostrum; even if this concern had to be bought at the price of less over the husband's distress in his reluctant admission of his own imperceptions. It is, however, more interesting to add the judgment of a leading Sovietologist: 'For what it is worth the evidence seems to be that Stalin really believed that the abolition of incomes from capital was the sole necessary principle of social morality, excusing any other action whatever' (Conquest 1968, p.67).

Here, and usually elsewhere too, this conclusion is mediated through the notion that the employment of labour by a private person or a private firm is necessarily exploitative, since any wage that can be paid cannot but involve an unfair exchange: ' . . . the term "exploitation" has an exact meaning. It describes precisely the process by which those who own the means of production draw off almost all the wealth . . . . They eat food, wear clothes, and live in houses produced by other men's labour and offer no product of their own labour in exchange. That is exploitation' (Strachey 1944, p.36). From this narrow and theory-loaded definition it follows that to nationalise 'all the means of production, distribution and exchange' is inevitably to put an end to every possible kind of exploitation.[22] It is, therefore, no wonder that the Coles were – and that so many other adherents of the same theories are – unable to discern any persistently protestable wrongs in socialist countries.

(b) The second of the two final examples is one of those many diagnoses of the British sickness which, by eschewing all use of the abominated word 'profit', contrives to conclude both that the main trouble is under-investment and that the sole solution is still more massive expenditure by government. It would have been easy to pick something similar from a well-known political or trades union leader. Hugh Scanlon, for instance, as President of the Amalgamated Union of Engineering Workers (AUEW) was ever eager to complain that there was 'an investment strike by the capitalists'. But it is more impressive to delineate the same deficiencies in a piece of academic writing, coming from a person who has stood as a candidate for parliament and is generally regarded as above average shrewd.

Laurence Silverman, a Senior Lecturer in Politics at Reading, presented 'Britain – The Crisis of Decline' as a contribution to an anniversary conference on *Britain's Crisis in Sociological Perspective*. It would not be quite true to say that in offering the familiar diagnosis, and proposing the favourite socialist panacea, Silverman had nothing whatever to say about profitability. For he does ask what has happened to the 'potential industrial innovators', and gives the answer (at first reluctant and qualified) that the reason why they have not in fact exercised their initiative and effected their innovations is that in Britain initiative and innovation have not been profitable (Silverman, p.15). A little later, and more boldly, he says: 'It is easy to show that conditions now obtaining in Britain . . . are such that it would not be profitable to engage in industrial investment on the scale everyone agrees to be necessary' (*Ibid.*, p.19).

Scanlon, by not uttering the horrid word, made it that much less likely that he would have to face nasty questions, either about what successive inflationary wage settlements have done to the general level of profitability, or about those notorious and it seems mainly public investments which have been going wholly or partly to waste, either because of inter-union disputes about manning or because of agreed all-union insistence on overmanning.

Silverman, by mentioning the same embarrassing, repugnant topic of profit only in abrupt parentheses, avoids having to ask himself these questions, or other questions about the impact on profitability and entrepreneurial incentives of socialist fiscal, educational, and social policies. Above all he manages to escape the central, fundamental question: 'How to ensure that the investment decisions made are maximally wealth-creating?' (McFadzean, pp.21-3).

Painful though this thought must be to Silverman, we have to reiterate the crucial point: investment – unless it is to be just still more scarce resources down the drain – has to be wealth-creating; and hence, whether privately or publicly, profitable. Perhaps it will make for some slight easing of the pain if I quote the man who might have become the second Stalin, had he not been too soon dismissed to the humbler task of running a power station beyond the Urals. Although this quotation refers to the management rather than the establishment of an enterprise, and despite its assumption of prices fixed by command rather than determined in a market, some part of the heart of the matter is in it. On 18 August 1953 Georgi Malenkov said to the Supreme Soviet of the USSR: 'Many enterprises which are still running at a loss exist in industry, enterprises in which production costs are higher than the prices laid down . . . factories, enterprises and mines which are running at a loss . . . living at the expense of leading enterprises . . .' (quoted Schwartz, p.65).

Perhaps at the times of the first editions of *The Acquisitive Society* and *Equality* it was all very well to write: 'The direction of investments is as important as their amount, and should equally be the concern of public policy. A prudent community . . . will follow the advice tendered to it by economists of unimpeachable propriety, and meet the danger that part of such supplies as are available may be wasted or misused by guiding the investments of capital into nationally desirable channels through the agency of a National Investment Board' (Tawney 1952, p.173). But it is quite another thing to remain so complacently cheerful in face of the long, almost uniformly black record of waste and misdirection now available. This is no place for an exhaustive examination of that record. It must suffice here simply to mention: the financial and environmental catastrophe of the Concord SST; the forced formation and ruinous rescues of British Leyland; the still more gigantic investment thrown into the massively unproductive pit of British Steel; and the general fact that 'In 1975 the British public corporations needed loans or subsidies of 58 pence for every pound's worth of net output they produced' (Eltis, p.124).

For us what is relevant is to point to a few studies of how these disastrous decisions on public investment were in fact made, and what pressures and incentives actually were effective upon the politicians, civil servants, and other persons involved in their making. So see, for instance, C. Jones, Broadway, and Bruce-Gardyne; and compare G. and P. Polanyi, Niskanen, and Tullock. What comes out with inescapable clarity from every study of the practical mechanics of these investments, and of public choice generally, is that all the supposed agents of the public interest are, being equally human, no more yet no less inclined than either capitalists or the rest of us to do the best they can for themselves. To put it more stuffily, they too try to maximise their own utilities.

The trouble is that there is no direct and necessary connection between these utilities and the choice of those investments promising to create most wealth. For, while great care is taken to ensure that our politicians and civil servants should not have any individual financial stake in the investments which they direct, their other personal utilities are often in fact such as to encourage not wealth-creation but wealth-destruction. For instance, large and long-established unions must, in the nature of the case, possess more political clout than others perhaps still unformed in industries not yet born. This makes politicians understandably eager to squander resources, that are not theirs, where these resources will be – and where those old and powerful unions will often help to make them – unprofitable (Joseph, p.42).

Even where they do have relevant interests, people will not

necessarily and always strive to satisfy these interests; and, especially in the present case, when they do try they may not succeed. Yet if wealth-creation is what we want, then we can afford to accept no substitute for arrangements ensuring that those who make the investment decisions have some proportionate interest in the resulting gains and losses – an interest big enough, relative to their own other interests, to be of major concern to them. As will become still clearer in Chapter VII, these are precisely the arrangements of 'the obvious and simple system of natural liberty'.

CHAPTER VII

Intended Actions and Unintended Consequences

But it is only for the sake of profit that any man employs
a capital in the support of industry; and he will always,
therefore, endeavour to employ it in the support of that
industry of which the produce is likely to be of the
greatest value .... But the annual revenue of every
society is always precisely equal to the exchangeable
value of the whole annual produce ..., or rather is
precisely the same thing with that exchangeable value.
As every individual, therefore, endeavours as much as
he can both to employ his capital ... and so to direct
... that its produce may be of the greatest value; every
individual necessarily labours to render the annual
revenue of the society as great as he can. He generally,
indeed, neither intends to promote the public interest,
nor knows how much he is promoting it ... he is in this,
as in many other cases, led by an invisible hand to
promote an end which was no part of his intention.
Adam Smith: The Wealth of Nations, IV, ii

The final Section 4 of Chapter VI considered one or two questions
about the connections and lack of connections between individual
interests and actual individual motivations. The whole of Chapter
VII will consist in a more extensive consideration of some
connections and lacks of connections between, on the one hand,
motives and intentions, and, on the other hand, the actual
outcomes of the operation of these motives and the pursuit of these
intentions. Let us start by first characterising, and thereafter
labelling, what is in the strictest sense a fallacy. It is to move,
direct and with no further premises given, from propositions about
intentions and motives to conclusions that, in the event, these and
only these will be fulfilled and satisfied. For this kind of invalid

move there is as yet no accepted name. So let it be called, a little tendentiously, the Planners' Fallacy.

1 The Planners' Fallacy and its converse

As always when the nerve of some fallacy has been exposed, it will seem to some that no one of any intelligence could possibly commit so obvious a mistake. We all know that conduct often has consequences which were not foreseen, and hence neither were nor could have been intended. We all know too that even the most careful and directed conduct is sometimes counterproductive: the actual outcome is flat contrary to the agent's intentions. But obviousness is essentially relative: what is obvious to us now may earlier have appeared impenetrably opaque; what is now obvious to you may not yet be obvious to me, and the other way about. So the fact that the nerve of the Planners' Fallacy is exposed as soon as it has been dissected in an abstract, clinical demonstration, does not ensure that things are or will remain obvious when the schematic outlines are obscured by concrete complications, or overwhelmed in the heat of the controversial kitchen.

(i) So consider two such real-life examples. The first occurred at Hillsdale College, Michigan, in an exchange between Tibor Machan, Professor of Philosophy from the State University of New York at Fredonia, and Ralph Nader, the hammer of the corporations. Nader had been advocating the establishment and extension of various legal controls and federal agencies intended to reduce air pollution. These proposals were challenged by Machan. Nader's response was the question: 'Have you ever seen anyone dying of emphysema?'

Whatever the merits and demerits of the main positions taken by either party to this particular debate, Nader was at fault in assuming that the only possible ground of objection to his own preferred policies must be an indifference, either ignorant or callous, to the incidence of emphysema. For policies can be, and very often are, ineffective to secure the intentions of their proponents. Even when effective they may also have, and normally do have, unintended consequences that give rise to unforeseen costs. Such costs may partly, or wholly, or more than offset the realised benefits.

A second example is provided by the commonest ways of contending that the entire national economy should be centrally planned and directed, because certain desired blessings can and will be realised only by this means. Again, for all that is to be said here the conclusion might be true; but the point is that it is not proved by these arguments.

It is for a start unsound to proceed from the premise that all sensible people to some extent plan and direct their own affairs straight to the conclusion that it must be sensible for many if not all of these affairs to be planned and directed for them by some central authority. The argument is superficially plausible (though on first thoughts surprising) but it both equivocates upon the word 'planning' and misprepresents the issue as 'Whether to plan?' rather than 'Who is to plan?' Like most if not all words used both about individuals and about collectives, 'planning' is systematically ambiguous as between those two different employments; the words have two different meanings, one in one case, and another in the other. This is the fundamental reason why Plato's proposal in *The Republic* to argue from justice writ large in the state to justice writ small in the individual will not do. That justice in the state is, as no doubt it is, in the public interest, does not prove – what is unfortunately not true – that it is always in the interests of every individual to act justly (Flew 1973b). Directly to the present point, the same is the reason why *The New York Times* was wrong to open an editorial with the overweening rhetorical question: 'Why is planning considered a good thing for individuals and business but a bad thing for the national economy?' (23 November 1975; quoted Hayek 1978, p.233).

After this bad start the usual, equally unsound next steps are: first, to assume that the actual central planners and directors will be guided by our values and our priorities, whatever these may be; and, second, to assume that they will in fact achieve the benefits intended, and this without an accumulation of more than offsetting costs. Since the first of these two assumptions is one regularly made by those proposing in any sphere to replace choice and spontaneity by direction and command, it is useful to have it labelled. So let us christen it for what it is – the Authoritarians' Assumption. People are forever calling for strong men, or for central committees, to dictate and to enforce authoritative orders; while all the time quietly and without argument assuming that, even if they are not themselves to be among those doing the dictating, still the sense of the dictators' dictations will turn out to be congenial.

That such assumptions are often false as well as unwarranted can be shown by telling a domestic tale from my time at the University of Keele. All Keele undergraduates were in those days required to read two subjects for honours, but permitted their choice of any two which were compatible on the university timetable. Naturally no faculty member was content with the distribution of these choices. So a majority formed on the Senate behind a proposal that we should somehow enforce a more satisfactory pattern. This illiberal legislation would certainly have gone through had not the opposition succeeded in securing an outline of that distribution which a sub-committee thought 'would result from the application of sound academic principles'. In the event the supporting majority disappeared the moment some of its members were thus forced to recognise how different their own notions of 'sound academic principles' were from those of others. The Authoritarians' Assumption was in this case not only unwarranted but also false.

The second of the two further assumptions amounts to a refusal to accept that the Planners' Fallacy is indeed a fallacy. That it is, has been shown already; but this refusal would not matter much if wholesale, central planning and direction were in fact always or normally successful in fulfilling all and only the intentions of the planners. In the middle thirties an intelligent and well-informed enthusiast for socialism could, I suppose, manage to find it 'impossible to believe that . . . , even if the planning authority is composed of the most fallible of fallible human beings, it can fail to provide for human needs to so gross an extent as does the capitalist principle of regulating production by profitability' (Strachey 1936, p.38). In face of various striking comparative records since World War II you could today scarcely say, much less believe, anything of the sort. Compare, for instance, the roaring progress of economic growth and popular enrichment in West Germany, Thailand and Japan with the – to put it modestly – more sluggish development of East Germany, Burma, and the USSR. Or, if entire countries appear too big and too far off for instructive comparison, turn up Jane Jacobs on *The Death and Life of Great American Cities*; and contemplate some of the unmitigated catastrophes of centrally-planned, wholesale, urban reconstruction.

Whatever comparisons anyone chooses to make ought, in any case, to be always of like with like. It will not do – even though this is what almost always is done – to compare a jaundiced picture of what actually happens when there is no central planning and direction, with an idealised sketch of what would happen if you or I were given dictatorial power, and we then produced a plan – as, of course, you or I would – which was effective in securing all and only the results intended. The relevant and crucial question is what will happen in reality when these total plans are made and implemented by those other less than perfect, less than omniscient people who do in practice obtain such positions and exercise such powers. 'Do you mean,' Alfred Marshall used to ask, 'Government all wise, all just, all powerful; or Government as it now is?'

(ii) The converse of the Planners' Fallacy may be christened the Creationist Fallacy. The former is the move, direct and with no further premises given, from propositions stating only intentions and motives to conclusions that in the event these and only these will be fulfilled and satisfied. The latter consists in the opposite move, again direct and with no further premises given, from propositions stating only that this is something which would fulfil certain possible intentions or satisfy certain possible motives, to conclusions that these are what did in fact bring it about.

Because, for instance, any halfway tolerable political order involves a measure of give and take, it is immediately inferred that every legitimate state must have originated in some kind of universal social contract between all concerned (or between their remote ancestors) with everyone having their own benefits and costs vividly in mind. Again, the same Creationist Fallacy is committed when people for whom everything seems to be going wrong insist, despite the lack of evidence, that some more or less anonymous 'they' are conspiring to impose these afflictions.

This will be a cue for someone to say: 'Ah, the Conspiracy Theory'. It is in both cases important, yet none too frequent, to recognise that to utter the phrases 'the Creationist Fallacy' or 'the Conspiracy Theory' is not by itself enough to refute any conclusion previously drawn. For there actually are both creations and conspiracies. No one, therefore, has the right to dismiss unheard every suggestion that what is under consideration may in fact have been produced by one or the other. This is obvious, once it has been clearly said; yet many, having learnt to speak of the Conspiracy Theory, like others who during the Vietnam War heard tell of the Domino Theory, have made, and made, and made again this obvious mistake. When I was in the USA during the academic year 1970/1 I must have had a dozen or more conversations with philosophical colleagues, in which my observation that an American withdrawal from Vietnam would be followed by the fall of Laos and Cambodia and increased pressure on Thailand and Malaysia, met with those comfortable words: 'Ah, the Domino Theory.' No one believed it necessary to contribute anything else in rebuttal of a forecast which, in the event, has proved all too true.

What is necessarily wrong with the Creationist and the Planners', as with all other fallacies, is not the actual conclusion drawn but the argument through which that conclusion is reached. The conclusion may just happen to be true, and someone may even have other good grounds for holding it to be so; but what we cannot say is that, given only the premises as offered, then that conclusion must follow. In the stricter sense in which it is a semi-technical logician's term of art, not a superfluous synonym for 'error' or 'misconception', that is what the word 'fallacy' by definition means (Flew 1975, Chapter 1 and passim).

2 Foundations of social science

Look now again, and more closely, at that famous, never too often quoted passage which serves as the text for our present sermon. It is one to which I was myself introduced as an undergraduate in a series of lectures by the then Chichele Professor of Social and Political Theory in the University of Oxford, G.D.H. Cole. Since there was much good elsewhere in those lectures, I regret to report that he was himself unable to see anything in the passage except factitious apologetic for something almost self-evidently scandalous. Like Max Lerner, the Editor of the 1937 Modern Library edition, Cole would have been happy to put down all *The Wealth of Nations* in Harold Laski's fastidiously donnish words: 'With Adam Smith the practical maxims of business enterprise achieved the status of a theology ... an unconscious mercenary in the service of a rising capitalist class ... He gave a new dignity to greed and a new sanctification of the predatory impulses ... ' (pp.ix-x). What especially incensed the principled and lifelong secularist Cole was the apparent suggestion in the final sentence quoted that spontaneous and unruled activities within 'the obvious and simple system of natural liberty' are in fact benevolently coordinated by the Invisible Hand of an All-wise Providence.

Section 4 of Chapter VI considered one aspect of Smith's present argument. The main relevant contention there was that investment decisions are most likely to turn out to be maximally wealth-creating where those who make those decisions are aware that they have strong individual interests in their so being; although it was also stressed that the fact that people are aware of having strong individual interests by no means necessitates that they act in pursuit of them, much less that those interests provide their sole motives for acting. It also emerged that – contrary to the assertions or insinuations of Cole, Lerner, Laski and the rest – Smith was not exclusively nor even especially devoted to the profits of capitalists. '*The Wealth of Nations*', as George Stigler so happily has it, 'is a stupendous palace erected on the granite of self-interest' (Skinner and Wilson, p.237). But it is precisely not the self-interest of any one group or class, as against that of others. Smith's characteristic practical concern is completely general: whatever is to be provided or achieved is provided or achieved most effectively and most satisfactorily when it is in the interests of those concerned.

The passage quoted here argues that, to effect the economically most efficient allocation of capital resources, the allocators should have strong individual interests in such allocation. Passages quoted earlier deployed similar arguments to support the parallel conclusion that, if consumers are to get the deals most satisfactory to them, there have to be competing would-be suppliers with strong individual interests in securing custom. For whatever the two points may be worth, it was then not merely allowed but insisted, both that suppliers who do have such strong individual interests may nevertheless be stirred, alternatively or additionally, by disinterested and benevolent motives, and that similarly disinterested and benevolent motives might (and no doubt at least equally often do) stir state and other monopoly suppliers who have no strong individual interest in consumer satisfaction.

In the latter case, however, even when such elevated motives are at work, the high-minded intention is almost sure to be to provide, not what consumers actually do want, but what it is thought best for them to have. The tale is told of a tolerant Roman Catholic chaplain, who said to his Protestant opposite number: 'Yes, we are both serving God: you in your way, and I in His.' The competing supplier might address a public-spirited monopolist in much the same terms: 'You are serving your customers in your way; and I in theirs.'

(i) Our business now is with a different aspect of the same passage. The self-interested investor, says Smith, 'generally . . .

neither intends to promote the public interest, nor knows how much he is promoting it . . . he is in this, as in many other cases, led by an invisible hand to promote an end which was no part of his intention.' To this Smith forthwith makes a dry addition, which the experience of his compatriots in recent decades has made vastly apposite: 'Nor is it always the worse for society that it was no part of it. By pursuing his own interest he frequently promotes that of the society more effectually than when he really intends to promote it. I have never known much good done by those who affected to trade for the public good.'

(a) By thus displaying the operations of a market as a mechanism through which intentional actions produce unintended consequences, Smith was making a major contribution to the development of social science. Certainly the outcomes of the operation of such mechanisms are not always and wholly happy. He himself, although never having enjoyed the benefit of seeing Charlie Chaplin's *Modern Times*, was extremely sensitive to the human costs of another economic institution of which he offered a similar account: 'The division of labour, from which so many advantages are derived, is not originally the effect of any human wisdom, which foresees and intends the general opulence to which it gives occasion. It is the necessary though very slow and gradual consequence of a certain propensity to truck, barter, and exchange one thing with another' (I, ii).

Smith might have added to his list a third economic mechanism, and one whose long-term effects appear to be wholly unfortunate. It is sometimes spoken of as 'the tragedy of the commons' (Hardin). Where there are no respected property-rights in some resource, no one has an individual interest in its economically efficient conservation. On the contrary: everyone who has an opportunity to exploit that resource has an individual interest in taking all they can before it is exhausted or destroyed by similarly interested, and similarly short-sighted, other people. Everyone's business is, notoriously, no one's.

For example: lions in Africa have in the past been treated as common property, and largely still are. They have been 'fair game' for anyone to kill and eat, or just to kill. The result has been, and is, a rapidly declining lion population. But now in the United Kingdom owned lions are effectively protected in parks and zoos; the population is rising; and some are being exported, it is said, even to Africa. Again, the great whales are being exterminated by an unholy combining of the arch-capitalists of Japan with the arch-socialists of the USSR. If only some were the property of the USSR and some of Japan, we could have much more hope for the survival of these splendid species. Finally, and of a different order of gravity, is the case of Sahel. There, as Kurt Waldheim has said, 'the encroachment of the desert threatens to wipe four or five African countries from the map.' Certainly other causes, such as a protracted drought, have exacerbated the problem. But the basic trouble is that on unenclosed land no one has an individual interest in doing what stops, or not doing what starts, desertification (Burton, pp.83-8).

(b) Because Smith did not see the effects of the workings of existing social institutions as always happy, and because he was concerned to explicate the mechanisms through which intelligible and intentional human action necessarily produces such unintended consequences, it is diametrically wrong to suggest that he was trying either to explain or to justify these as the miraculous deeds of a beneficent Providence. The truth is that Smith, confronted with formations which look very much as if they might have been designed, still studiously eschewed the Creationist Fallacy, and was instead labouring to show that these formations might arise and continue without any design or intention, whether human or Divine.

Nowhere in his writings is there the whisper of an appeal to any miraculous overriding of the usual course of nature. The only 'economic miracles' which Smith either knew or expected had been or would be achieved – like those of our own time – by wholly natural and this-worldly means. Nor is there in his work any special paean to the enterpriser (*Enterpriser*, not *entrepreneur*: it is overtime for the people whose ancestors made the first industrial revolution to have a native word for members of the class which led it! Compare Seldon 1980, passim).

So the sober quotation which follows is drawn from Dr Goh Keng Swee, Minister of Finance in what, perhaps perversely, describes itself as the socialist government of the city-state of Singapore. I copied it in 1969 from a plaque erected in the central market place: 'A society which wishes for economic growth should nurse the creative talent which its enterprising members possess, and should encourage the development of such talent to its full stature.'[23]

(c) In his accounts of the mechanics of economic institutions

Smith revealed an insight common to, and characteristic of, the group of thinkers whom Hayek has taught us to honour as the Scottish founding fathers of social science (Hayek 1967, Chapter 6). This insight had been expressed in more general terms nine years earlier by a sometime Chaplain of the Black Watch, and later Edinburgh University Professor: 'Mankind in following the present sense of their minds, in striving to remove inconveniences, or to gain apparent and contiguous advantages, arrive at ends which even their imagination could not anticipate . . . and nations stumble upon establishments, which are indeed the result of human action but not the execution of human design' (Ferguson 1767, pp.122-3). Earlier still David Hume, inspired in part by Bernard Mandeville, had investigated other and even more fundamental formations; arguing not merely that these were not in fact planned and intended products, but that some at least could not have been (Flew 1978b, pp.135-9).

In this historical perspective it is difficult to discern anything for aspiring social scientists to do which is not either, on the one hand, the collection, collation and criticism of the accounts people give of their conduct and their own reasons for it, or, on the other hand, a study of the unintended and perhaps unrecognised consequences of these conscious and intended actions. It becomes in that same perspective possible to provide intelligible, non-mystificatory accounts of how and in what sense a social whole can be greater than the sum of all its parts.

(ii) One of the many paradoxes of the history of thought is that the developments just described occurred first in the fields of the human rather than of the natural and biological sciences. What these great Scots were discovering was the way in which certain phenomena, looking as if they must have been the products of design, instead could – sometimes indeed must – have been the outcome of non-intentional processes. Just as, in the following century, Charles Darwin argued for the origin of species by natural selection, so they too in their different spheres contended earlier for progressive evolution as opposed to special creation.

In consequence, those shadowy demigods and mythical culture-heroes, whose existence as single-handed inventors and wholesale creators of social institutions and political constitutions had once been postulated, now began to be replaced by long stories of piecemeal historical development, or by revealing accounts of the operations of mechanisms blind, undesigning, and undesigned.

Lycurgus, for instance, despite the lack of any direct historical evidence, had been postulated as the creator of the constitution of Sparta; a constitution much admired by Plato and by pro-Spartan contemporaries in his native Athens, as well as by many later generations of temperamental authoritarians and actual or would-be Guardians. It was with reason that, in his essay on 'Montesquieu and Rousseau, precursors of sociology', Durkheim maintained that the myth of the inspired and revolutionary legislator had been the greatest hindrance to the development of the subject.

Given that these Scottish social scientists were in that sense evolutionists rather than creationists, the question must arise why their work and their teaching met little or no opposition from religious conservatives. The best available answer is that there were three relevant differences between an evolutionary account of the origin of biological species and the same sort of account of the origins of certain social institutions.

First, in few if any cases was any Biblical story perceived as a revealed rival to the findings of social science. The story of the Tower of Babel accounted not for the first origin but for the later diversification of languages; while the children of Israel had not in their earliest days been sufficiently aware of either the division of labour or the capital market to invent any aetiological myths to explain the origins of these establishments!

Second, the hypothetical social and political inventors made redundant by the advance of social science were men. Lycurgus and Romulus may indeed never have existed at all; but certainly, if they did, they were men born of no longer virgin women. But in *Genesis* it was God himself who was supposed to have created biological species directly and immediately.

Third, the sociological work of the Scots had no relevance, or appeared to have no relevance, to natural theology. The centre-piece of that was for everyone in Britain, and at least for all plain persons everywhere, the Argument to Design. By far and away the most impressive premises for that argument were provided by the facts of biology, not of social life. If all the integration and all the complexity of organisms could be accounted for by natural selection operating on chance variations, then what need remained for what, with such mischievous care and niceness, Hume had labelled 'the religious hypothesis' (Hume 1748, Section XI; and compare Flew 1966, Chapter 3 and Flew 1976b, Chapter 3)?

3 Constructivism, revolution and reform

The previous section on the theoretical foundations of social science may or may not have been interesting in itself. But its relevance for us lies in the practical morals. The first of these is that it makes clear that the kind of thinking constructively picked out and labelled as constructivistic is fallacious (Hayek 1978, Chapter 1). The fallacy here consists in arguing that, because all human social institutions have to be generated by nothing else but human activity, therefore it must be possible for us, acting collectively, totally to reshape any or all of these institutions to accord better with whatever may be or become our hearts' desires. The crux, of course, is that what is brought about by nothing else but human activity is not necessarily the *intended* consequence of that activity. Still more to the point, although this consequence comes from the activities of large numbers of people, these activities need not be (and often are not) consciously coordinated. What then results from those activities is not the product of collective intention and decision. So we are not entitled to assume that it can be restructured at will by a change of such intention and a fresh decision. Having said this one has to add that the opposite mistake, to which in fact few nowadays are much inclined, is equally wrong – to bow down without discrimination before all the unintended institutional consequences of intended action, seeing every one in its every aspect as a precious and irreformable product of 'the cunning of reason' (Hegel).

(i) The correct response, surely, is to be always the piecemeal, realistic reformist, never the wholesale, utopian revolutionary (Popper 1965, Chapter 9). Whatever social policies we adopt ought to be introduced tentatively and reviewed regularly in the light of actual experience, with a readiness to change or to reverse any measures if they are found not to be yielding the promised balance of advantage. Any unwillingness thus to monitor progress, and to make whatever reversals may prove to be necessary, can only, and should, be construed as a sign that our concern is really rather more for our privately cherished nostrums than for the public goods which these nostrums were originally recommended to promote. The wholesale, utopian, social engineer, by contrast, determined to impose his long-term policies no matter what the immediate discontents, is by his cloth precluded from learning from his mistakes. Nor can he take account of the insight that there will always be unintended consequences, whether good, or bad, or mixed (Lasky, and Szamuely, passim).

This application of a Popperian antithesis includes something which is not in Popper himself. He has taught us that to deserve the name of 'rational' any method of inquiry, and any social policy, must provide for the recognition and correction of mistakes. I add a harsher note. The same provision is just as necessary if it is to be allowed either that the inquirer is sincere in the claim to be a seeker after truth, or that the advocate of a policy is sincerely pursuing its pretended aims.

Suppose, for instance, that someone proclaims a Quest for the Holy Grail. Suppose too that, almost as soon as the fanfares have died, they settle for the first antique-seeming mug pushed forward by the first fluent rogue in the local bazaar. Then we surely have to say that this neglect of any serious and systematic inquiry, this total lack of interest in either the history of the purchase put in the place of honour on the mantelpiece or the evidence that the real thing does after all survive somewhere else, conspire together to show that, whatever else the intention may have been, most certainly it was not to unearth and to acquire the vessel actually used in the original Last Supper. Sincerity of purpose absolutely presupposes a steady concern to know whether the purpose entertained has been or is being achieved (Flew 1976a, Chapter 6 and Flew 1979).

That there is this universal and necessary connection between sincerity of purpose and the monitoring of progress is, once it has been pointed out, so manifest a logical fact as to require no further illustration or proof. It is, nevertheless, one of those manifest logical facts from which it is easy to derive exciting, contested conclusions. In particular, but still for once not naming names, those who profess to be trying to teach or to learn, and yet repudiate every attempt to monitor what, if anything, has in truth been either taught or learnt, thereby supply indubitable proof of the insincerity of their own educational professions. (So much for the objections to the independent public examining of the work done or not done in our schools; and the suppressions of the findings of such examinations!)

In general, and in sum, any person or any party pressing some programme while refusing to monitor its success or to revise it in the light of demonstrated failure, necessarily reveals that the true commitment either always was, or has become, not to the values which it was originally supposed to realise, but rather, either to that programme itself for its own sake, or else to some other less openly proclaimed values which its enforcement perhaps actually is realising.

(ii) Consider, as a comparatively unpolitical and uncontroversial illustration of both the fallacy of constructivism and the practical morals to be drawn from it, the natural languages. We can be sure that every natural language is a social product, the offspring of nothing else but human activity. It is even more certain that no natural language either was or could have been the intended product of intended action: indeed the point of inserting the qualification 'natural' exactly is to rule out such 'artificial languages' as chess or chemical notation. We are, therefore, by no means entitled to infer that any society which has produced its own natural language could, acting in a coordinated and collective way, create some new and vastly improved language, designed and better designed to fulfil the purposes of an actual controlling élite of planners, politicians or whoever else.

In fact every natural language is an instrument of enormous richness and subtlety. In his *Principles of Moral and Political Science* Ferguson becomes lyrical about: 'This amazing fabric . . . which, when raised to its height, appears so much above what could be ascribed to any simultaneous effort of the most sublime and comprehensive abilities.' Indeed, he goes on, 'The speculative mind is apt to look back with amazement from the height it has gained; as a traveller might do, who, rising insensibly on the slope of a hill, should come to look from a precipice of almost unfathomable depth, to the summit of which he could scarcely believe himself to have ascended without supernatural aid' (Ferguson 1792, I p.43). He was perhaps thinking of statements made a generation earlier by the gruffly witty, studiously old-fashioned eccentric who was perhaps of all contemporary compatriots most expert in linguistics; and who could 'hardly believe but that in the first discovery of so artificial a method of communication, men had no supernatural assistance.' So he was 'much inclined to listen to what Egyptians tell us of a God, as they call him, that is, an intelligence superior to man, having first told them the use of language' (Monboddo, IV, p.484).

Even the most careful and competent masters of natural languages would fail a challenge to provide explicit accounts of all the refinements of distinction which they themselves so regularly and so fruitfully employ. The best demonstration of this truth is John Austin's methodological masterpiece, 'A Plea for Excuses'. It is of especial interest to us here because it is so often, none too scrupulously, attacked by members of the largely Leninist Radical Philosophy Group. After displaying some of the rarely recognised richness of our everyday vocabulary of extenuation and excuse, Austin continues: ' . . . our common stock of words embodies all the distinctions men have found worth drawing, and the connections they have found worth making, in the lifetimes of many generations: these surely are likely to be more numerous, more sound, since they have stood up to the long test of the survival of the fittest, and more subtle, at least in all ordinary and reasonably practical matters, than any that you or I are likely to think up in our armchairs of an afternoon – the most favoured alternative method' (Austin 1970, p.182).

This passage is quoted, for instance, in one of the well-nicknamed Penguin *Red Papers* on education; although the writer is careful to omit both the reference to 'the survival of the fittest' and the qualification 'at least in all ordinary and reasonably practical matters'. He then comments: 'To others of us it is at least equally reasonable to think that new and unfamiliar experiences or ways of seeing the world and human nature may require the formulation of new concepts and new theories, rather than efforts to cram them into old and established categories. Yet it has been left to "outsiders" like Ernest Gellner . . . and Herbert Marcuse . . . to expose the conservatism of the linguistic orthodoxy in philosophy; and their criticisms have in general been ignored with patronage or contempt by "professionals" in the field' (Rubinstein and Stoneman, pp.36-7; and compare Flew 1976a, Chapter 8).

Certainly there is some ignoring going on; and some patronage and contempt – or worse. For anyone so patient and so conscientious as to read on in Austin will find that three pages later he glosses those carefully omitted clauses. He says: 'If a distinction works well for practical purposes in ordinary life . . . then there is sure to be something in it, it will not mark nothing: yet this is likely enough not to be the best way of arranging things if our interests are more extensive or intellectual than the ordinary. And again, that experience has been derived only from the sources available to ordinary men throughout most of civilized history: it has not been fed from the resources of the microscope and its successors. Certainly then, ordinary language is *not* the last word: in principle it can everywhere be supplemented and improved upon and superseded. Only remember, it *is* the *first* word.' Having thus put appreciation of the actual situation before formulation of proposals for change, Austin goes on, four pages later still, to give as his own example of an area where there is room for supplementation and improvement one which is also a favourite with the *enragés*: 'There is real danger in contempt for the "jargon" of psychology, at least when it sets out to supplant the language of ordinary life' (Austin 1970, pp.185 and 189: italics and quotes original).

Austin's position on language reform, as shown in the two statements quoted, constitutes a model of (and for) the piecemeal reformist. He is fully aware that something which has survived and evolved over the centuries is neither to be understood at first glance nor to be dismissed unexamined as an obviously outdated and ineffective instrument. Such an evolved institution can be deliberately improved only by those who have laboured to comprehend it as it is; and who have the patience and the sincerity to move tentatively, with a continuing willingness both to learn and to unlearn.

(iii) Hayek traced the philosophical inspiration of the opposite, wrong approach back to Descartes. In Part II of the *Discourse on the Method*, his first most devastating publication, Descartes asserts that things are (almost) always better when their design and construction has been from the beginning the work of a single master. So in Part IV he proceeds to launch his own programme of wholesale and simultaneous doubt, in order thereafter to erect, on the basis of whatever this Cartesian bulldozer cannot raze, a really secure structure of indubitable knowledge: 'My design', the modest explanation runs, 'has never extended beyond trying to reform my own opinions and to build upon a foundation which is entirely my own.'

It was left to successors in later centuries to press this constructivistic Cartesian approach into the field of social policy. Voltaire, for instance, expressed the whole spirit of the French Enlightenment when in the article on 'Law' in the great *Encyclopaedia* he wrote: 'if you want good laws, burn those you have and make yourselves new ones.' It was in this same spirit that the men of 1789 and also the Bolsheviks in October 1917 tried to live each day as if their first, in one blind bound remaking all things new. Such phrases to some will now recall the student *émeutes* of 1968 and the following years: did not Marx himself say, in *The*

Eighteenth Brumaire of Louis Buonaparte, that history does repeat itself – only the second time as farce? (It is, by the way, surely significant either of some neglect of their studies or of grave deficiencies in the diet there provided that so many of those utopian militants came from Departments of Sociology.)

In Section 2 (i) of Chapter V Kai Nielsen served as a paradigm case of a philosopher aspiring to be a Guardian. He is equally a paradigm of what Popper calls the revolutionary utopian social engineer. Nielsen's apologia 'In Defence of Radicalism' starts by mentioning, but scarcely describing, 'a new model of life for a transformed society'; and always Nielsen insists that the transformation required is holistic and total. He goes on to the perhaps surprising admission: 'We socialists have a programme and a critical analysis of society, but we have no convincing account of effective vehicles for transforming society' (*Ibid.,* p.61). However, 'There is no need or indeed justification for intellectuals to get themselves into such a state that they are incapable of acting politically because they are caught up in ... a Popperian scepticism engendered by worries over the unintended social consequences of adopting different policies or strategies' (*Ibid.,* p.62).

It strains both my credulity and my charity to believe that a philosopher as able as Nielsen really misunderstands Hayek and Popper so completely; and that he is in truth convinced that, on the basis of a general scepticism about the possibility of social science, either or both advocate universal political inertia. Certainly the present chapter has already shown that Hayek thinks, and that he is right in thinking, that the unintended consequences of intended action are part of the subject-matter of the social sciences, and not a reason for supposing them impossible.

It is sufficient, and perhaps necessary, to add that what Popper is against, and what he believes that we do not and are never likely to have sufficient social science to do, is wholesale utopian social engineering, involving total transformation in accordance with some blueprint for the universal good; whereas what he unreservedly favours are strenuous but piecemeal attempts to remove particular recognised evils – attempts whose results are continually monitored, and whose effectiveness is thus continually improved. Popper is well aware also that the road to Utopia has in fact too often led through Hell; and that 'the Utopian attempt to realize an ideal state, using a blueprint of society as a whole, is one which demands a strong centralised rule of a few . . . ' (Popper 1965, I, p.159). As they used to say in Yorkshire: 'He saw Nielsen coming.'[24] The misrepresentation of Popper as a prophet of political and social inertia suggests that Nielsen in his turn saw Popper coming; and, seeing, recognised his own inability to meet the arguments actually put.

CHAPTER VIII

Epilogue

And though a philosopher may live remote from business, the genius of philosophy, if carefully cultivated by several, must gradually diffuse itself throughout the whole society, and bestow a similar correctness on every art and calling. *David Hume: Enquiry concerning Human Understanding, I*

My Prologue promised to 'examine and assail presuppositions and implications of two master notions in the contemporary climate of opinion'. I did not, of course, undertake to deal with all these presuppositions and implications, but rather those that are most closely associated with the Procrustean ideal, a centrally enforced equality of outcome.

The Prologue went on at once to make two other things clear: that the examinations and the attacks were to be directed at these ideas as they have appeared in the writings of sociologists, economists, social and political philosophers, and other professional men of thought; and that always 'the hope is that any rectification of ideas which have captivated so many of our intellectuals will in the not too distant future spread out into broader circles.' So there has at no stage been any hesitation about drawing illustrations from, or making applications to, what are matters of current controversy outside the academic cloisters. Thus it would, as was argued in Section 2 of that same Prologue, be irresponsible and obscurantist to propose and adopt a meaning for the word 'socialism' without taking most explicit account of the way in which it is implicitly defined by those who advocate it – in Britain chiefly the Labour Party, the TUC, and most of their important separate constituents. Again, to have eschewed in the next six chapters all topical examples and all partisan commentary would have been to present material in an unnecessarily obscure and abstract fashion, and to give a quite false impression of triviality and remoteness.

There is, however, now no longer any call for even that much rather unapologetic apology for practical involvement. The time has come to bring the whole act together before putting it onto the road.

1 *What has been done*

Chapter II distinguished this Procrustean ideal, on the one hand, from any claims purporting to be statements of comparative fact about individual human beings, and, on the other hand, from two other more ancient and more admirable ideals of equality – themselves both ultimately incompatible with this one. Chapter III argued that it is perverse and preposterous to represent such essentially forward-looking Procrusteanism, as it almost always is represented, as if it either were or could be the supreme imperative of what is the essentially backward-looking authority of justice. Chapter IV brought out that this misconception itself presupposes that we are all, at any rate from a properly moral point of view, 'as interchangeable as ants'. It is doubtful if this assumption is even compatible with the conception of beings endowed with rights, and themselves both capable of recognising, and morally required to recognise, the rights of others.

At this point the book ceased to concentrate upon ideas and ideals of equality, in order to move on to socialism; or rather, more particularly, to those supposed superior motives and higher intentions which to many appear to give socialism a legitimacy greater than can characterise any perceived rival. Inasmuch as it linked the enforcers of 'equality and social justice' with those who give the orders in a socialist command economy, Chapter V was a bridge. It displayed the enormous appeal to all authoritarians of the notion of need; a notion in terms of which actual or would-be Guardians may supply to, or enforce upon, us their subjects whatever in their wisdom (though, of course, in nothing but our own interests) they themselves may determine to be for the best.

Chapter VI examined competition, and the nowadays so much and so sanctimoniously execrated profit motive. A principal contention was that it is ridiculous to try to maintain the usual night-against-day, neo-Manichean antithesis between the profit motive and the altogether nobler motives which – it is assumed – are typically engaged in socialist production and socialist distribution. Chapter VII, the third of these second three, developed a general offensive against the practice of judging economic systems, social policies, political parties or whatever else by reference either to the putative (or even actual) motives, purposes, intentions or interests of persons involved in their initiation and operation.

Save in so far as any of these may happen to connect with what primarily concerns the practical person conducting a life in this world, they should all be left either to God and the Last Judgement or to the historians. For any one of us living our ordinary non-theoretical lives, that primary concern must be with how these systems, policies, parties or what have you do or may impinge upon those things which we ourselves are concerned about. There are, in a word, no regular, universal, or necessary connections between our concerns and the putative or actual motives, purposes or interests of the policy makers. We should look always, not to what is or was supposedly intended, but to what actually happens.

(i) In that perspective let us for a moment, before proceeding to a final Section 2, contemplate two menacing intellectual manifestos. The first comes from the very end of the last paragraph of a discussion of 'Socialism and Equality' in a book of papers on *The Socialist Idea*. The author, Steven Lukes (a Fellow in Politics of Balliol College, Oxford) admits to being a strong egalitarian socialist. His conclusion is: 'that the argument that the costs of implementing equality are too high is the most crucial question facing any socialist today. And it is perhaps the inclination to see the accumulated weight of historical evidence for the apparent need to pay such costs – from the rise of Stalin to the fall of Allende – as a challenge rather than a source of despair that is, in the end, the distinguishing mark of an egalitarian socialist' (Kolakowski and Hampshire, p.94).

Of Lukes and his like, therefore, we cannot, as we might wish, cry in charity: 'They know not what they do.'

(ii) The second author is a Lecturer in Politics at Hull. He is more equivocal about his own commitments. He appears nevertheless equally insensitive to the extreme inequalities, under what he too describes as egalitarian socialism, between the party élite of equalisers and the broad masses of those who are equalised. With particular reference to Cuban militarism he contends that 'there are certain things for which it makes no sense to criticise egalitarian societies, such as their austerity, their relative lack of charity, their intolerance, their drabness and poverty, their failure to allow public protest or "dissent". Egalitarian ideals command the highest respect; egalitarian practice must always be treated

with caution. The price of egalitarianism is sublimated suffering. . .'
(Berki, p.135).

It is clear that the sneer quotes are inserted to express his
socialist contempt for any liberal tolerance of public protest and
dissent. But it is difficult to conjecture why he thinks that 'it makes
no sense to criticise egalitarian societies' on such counts. The
subsequent heavy contrast between 'egalitarian ideals' and 'egalitarian practice' forces us to reject the obvious suggestion that this
might be because he takes them to be all essential features. For
why ever should we be asked to pay the 'highest respect' to anyone
who, construing all these things as part of what the expression
'egalitarian socialism' means, nevertheless conspires and contrives
with the conscious and deliberate aim of imposing such a slum
totalitarianism?

2 *The relevance of it all*

In this final section I try to display the practical relevance of
previous theorising in as vivid and persuasive a fashion as I can.
To do this I apply a few of the points already made to four
newspaper clippings, the first three appearing in *The Times* of
London during the month when I was beginning to work on the
present chapter.

(i) Number one is a meditation upon that old faithful theme
'How the British have kept up their class barriers' (9 January
1980). At the start of a long and reverential review two reports of a
massive sociological survey are said to 'make depressing reading
for all those who hoped that . . . the social and educational policies
pursued by successive governments since the war would lead to a
greater equality of opportunities and chances between those born
into different social classes.' (The reports discussed were Halsey,
Heath and Ridge; also Goldthorpe.)

It may be that the truth is depressing, but it is not shown to be so
(nor indeed is it revealed just what the truth is) by any of the evidence
redeployed in *The Times*. For it appears that the several investi-
gators attended only to what careers were eventually pursued, after
receiving different forms of education, by the offspring of members
of the various classes distinguished. Such achievements were, very
properly, construed as sufficient demonstration of corresponding
opportunities. But, most unreasonably, the *absence* of any achievement was then interpreted as an equally knock-down decisive
proof of the absence of any corresponding opportunity.

Again, what are no doubt sound calculations and accurate estimates of the always unequal probabilities of various sorts of success within the various groups contrasted were paraded as showing exactly the same degrees of either inequality in access to, or unfairness in the conduct of, the various competitions concerned. No account at all was taken of the possibility – indeed, surely, the certainty – of some relevant differences in respect both of eagerness to compete and of capacity to win. Even the plainest of plain persons most certainly would expect such average and relevant differences between any groups which sociologists find sufficient reason to distinguish as social classes – while the professionals still more certainly should.

These gross yet pervasive methodological deficiencies vitiated the arguments of the reviewer and undermined all the support offered for his excited and exciting conclusions. Had he seen this, then he might well have tried to establish the same conclusions in some other way; and perhaps he would have been successful. But anyone who has taken on board the contents of the previous paragraph ought, I think, to pause for a moment to ask themselves whether they really do believe it imperative to work for a society so completely homogeneous that there would be no such differences, even on average, between any groups distinguishable as social classes; and whether, if they themselves were eventually able to live in such a society, they would expect to be happy.

Whatever my answer or the reader's answer to these questions, it is clear that, to the first at least, that of the Director of this research programme would be in the affirmative. For the man responsible was Professor A.H. Halsey, identified earlier as an obsessional Procrustean, unable to divine any reason other than 'malevolence' why anyone should want to stand in his way. (See the beginning of Section 1, i of Chapter II.)

(ii) The second item, also a review, was presented as 'A damning indictment of Labour' (28 January 1980). This time the subject was a volume of essays, entitled *Labour and Equality: A Fabian Study of Labour in Power 1974-79* (Bosanquet and Townsend). 'Perhaps the most damning indictment in a devastating critique is', we are told, 'that the Labour government abandoned its traditional concern with equality.' Yet the only kind of evidence marshalled is totally irrelevant to the thesis proposed. For instance, the claim is made: 'Thus a Labour Government ... within months of taking office had set in train economic policies which led to average cuts in the standard of living of 7 per cent between 1974 and 1977.'

It should have been obvious, both to the reviewer and to the book's contributors, that statistics of this kind have on their own absolutely no bearing upon the essential relativities of equality. Yet neither the one nor the other seems to have had a moment to consider whether (or how far) the gaps between the better off and the worse off were diminished, and equality therefore increased, by additional taxation designed – as the then shadow Chancellor explained to exultant applause at the 1973 party conference – 'to make the rich howl in agony'. (The top rates on ordinary income were raised to 83 per cent, and on investment income to a grotesque 98 per cent; while the thresholds for these top rates, already very low by North Atlantic standards, were through a period of 100 per cent inflation kept steady in money terms. Hence, in real terms, they were in each successive year significantly lowered. There were also new and equally onerous taxes on capital.)

There is an equally remarkable obverse to this ostensible inability to seize and to hold the crucial distinction between questions about absolute positions and questions about gaps between floors and ceilings. We noticed long since that outcome egalitarians are inclined to assume that no one consciously rejecting their ideal can be anything but an inegalitarian, cherishing inequalities for their own sake and regardless of consequences: knee-jerk reactions of this sort are reminiscent of those who used to believe that anyone repudiating their God must be by the same token a worshipper of their Devil. Outcome egalitarians are also almost invincibly reluctant to acknowledge that nearly if not quite all those who revolt against their own longings to bring floors and ceilings ever closer together are in fact just as dedicated as themselves, perhaps more so, to the proposition that there must be firm floors.

For instance: in American Milton Friedman has been a long-time advocate of the direct abolition of poverty by a negative income tax; while in England a very similar (if not exactly the same) line is taken by those whom their opponents describe as the most right-wing of Conservatives. Selsdon Group Brief No. 18, *A Beginner's Guide to Public Expenditure Cuts*, thus states: 'Only by cutting out some state activities altogether can this or any government concentrate sufficiently on that very limited list –

defence, preservation of the value of the currency, maintenance of
order, guaranteeing a minimum standard of life to the poorest – of
activities which, arguably at least, the state and only the state can
perform. The last-mentioned is, of course, not the least important
duty of the state . . . . Poverty is a lack of money, and its cure is and
always has been more money, not state services of questionable
value provided free (or at artificially low prices) at the point of
consumption' (p.7).

(iii) The third item was a centre page feature article by Dr David
Owen, a former Labour Foreign Secretary, entitled 'This serious
challenge Labour must fight'. His starting point is 'the Labour
Party's hitherto unchallengeable role as the most concerned and
compassionate party'; and he makes it extraordinarily clear that
for him all its actions and policies are seen, or for the most part
simply not seen, through these blinkers. Thus for Owen, as for so
many others, the attributed motivational and intentional image is
all. Works and deeds, the actual effects of laws passed and of
policies implemented – indeed, one is in this case tempted to add,
even the actual motives and intentions of flesh and blood
colleagues – all of these are, compared with this image, irrelevant
nothings.

Totally in its thrall he is so ingenuous as to resent, in his words,
'a skilfully conducted campaign to descredit the ideals of socialism,
identifying the Labour government with bureaucratic statist
insensitivity and the stifling of individual liberty'. He never thinks
even to try to deny or explain away any of the most obvious facts,
to which any such campaign could not but refer. For instance, that
same government forced through, always with Owen's vote, what
the Shadow Chancellor at that 1973 party conference had
correctly described as 'a massive extension of nationalisation'.
Again, his government forced through, as always with Owen's
own vote, unparalleled extensions of legal privilege for the labour
unions – including above all legal sanction for vast extensions of
the closed shop, which in Britain means, as has been remarked
earlier, compulsory membership of organisations with constit-
utionally specified political aims. And so on.

Self-blinded and intellectually paralysed by the same radically
misleading image of compassionist motivation, and consequently
without any thought here either of the ever reiterated theoretical
and practical commitment to socialism or of the fact that nearly all
the party's funds are provided by the labour unions and nearly all

its conference votes are cast in their name, Owen proceeds to warn of another manifestly sinister and twisted propaganda exercise. 'Between now and 1983 or 1984', he writes, 'there will be persistent attempts to associate the Labour Party with envious, authoritarian, insensitive, bureaucratic control. To depict it as the advocate of all-pervading state power, impersonal national institutions, and as being dominated by the trade unions.' No wonder that a growing group on the National Executive of the Labour Party is eager to bring a press capable of such misrepresentation under their direction!

(iv) The fourth and final news item is a reported statement by Mr Dennis Gee. He is both Headmaster of a state school in Ashford, Kent and Secretary of the local branch of the National Union of Teachers. Without embarrassment and brazenly he demands power for himself and for his fellow Guardians, power to provide what and only what, as those Guardians shall determine, all their subjects must ideally need; and let no one – with some 'sticky little piece of paper in their hands' – dare to ask and to offer to pay for some different service which they themselves may happen actually to want. Here we can see the vivid drama of individual choice confronting collective control, the freedoms of the market threatening the pompous commands of authority. The occasion of this Headmaster's pronouncement was a proposal to experiment with a system of educational vouchers. Speaking presumably both as a Headmaster and as the Secretary of the local branch of a labour monopoly, Dennis Gee said: 'We see this as a barrier between us and the parent – this sticky little piece of paper in their hands – coming in and under duress – you will do this or else. We make our judgement because we believe it's in the best interest of every Willie and every little Johnny that we've got – and not because someone's going to say "If you don't do it, we will do that." It's this sort of philosophy of the market place that we object to' (Quoted M. and R. Friedman 1980, pp.173-4).

Just so. It is the friends of the educational voucher, and of the market generally, who are in truth the friends of individual liberty and of individual choice as well as being protagonists of, in the most genuine sense, power for the people. Those who shout 'Power for the people!' in practice advance the power only of the leaders and directors of those who shout 'Power for the people!'.

Notes

1   The first German edition of 1937, with its author's Preface stressing that his own 'theory of aggregate production . . . can be much more easily adapted to the conditions of a totalitarian state than the theory . . . put forth under the conditions of free competition and a large degree of laissez-faire', showed tact also by silently suppressing the final sentence quoted above.

2   But compare and contrast Crosland 1956. Apparently then agreeing with the vulgar 'that an individual's genes are his, and . . . entitle him to whatever advantages he can get from them', Crosland there allowed that 'extra responsibility and exceptional talent require and *deserve* a differential reward' (p.149: italics supplied).

3   British readers may wish to note that his *The Conservative Enemy*, first published in 1962, gives several hints – on pp.15, 16 and 33 – that direct taxes on marginal earnings were already at or over the limit of fiscal and economic prudence. But that did not hold him back from contented participation in two later Labour governments. These imposed further direct taxes and even higher top rates. Also, in the face of a plummeting collapse of the real value of sterling, they stubbornly maintained for these higher rates the same nominal thresholds.

     The reluctance actually to concede any trade-offs against equality comes out again in some remarks made by an Australian expatriate in Cambridge, England. Writing immediately after the latest Labour Chancellor of the Exchequer had introduced increases designed, in his own characteristically sadistic words, to 'make the rich howl in agony', this not untypical modern socialist 'moderate' insisted: 'There is *nothing* to be said in favour of greater-than-present inequalities.' He then went on to dismiss talk about incentives to acquire and employ skills, or to make and maintain productive investments, as intolerably right-wing (Stretton, pp.169 ff: italics supplied).

4   I mined this treasure from *The Wall Street Journal* for 25 October 1978, from an editorial entitled 'A Sense of Proportion'. No doubt Cicero was in his own day, but not today, on target when he wrote: 'We do not speak of justice in the case of horses or lions' (quoted Grotius, p.23).

5   See: as an introduction to the constitutional question, Chapter 1 of Watkins; and, on electoral reform, either Mayhew or – much fuller – Finer. The issue of giving all votes equal weight ought to appeal to those who cherish the first of the three ideals of equality distinguished in Chapter II, above; although, significantly, it seems usual for enthusiasts for the third – an enforced equality of outcome – to be firmly wedded to the present system. (Presumably the attraction to them is that it offers such promise that their fellow Procrusteans will achieve elective dictatorship.)

6   Quoted in *The Economist* for 17 June 1972, p.23; thanks to Robert Moss I now possess a photocopy of the original Russian text.

7   Issues of the *Los Angeles Times* while I was writing Section 4 of Chapter II described as liberals – among others – Bella Abzug, J.K. Galbraith, and Jane Fonda; notwithstanding that all three are in fact socialists. Galbraith for one is on record with a chilling, bold confession: 'I am not particular about freedom.'

   This nugget was one of several extracted by Sir Keith Joseph from an interview given to *Die Zeit*, and shared by him with readers of *The Times* of London in letters published on 1 April and 4 May 1977. Asked by his interviewer how he could say such things within sight of the Berlin Wall, Galbraith showed that he at least suffered no hesitations in *The Age of Uncertainty*: 'I think the Wall is a good thing; at least it has maintained the peace.'

8   A review of what seems to have been the only major sociological study of social stratification in a fully socialist country, a study completed as it was reoccupied by the tanks of Russian imperial 'normalisation', remarks: 'There are reasons for suspecting that the working class entry into higher education suffered from the egalitarianism, by diminishing incentives for undergoing it, and thus encouraging the self-recruitment of those oriented towards it as an end in

itself.' And, apropos the attempts to exclude the children of the class enemy, it suggested: 'My suspicion is that the effects of this policy were relatively small in the long run – those who wanted education in the end obtained it.', although 'This of course in no way excuses these repellent measures, nor does it constitute much consolation for those 'who had to suffer from them, least of all for those who never recovered' (Gellner, p.167).

9   See note 7, above.

10   The following unblushing statement was actually published in 1975 in, of all countries, Britain: 'The legal arrangements of capitalism provide employers with definite advantages in bargaining' (Hollis and Nell, pp.210-11). The true situation even in the much less union-dominated USA has been soberly described as follows: 'If A is bargaining with B over the sale of his house, and if A were given the privileges of a modern labour union, he would be able (1) to conspire with all other owners of houses not to make an alternative offer to B . . . (2) to deprive B himself of access to any alternative offers, (3) to surround the house of B and cut off all deliveries, . . . (4) to stop all movement from B's house, . . . and (5) to institute a boycott of B's business. All of these privileges, if he were capable of carrying them out, would no doubt strengthen A's position. But they would not be regarded by anyone as part of "bargaining" – unless A were a labour union' (Chamberlin, pp.41-2: compare for instance, Hutt 1973 and 1975, and Ward).

11   Compare, for instance, a working paper 'on the scope and aims of social policies' commissioned by the National Economic and Social Council of the Republic of Ireland. This Council is by its terms of reference required to promote 'social justice'; which apparently either involves, or is, the 'fair and equitable distribution of the income and wealth of the nation'. That final Rawlsian phrase, whether or not this was intended, clearly covers all the wealth held by citizens resident within the national frontiers and all the income at any time acquired.

       The actual writer of this particular report does distance himself from one assumption of his employers; the assumption that 'social policy' must be specifically defined in terms

of the aim to promote 'social justice', construed as equalisation. 'What', he says, 'distinguishes a policy as "social" is
not these putative consequences but the fact that it deals with
the distribution of resources, opportunities, and life-chances
between different groups and categories of people' (Donnison,
1975a, p.26).

However, presumably because he is himself – like almost
all established advisors on social policy and social administration – both a socialist and an *aficionado* of social justice
as here construed, he does not point out how these commitments are built into the Council's mandate: ' . . . the achievement of social justice . . . fair and equitable distribution *of
the income and wealth of the nation*' (*Ibid.*, p.7: italics
supplied).

12 I do not know whether there is any significance in the fact
that this passage was to be heard in the original talks and read
in *The Listener* thereafter, but is not to be found in the book
of the broadcasts.

13 The difficulties of enforcing such determinations are reviewed
in Schuettinger and Butler. The nineteenth century French
utopian socialist Etienne Çabet was egregiously mistaken in
his fundamental belief that ' . . . nothing is impossible for a
government that *wants* the good of its citizens' (Quoted by
Kristol, p.164: italics original).

14 Speaking of the 1973 oil crisis, and the consequent British
miners' strike, the future Prime Minister Callaghan said: 'If
this means hardship it has to be fairly shared, and Labour
intends that the wealthy who are best able to take the burden
should bear more than their fair share of sacrifices.' I borrow
this nugget from Terry Arthur's robustly titled anthology of
current British political thought.

15 Both Aristotle and Mill appear to have accepted this
principle; though at any rate Aristotle would surely have
been willing to concede a category of the neither deserved
nor undeserved. The *Rhetoric* says: 'Pain at unmerited good
fortune is, in one sense, opposite to pain at unmerited bad
fortune, . . . Both feelings are associated with good moral
character; it is our duty both to feel sympathy and pity for
unmerited distress, and to feel indignation at unmerited
prosperity; for whatever is undeserved is unjust, . . . ' (1386
B 10-15).

Utilitarianism is even more emphatic: 'It is universally considered just that each person should obtain that (whether good or evil) which he *deserves*; and unjust that he should obtain a good or be made to undergo an evil, which he does not deserve. This is, perhaps, the clearest and most emphatic form in which the idea of justice is conceived by the general mind' (p.41).

16 Nisbet 1974 brings out how much Rawls is a 1700s French *philosophe redivivus*. So we should not be surprised that *An Appeal from the New to the Old Whigs* has a rod in pickle for him: 'Who are they that presume to assert that the land which I purchased of the individual, a natural person, and not a fiction of state, belongs to them who in the very capacity in which they make their claim can only exist as an imaginary being, and in virtue of the very prescription which they reject and disown. . . . By what they call reasoning without prejudice, they leave not one stone upon another in the fabric of human society. They subvert all the authority which they hold as well as all that which they have destroyed' (p.103).

17 This could be part of what, if anything, was in the mind of the person who wrote: 'The equality to which it may be rational to aspire is not uniformity but the state of affairs in which differences due to taste, talent, or luck, are as nearly as possible randomly distributed' (Donnison 1975a, p.32). But this is one occasion when I am happy to concede the truth of his remark that the egalitarian ideology of which he is a mouthpiece is 'muddled'. That at least is clear. (See Chapter II 5, ii, b, above.)

18 I should perhaps mention that Kharume, who has since been assassinated, was a Zanzibari, and that, while mainland Tanzania had leanings towards China, his Afro-Shirazi Party, which maintained tight monopoly control of the islands, has been much advised and influenced by Soviet Germany. I certainly want to add that I myself have no difficulty at all in sympathising with those who preferred to go on scratching a wretched living among the not so very bright lights of Dar, rather than to be forcibly bundled back to the excruciating boredom of the villages from which they came.

20 I thank Sidney Hook for this reference, as also for that to

Janos Kadar, in the text at the beginning of Chapter V. Lewis Feuer *Marxism and the Intellectuals* is full of material showing how its appeal has been to would-be vanguard members from almost everything but the classical proletariat in the most advanced industrial countries. What proletariat was there, for instance, in either Ethiopia or Afghanistan before the coups which brought those countries into the Socialist Bloc?

21   It is a mark of both frivolity and bigotry that the 'heartless laissez-faire policies' here denounced are forthwith specified: not as those of what Adam Smith called 'the system of natural liberty', but as those of what Marx and others labelled 'oriental despotism'. The two following sentences read: 'If a ruler owns all the land and means of production, he need not burden his people with a multitude of laws and taxes. He need not make explicit demands, because his subjects have no choice but to sell him their labour in order to survive' (Gibbs, p.24). Compare also in the text of Section 3 of Chapter V, Trotsky on practical socialism; the new and (in historicist terms) higher form of oriental despotism.

    It is most odd that some people who are not in principle unfriendly to all private capital should argue that anything necessary for the sheer survival of others ought on that account always to be owned, not plurally and privately, but singly and exclusively by the most formidable of all mono-polists – the state. (See, for instance, Becker, p.78; and contrast Locke, II(xi) 137.)

22   He was, of course, also fully seized of the point that we are all naturally inclined to cooperate to escape the discipline of competition: 'People of the same trade seldom meet together, even for merriment and diversion, but the conversation ends in a conspiracy against the public, or in some contrivance to raise prices' (Smith, I, x). Consider here the political initiatives, in which it is usual for employers and employed to combine, demanding tariff and other protection for inefficiency and restrictive practices.

23   A parallel definition of 'wage-labour' makes it a 'tautology' in the *Manifesto* 'that there can no longer be any wage-labour when there is no longer any capital' (Marx and Engels, p.99). It should be remarked much more often than it

is that this proof that socialism must mean an end to wage-labour is no more than an empty demonstration in verbal sleight of hand; and one would like too to hear some trades union voices asking whether it is being promised that under socialism all work will be unpaid!

24 I might instead have used another never too often quoted or sufficiently understood description of 'the gale of creative destruction', which follows the unleashing of the enterprisers: 'Capitalism . . . is by nature a form or method of economic change, and not only never is but never can be stationary' (Schumpeter, Chapter 7). That other more familiar purple passage runs: 'The bourgeoisie cannot exist without constantly revolutionising the instruments of production. . . . The cheap prices of its commodities are the heavy artillery with which it batters down all Chinese walls. . . . It has created enormous cities . . . more massive and more colossal productive forces than have all previous generations together' (Marx and Engels 1848, pp.83-5).

25 Popper had after all as a young man known Otto Neurath, a foundation member of the old original Vienna Circle of Logical Positivists, and watched his reluctant disillusionment (Neurath and Cohen, pp.52ff). Neurath in 1919 certainly could have served as a – indeed the – paradigm case. Over the title 'Utopia as a Social Engineer's Construction' he wrote: 'Successful socialisation is possible only of the whole and from above. If one wants to socialise at all it should be done at once and quickly' (*Ibid.*, p.150).

References

Acton, H.B., *The Morals of Markets* (London: Longman, 1971).

Andreski, S. (ed.), *Reflections on Inequality* (London: Croom Helm, 1975).

Aristophanes, *Comedies*, translated by B.B. Rogers (London, and New York: Heinemann, and Putnam, 1924).

Aristotle, *The Basic Works of Aristotle*, edited by R. McKeon (New York: Random House, 1941).

Arthur, T., *Ninety Five Per Cent is Crap: A Plain Man's Guide to British Politics* (Bedford: Libertarian Books, 1975).

Atkinson, A.B., *Unequal Shares: Wealth in Britain* (Harmondsworth and Baltimore: Penguin, Revised Edition 1974).

Attlee, C.R., *The Labour Party in Perspective* (London: Gollancz, Left Book Club Edition 1937).

Austin, J.L., 1962, *Sense and Sensibilia* (Oxford: Clarendon, 1962).

Austin, J.L., 1970, *Philosophical Papers* (Oxford: OUP, Second Edition 1970).

Bambrough, R., 'Plato's Political Analogies', in R. Bambrough (ed.) *Plato, Popper and Politics* (Cambridge, and New York: Heffer, and Barnes and Noble, 1967).

Barry, B., 1965, *Political Argument* (London: Routledge and Kegan Paul, 1965).

Barry, B., 1967, 'Justice and the Common Good', in A.M. Quinton (Ed.) *Political Philosophy* (London: OUP, 1967).

Barry, B., 1971, 'Reflexions on "Justice as Fairness"' in, H.A. Bedau (Ed.) *Justice and Equality* (Englewood Cliffs, N.J.: Prentice Hall, 1971).

Barry, B., 1973, *The Liberal Theory of Justice* (Oxford: OUP, 1973).

Bauer, P., 1976, *Dissent on Development* (Cambridge, Mass.: Harvard UP, Revised edition 1976).

Bauer, P., 1980, 'Ali Mazrui, A Prophet out of Africa', in *Encounter* for June 1980 (Vol.LIV, No.6)

Bay, C., 'Needs, Wants and Political Legitimacy', in the *Canadian Journal of Political Science* for 1968 (Vol.I, No.3).

Becker, L.C., *Property Rights* (London: Routledge and Kegan Paul, 1977).

Beer, S.H., *British Politics in the Collectivist Age* (New York: Knopf, 1965).

Benn, S., 'Human Rights – for whom and for what?' in E. Kamenka and A.E.-S. Tay, *Human Rights* (London: Edward Arnold, 1978).

Bentham, J. *Works*, edited by J. Bowring (London: 1843).

Bentham, J., *A Fragment on Government and An Introduction to the Principle of Morals and Legislation*, ed. W. Harrison (Oxford: Blackwell, 1948).

Berki, R.N., *Socialism* (London: Dent, 1974).

Berlin, I., 1956, 'Equality', in *Proceedings of the Aristotelian Society* for 1955-6 (Vol.LVI).

Berlin, I., 1969, *Four Essays on Liberty* (Oxford: OUP, 1969).

Blackburn, R. (Ed.) *Ideology and Social Science* (London: Collins Fontana, 1972).

Blatchford, R., *Merrie England* (London: Clarion, 1894).

Bosanquet, N., and Townsend, P. (eds), *Labour and Equality: A Fabian Study of Labour in Power 1974-79* (London: Heinemann, 1980).

Boudon, R., 1969, *The Logic of Sociological Explanation*, translated by T. Burns (Harmondsworth: Penguin, 1969).

Boudon, R., 1974, *Education, Oportunity, and Social Inequality (New York: Wiley, 1974).*

Brittan, S., 1973, *Capitalism and the Permissive Society* (London: Macmillan, 1973).

Brittan, S., 1975, 'The Economic Contradictions of Democracy', in K.J.W. Alexander (Ed.) *The Political Economy of Change* (Oxford: OUP, 1975).

Brittan, S., 1979, *Participation without Politics* (London: Institute of Economic Affairs, 1979).

Broadway, F., *Upper Clyde Shipbuilders* (London: Centre for Policy Studies, 1976).

Bruce-Gardyne, J., *Meriden: Odyssey of a Lame Duck* (London: Centre for Policy Studies, 1978).

Burke, E., 1757, *Philosophical Enquiry into the Origin of Our Ideas of the Sublime and the Beautiful*, Edited by L.B. Boulton (Notre Dame, Ind.: Notre Dame UP, 1968).

Burke, E., 1791, *An Appeal from the New to the Old Whigs,* edited by J.M. Robson (Indianapolis: Bobbs-Merrill, 1962).

Burton, J., 'Epilogue', in S.N.S. Cheung (Ed.) *The Myth of Social Cost* (London: Institute of Economic Affairs, 1978).

Carr, E.H., *The Bolshevik Revolution 1917-23* (Harmondsworth: Penguin, 1966).

Chamberlin, E.H., *The Economic Analysis of Labour Union Power* (Washington, D.C.: American Enterprise Association, 1958).

Chomsky, N., *American Power and the New Mandarins* (Harmondsworth: Penguin, 1969).

Cole, M., *The Life of G.D.H. Cole* (London: Macmillan, 1972).

Coleman, J.S. and Others, 1966, *Equality of Educational Opportunity* (Washington, D.C.: US Government Printing Office, 1966).

Coleman, J.S., 1974, 'Inequality, Sociology and Moral Philosophy', in the *American Journal of Sociology* for 1974 (Vol. LXXX No. 3).

Confucius (K'ung Fu-tzu), *The Analects*, translated and edited by W.E. Soothill (Taiyuanfu, Shansi: Soothill, 1910).

Conquest, R., 1968, *The Great Terror* (London: Macmillan, 1968).

Conquest, R., 1972, *Lenin* (London: Collins Fontana, 1972).

Cox, C.B. and Dyson, A.E. (Eds), 1970, *Fight for Education: A Black Paper* (London: Critical Quarterly, 1969).

Cox C.B. and Dyson, A.E. (Eds), 1970, *Black Paper Two* (London: Critical Quarterly, 1970).

Cox, C.B. and Dyson, A.E. (Eds), 1971, *Black Paper Three: Goodbye Mr Short* (London: Critical Quarterly, 1971).

Cranston, M., 1967a, 'Human Rights, Real and Supposed', in D.D. Raphael (Ed.) *Political Theory and the Rights of Man* (Bloomington, Ind., and London: Indiana UP, 1967).

Cranston, M., 1967b, 'Reply to Raphael', in D.D. Raphael (Ed.) *Political Theory and the Rights of Man* (Bloomington, Ind., and London: Indiana UP, 1967).

Crosland, C.A.R., 1956, *The Future of Socialism* (London: Cape, Revised Edition 1963).

Crosland, C.A.R., 1962, *The Conservative Enemy* (London: Cape, 1962).

Crosland, C.A.R., 1975, *Social Democracy in Europe* (London: Fabian Society, 1975).

Dearden, R.F., '"Needs" in Education', in R.F. Dearden, P.H. Hirst, and R.S. Peters (Eds) *Education and the Development of Reason* (London: Routledge and Kegan Paul, 1972).

Descartes, R., *The Philosophical Works of Descartes*, translated by E.S. Haldane and G.R.T. Ross (Cambridge: CUP, 1911).

Donnison, D.V., 1975a, *An Approach to Social Policy* (Dublin: Stationery Office, 1975).

Donnison, D.V., 1975b, 'Equality' in *New Society* (London) for 20 November 1975, pp.422-4.

Dworkin, R., *Taking Rights Seriously* (Cambridge, Mass.: Harvard UP, 1977).

Dylan, R., *Writings and Drawings* (London: Panther, 1974).

Edwards, P. (Ed.) *Encyclopaedia of Philosophy* (New York: Collier-Macmillan, 1967).

Eltis, W., 'Public Policy', in R. Harris (Ed.) *Job 'Creation' – or Destruction* (London: Institute of Economic Affairs, 1979).

Ericsson, L., *Justice in the Distribution of Economic Resources* (Stockholm: Almquist and Wiksell, 1976).

Ferguson, A., 1967, *An Essay on the History of Civil Society,* edited by D. Forbes (Edinburgh: Edinburgh UP, 1966. First published 1767).

Ferguson, A., 1792, *Principles of Moral and Political Science* (Edinburgh, 1792).

Feuer, L., *Marxism and the Intellectuals* (New York: Doubleday Anchor, 1969).

Feuerbach, L., *The Essence of Christianity*, translated by G. Eliot (New York: Harper, 1957).

Field, F., 1973, *Unequal Britain* (London: Arrow, 1973).

Field, F. (Ed.), 1979, *The Wealth Report* (London: Routledge and Kegan Paul, 1979).

Finer, S.E. (Ed.), *Adversary Politics and Electoral Reform* (London: Wigram, 1975).

Firth, C.H. (Ed.), *The Clarke Papers* (London: Clarendon for the Camden Society, 1891).

Fitzgerald, R. (Ed.) *Human Needs and Politics* (Rushcutters Bay, N.S.W.: Pergamon, 1977).

Flew, A.G.N., 1966, *God and Philosophy* (London, and New York: Hutchinson, and Harcourt Brace, 1966).

Flew, A.G.N., 1971, *An Introduction to Western Philosophy* (Indianapolis, and London: Bobbs-Merrill, and Thames and Hudson, 1971).

Flew, A.G.N., 1973a, *Crime or Disease?* (London, and New York: Macmillan, and Barnes and Noble, 1973).

Flew, A.G.N., 1973b, 'What Socrates should have said to Thrasymachus', in C. Carter (Ed.) *Scepticism and Moral Principles* (Evanston, Illinois: New UP, 1973).

Flew, A.G.N., 1975, *Thinking about Thinking* (London: Collins Fontana, 1975). Also as *Thinking Straight* (Buffalo: Prometheus Unbound, 1977).

Flew, A.G.N., 1976a, *Sociology, Equality and Education* (London, and New York: Macmillan, and Barnes and Noble, 1976).

Flew, A.G.N., 1976b, *The Presumption of Atheism* (London, and New York: Elek/Pemberton, and Barnes and Noble, 1976).

Flew, A.G.N., 1978a, *A Rational Animal* (Oxford: Clarendon, 1978).

Flew, A.G.N., 1978b, 'Adam Smith y los fundatores escoses de las ciencias sociales' in R. Orayen (Ed.) *Ensayos Actuales Sobre Adam Smith y David Hume* (Buenos Aires: Instituto Torcuato Di Tella, 1978).

Flew, A.G.N., 1979, 'Sincerity, Criticism and Monitoring', in *The Journal of the Philosophy of Education* for 1979 (Vol. XIII).

Flew, A.G.N., 1980, 'What are Rights?' in *The Georgia law Review* for 1979 (Vol. XIII).

Floud, J., 'Making Adults More Equal: The Scope and Limitations of Public Educational Policy', in P.R. Cox, H.B. Miles, and J. Peels (Eds) *Equalities and Inequalities in Education* (London New York and San Francisco: Academic Press, 1975).

Floud, J., Halsey, A.H. and Martin, F.M., *Social Class and Educational Opportunity* (Westport, Conn.: Greenwood, 1973).

Frankena, W., 'The Concept of Social Justice', in N. Daniels (Ed.) *Reading Rawls* (Oxford: Blackwell, 1975). Previously in R.B. Brandt (Ed.) *Social Justice* (Englewood Cliffs, N.J.: Prentice Hall, 1965).

Friedman, M., 1955, 'The Role of Government in Education', in R.A. Solo (Ed.) *Economics and the Public Interest* (Newark, N.J.: Rutgers UP, 1955).

Friedman, M. and R., 1962, *Capitalism and Freedom* (Chicago: Chicago UP, 1962).

Friedman, M. and R., 1980 *Free to Choose* (London: Secker and Warburg, 1980).

Fromm, E., *The Sane Society* (London: Routledge and Kegan Paul, 1973).

Gaitskell, H., *Socialism and Nationalisation* (London: Fabian Society, 1956).

Galbraith, J.K., 1958, *The Affluent Society* (New York: Houghton Mifflin, 1958).

Galbriath, J.K., 1977, *The Age of Uncertainty* (Boston: Houghton Mifflin, 1977).

Gellner, E.A., 'The Pluralist Anti-levellers of Prague', in his *Contemporary Thought and Politics* (London and Boston: Routledge and Kegan Paul, 1974).

Gewirth, A., 1972, *Moral Rationality,* The Lindley Lecture, given and printed in 1972 at the University of Kansas.

Gewirth, A., 1974, 'The *Is-Ought* Problem Resolved', in *Proceedings and Addresses of the American Philosophical Association* for 1974 (Vol.XLVII).

Gewirth, A., 1978, *Reason and Morality* (Chicago: Chicago UP, 1978).

Gibbs, B., *Freedom and Liberation* (London: Sussex UP, 1976).

Goldthorpe, J.H., *Social Mobility and Class Structure* (Oxford: OUP, 1980).

Greenberg, E., 'In Defence of Avarice', in *Social Policy* for 1976.

Grotius, H., *The Law of War and Peace*, translated by F.W. Kelsey and edited by J.B. Scott (Indianapolis: Bobbs-Merrill, 1925).

Halsey, A.H., 1975, 'Sociology and the Equality Debate', in the *Oxford Review of Education* for 1975, No. 1.

Halsey, A.H. (Ed.), 1977, *Heredity and Environment* (London: Methuen, 1977).

Halsey, A.H., Heath, A.F. and Ridge, J.M., *Origins and Destinations: Family Class and Education in Modern Britain* (Oxford: OUP, 1980).

Hampshire, S.N., 1972a, Critical Notice of J. Rawls' *A Theory of Justice*, in *The New York Review of Books* for 1972.

Hampshire, S.N., 1972b, 'Russell, Radicalism, and Reason', in V. Held, K. Nielsen, and C. Parsons (Eds) *Philosophy and Political Action* (New York: OUP, 1972).

Hardin, G., 'The Tragedy of the Commons', in G. Hardin and J. Baden (Eds) *Managing the Commons* (San Francisco: W.H. Freeman, 1977).

Hare, R.M., Critical Notice of John Rawls' *A Theory of Justice*, in *The Philosophical Quarterly* for 1973 (Vol. XXIII, Nos 91 and 92).

Harris, R. and Seldon, A., 1963, *Choice in Welfare* (London: Institute of Economic Affairs, 1963).

Harris, R. and Seldon, A., 1978, *Not from Benevolence Alone* (London: Institute of Economic Affairs, 1963).

Harris, R. and Seldon, A., 1979, *Over-ruled on Welfare* (London Institute of Economic Affairs, 1979).

Hartley, L.P., *Facial Justice* (London: Hamilton, 1960).

Harvard Educational Review Editors *Equal Educational Opportunity* (Cambridge, Mass.: Harvard UP, 1969).

Hayek, F.A., 1944, *The Road to Serfdom* (London: Routledge and Kegan Paul, 1944).

Hayek, F.A., 1960, *The Constitution of Liberty* (London: Routledge and Kegan Paul, 1960).

Hayek, F.A., 1967, *Studies in Philosophy, Politics and Economics* (London: Routledge and Kegan Paul, 1967).

Hayek, F.A., 1978, *New Studies in Philosophy, Politics, Economics and the History of Ideas* (London: Routledge and Kegan Paul, 1978).

Hegel, G.F.W., *Reason in History*, translated and edited by R.S. Hartman (New York: Liberal Arts, 1953).

Hobbes, T., *Leviathan*, edited by A.D. Lindsay (London, and New York: Dent, and Dutton, 1914).

Hodgson, G., 'Do Schools Make a Diference?', in D.M. Levine and M.J. Bane (Eds) *The 'Inequality' Controversy* (New York: Basic Books, 1975).

Hollis, M. and Nell, E., *Rational Economic Man* (Cambridge: CUP, 1975).

Honderich, T. *Political Violence* (Ithaca, N.Y.: Cornell UP, 1976).

Hook, S. *The Hero in History* (Boston: Beacon, 1935).

Housman, A.E. *Juvena Saturae* (Cambridge: CUP, Revised Edition 1931).

Hume, D., 1739-40, *A Treatise of Human Nature*, edited by L.A. Selby-Bigge (Oxford: Clarendon, 1896. First published 1739-40).

Hume, D., 1748 and 1751, *Enquiries concerning Human Understanding and concerning the Principles of Morals*, edited by L.A. Selby-Bigge, and P. Nidditch (Oxford: Clarendon, Third Edition 1975. First published 1748 and 1751).

Hutt, W.H., 1973, *The Strike-Threat System* (New York: Arlington House, 1973).

Hutt, W.H., 1975, *The Theory of Collective Bargaining 1930-75* (London: Institute of Economic Affairs, 1975).

Illych, I. *Deschooling Society* (Harmondsworth: Penguin, 1976).

Ivens, M. (Ed.) *Prophets of Freedom and Enterprise* (London: Kogan Page, 1975).

Jacobs, J. *The Death and Life of Great American Cities* (New York: Random House, 1961).

Jay, D. *Socialism in the New Society* (London: Longman, 1962).

Jefferson, T., 1787, *Notes on the State of Virginia*, edited by W. Peden (Chapel Hill, N.C.: North Carolina UP, 1955).

Jefferson, T. *Papers*, edited by J.P. Boyd, L.H. Butterfield, etc. (Princeton: Princeton UP, 1950-).

Jencks, C. and others *Inequality* (London: Allen Lane, 1973).

Jones, A. (Ed.) *Economics and Equality* (Oxford: Philip Allan, 1976).

Jones, C. *The £200,000 Job!* (London: Centre for Policy Studies, 1977).

Joseph, K. *Stranded on the Middle Ground* (London: Centre for Policy Studies, 1976).

Joseph, K. and Sumption, J. *Equality* (London: John Murray, 1979).

Kant, I. *Groundwork of the Metaphysic of Morals*, in *The Moral Law*, translated by H. J. Paton (London: Hutchinson, 1948).

Keynes, J.M. *The General Theory of Employment, Interest and Money* (London: Macmillan, 1936).

Kolakowski, L. and Hampshire, S.N. (Eds) *The Socialist Idea* (London: Weidenfeld and Nicolson, 1974).

Kristol, I. *Two Cheers for Capitalism* (New York: Basic Books, 1978).

Langford, G. *Teaching as a Profession* (Manchester: Manchester UP, 1978).

Lasky, M.J. *Utopia and Revolution* (London: Macmillan, 1976).

Laslett, P. and Runciman, W.G. (Eds) *Politics, Philosophy and Society: Second Series* (Oxford: Blackwell, 1962).

Levine, D.M. and Bane, M.J. (Eds) *The 'Inequality' Controversy* (New York: Basic Books, 1975).

Lewis, W.A. *The Principles of Economic Planning* (London: Fabian Society, 1949).

Lichtheim, G. *A Short History of Socialism* (London: Collins Fontana, 1975).

Lloyd-Thomas, D.A., 1977, 'Competitive Equality of Opportunity', in *Mind* for 1977 (Vol. LXXXVI, No. 343).

Lloyd-Thomas, D.A., 1979, 'The Ones in Darkness', in *Philosophy* for 1979 (Vol. LIV, No. 209).

Locke, J. *Two Treatises of Government*, edited by P. Laslett (Cambridge: CUP, 1960).

Lothstein, A. (Ed.) *All we are saying . . . the philosophy of the new left* (New York: Putnam, 1971).

Lucas, J.R., 1971, 'Against Equality', in H. Bedau (Ed.) *Justice and Equality* (Englewood Cliffs, N.J.: Prentice Hall, 1971).

Lucas, J.R., 1977, 'Against Equality Again', in *Philosophy* for 1977 (Vol. LII, No. 201).

Macdiarmid, H. *Selected Poems*, edited by D. Craig and J. Manson (Harmondsworth: Penguin, 1970).

McFadzean, G. *The Economics of John Kenneth Galbraith*

(London: Centre for Policy Studies, 1977).

Macpherson, C.B., 1966, *The Real World of Democracy* (Oxford: OUP, 1966).

Macpherson C.B., 1977, *The Life and Times of Liberal Democracy* (Oxford: OUP, 1977).

Magee, B. *Popper* (London: Collins Fontana, 1973).

Mandeville, B. de *The Fable of the Bees*, edited by P. Harth (Harmondsworth: Penguin, 1970).

Marcuse, H., 1968, 'Liberation from the Affluent Society', in D. Cooper (Ed.) *The Dialectics of Liberation* (Harmondsworth: Penguin, 1968).

Marcuse, H., 1969, 'Repressive Tolerance', in H. Marcuse, B. Moore, and R. Wolff *A Critique of Pure Tolerance* (London: Cape, 1969).

Marx, K., 1844, *The Economic and Philosophical Manuscripts of 1844*, edited by D.J. Struik (New York: International, 1964).

Marx, K., 1852, *The Eighteenth Brumaire of Louis Buonaparte*, no translator named (Moscow: Progress, 1934).

Marx, K., 1859, *A Contribution to the Critique of Political Economy*, edited by M. Dobb (New York: International, 1971).

Marx, K., 1867, *Capital*, edited by F. Engels (New York: International, 1967).

Marx, K., 1891, *Critique of the Gotha Programme*, in K. Marx and F. Engels *Selected Works* (Moscow: Foreign Languages Publishing House, 1949), Vol.II.

Marx, K. and Engels, F., 1846, *The German Ideology*, edited by S. Ryazanskaya, no translator named (Moscow: Progress, 1964).

Marx, K. and Engels, F., 1848, *The Communist Manifesto*, translated by S. Moore and edited by A.J.P. Taylor (Harmondsworth: Penguin, 1967).

Marx, K. and Engels, F. *Collected Works*, various translators (Moscow: Progress, 1975).

Matson, W. 'What Rawls Calls Justice', in *The Occasional Review* for Autumn 1978, No. 8/9 (San Diego: World Research, 1978).

Mayhew, C. *The Disillusioned Voter's Guide to Electoral*

Reform (London: Hutchinson Arrow, 1976).

Maynard, A. *Experiment with Choice in Education* (London: Institute of Economic Affairs, 1975).

Menninger, K. *The Crime of Punishment* (New York: Viking, 1968).

Mill, J.S., 1859, *On Liberty*, in *Utilitarianism, Liberty and Representative Government* (London, and New York: J.M. Dent, and Dutton, 1910).

Mill, J.S., 1861, *Utilitarianism*, in *ibid.*

Miller, D. *Social Justice* (Oxford: OUP, 1976).

Minogue, K. *The Liberal Mind* (London: Methuen, 1963).

Monboddo, James Burnet, Lord *Origin and Progress of Language* (Edinburgh, Second Edition 1774).

Moss, R. *Chile's Marxist Experiment* (London: David and Charles, 1973).

Moynihan, D.P., 1972, 'Equalising Education: in Whose Benefit?', in *The Public Interest* for 1972 (No. 29). Reprinted in Levine and Bane.

Musgrave, F. *The Family, Education and Society* (London: Routledge and Kegan Paul, 1966).

Neurath, M. and Cohen, R.S. (Eds) *Otto Neurath: Empiricism and Sociology* (Dordrecht and Boston: Reidel, 1973).

Nielsen, K., 1972, 'Is Empiricism an Ideology?', in *Metaphilosophy* for 1972 (Vol.III, No.4).

Nielsen, K., 1974, 'In Defence of Radicalism', in H. Hawton (Ed.) *Question Seven* (London: Pemberton, 1974).

Nisbet, R., 1974, 'The Pursuit of Equality', in *The Public Interest* for 1974 (No. 35).

Nisbet, R., 1975, *The Twilight of Authority* (Oxford: OUP, 1975).

Nisbet, R., 1976, 'The Fatal Ambivalence', in *Encounter* for December 1976 (Vol. XLVII, No. 6).

Niskanen, W.A. *Bureaucracy: Servant or Master?* (London: Institute of Economic Affairs, 1973).

Nozick, R. *Anarchy, State, and Utopia* (New York, and Oxford: Basic Books, and Blackwell, 1974).

Okun, A.M. *Equality and Efficiency: The Big Tradeoff* (Washington: Brookings, 1975).

Orwell, G. *1984* (London: Secker and Warburg, 1949).

Parkin, F. *Class Inequality and Political Order* (London: Paladin, 1972).

Peacock, A.I. and Wiseman, J. *Education for Democrats* (London: Institute of Economic Affairs, 1964).

Plato *Dialogues*, translated by B. Jowett (New York: Random House, 1937).

Polanyi, G. and P. *Failing the Nation* (London: Ansbacher, 1974).

Polanyi, G. and Wood, J.B. *How Much Inequality?* (London: Institute of Economic Affairs, 1974).

Pole, J.R. *The Pursuit of Equality in American History* (Berkeley, Los Angeles, and London: California UP, 1978).

Popper, K.R., 1957, *The Poverty of Historicism* (London: Routledge and Kegan Paul, 1957).

Popper, K.R., 1963, *Conjectures and Refutations* (London: Routledge and Kegan Paul, 1963).

Popper, K.R., 1965, *The Open Society and its Enemies* (London: Routledge and Kegan Paul, Fifth Edition, 1965).

Posner, R. 'Economic Justice and the Economist', in *The Public Interest* for 1973 (No. 33).

Quinton, A.M. *Utilitarian Ethics* (London: Macmillan, 1973).

Rawls, J., 1958, 'Justice as Fairness', in *The Philosophical Review* for 1958 (Vol.LXVII); also reprinted in P. Laslett and W.G. Runciman.

Rawls, J., 1969 *'The Justification of Civil Disobedience'*, in H.A. Bedau (Ed.) *Civil Disobedience* (New York: Pegasus, 1969).

Rawls, J., 1971, *A Theory of Justice* (Cambridge, Mass., and Oxford, England: Harvard UP, 1971 and Clarendon, 1972).

Robbins, L.C. *Liberty and Equality* (London: Institute of Economic Affairs, 1977).

Rogge, B.A. *Can Capitalism Survive?* (Indianapolis: Liberty Press, 1979).

Roover, R. de 'The Concept of the Just Price', in *The Journal of Economic History* for 1958 (Vol.XVIII).

Ross, A. *On Law and Justice* (Berkeley and Los Angeles: California UP, 1959).

Rothbard, M.N. *Egalitarianism as a Revolt against Nature* (Washington, D.C.: Libertarian Review, 1974).

Rousseau, J. - J. *The Social Contract*, translated by G.D.H. Cole (London, and New York: Dent, and Dutton, 1913).

Rubinstein, D. and Stoneman, C. (Eds) *Education for Democracy* (Harmondsworth and Baltimore: Penguin, Second edition, 1972).

Runciman, W.G. *Relative Deprivation and Social Justice* (London: Routledge and Kegan Paul, 1966).

Runyon, D. *Runyon on Broadway* (London: Constable, 1950).

Ruskin, J. *Unto this Last* (London: G. Allen, 1899).

Sachs, D. 'A Fallacy in Plato's *Republic*', in G. Vlastos (Ed.) *Plato: Ethics, Politics and Philosophy of Art and Religion* (New York, and London: Doubleday, and Macmillan, 1971 and 1972).

Schaar, J.H. 'Equality of Opportunity and Beyond', in J.R. Pennock and J.W. Chapman (Eds) *Equality* (New York: Atherton, 1967).

Schoeck, H. *Envy: A Theory of Social Behaviour*, translated by M. Glenny and B. Ross (London: Secker and Warburg, 1969).

Schopenhauer, A. *On the Basis of Morality*, translated by E.F.J. Payne (Indianapolis: Bobbs-Merrill, 1965).

Schuettinger, R.L. and Butler, E.F. *Forty Centuries of Wage and Price Controls* (Washington, D.C.: Heritage Foundation, 1979).

Schumpeter, J.A. *Capitalism, Socialism and Democracy* (London: Allen and Unwin, 1943).

Schwartz, G. *Bread and Circuses* (London: Sunday Times, 1959).

Seldon, A., 1977, *Charge* (London: Temple Smith, 1977).

Seldon, A., 1980, *Prime Mover of Progress* (London: Institute of Economic Affairs, 1980).

Selsdon Group *A Beginner's Guide to Public Expenditure Cuts* (London: Selsdon Group, 1980).

Sennett, R. and Cobb, J. *The Hidden Injuries of Class* (New York: Knopf, 1972).

Sidgwick, H. *The Methods of Ethics* (London: Macmillan, Sixth Edition, 1901).

Silverman, L. 'Britain – The Crisis of Decline', in M.B. Hamilton and K.G. Robertson (Eds) *Britain's Crisis in Sociological Perspective* (Reading: University of Reading, 1976).

Sjöstrand, W. *Freedom and Equality as Fundamental Educational Principles in Western Democracy from John Locke to Edmund Burke* (Stockholm: Almquist and Wiksell, 1973).

Skinner, A.S. and Wilson, T. (Eds) *Essays on Adam Smith* (Oxford: Clarendon, 1976).

Skinner, B.F. *Beyond Freedom and Dignity* (New York and London: Knopf, and Cape, 1971 and 1972 respectively).

Smith, A. *The Wealth of Nations*, introduced by E.R.A. Seligman (London, and New York: Dent, and Dutton, 1904).

Solzhenitsyn, A. *The Gulag Archipelago* (London: Collins Fontana, 1976-8).

Stephen, J.F. *Liberty, Equality and Fraternity* (London: Smith and Elder, 1873).

Strachey, J., 1936, *The Theory and Practice of Socialism* (London: Gollancz, 1936).

Strachey, J., 1944, *Why You should be a Socialist* (London: Gollancz, Revised Edition 1944).

Stretton, H. *Capitalism, Socialism, and the Environment* (Cambridge: CUP, 1976).

Szamuely, T. *The Russian Tradition*, edited by R. Conquest (London: Secker and Warburg, 1974).

Talmon, J.L. *The Origins of Totalitarian Democracy* (London: Secker and Warburg, 1952).

Tawney, R.H., 1921, *The Acquisitive Society* (London: G. Bell, 1921).

Tawney, R. H., 1938, *Religion and the Rise of Capitalism* (Harmondsworth: Penguin, 1938).

Tawney, R.H., 1952, *Equality* (New York: Capricorn, 1962. A reprint of the edition finally revised by the author in 1951, and published 1952).

Thurrow, L. 'Toward a Definition of Economic Justice', in *The Public Interest* for 1973 (No. 31).

Trotsky, L. *The Revolution Betrayed* (New York: Pioneer, 1937).

Tullock, G. *The Vote Motive* (London: Institute of Economic Affairs, 1976).

Vazey, J. 'Whatever Happened to Equality?', in *The Listener* for 5 May 1974.

Vieira, E. 'Rights and the American Constitution', in *The Georgia Law Review* for 1979 (Vol.XIII).

Viner, J. 'The Intellectual History of Laissez-Faire', in *The Journal of Law and Economics* for 1960.

Vonnegut, K. *Welcome to the Monkey House* (New York: Dell, 1950).

Ward, G. *Fort Grunwick* (London: Temple Smith, 1977).

Watkins, K.W. (Ed.) *In Defence of Freedom* (London: Cassell, 1978).

Weale, A. *Equality and Social Policy* (London: Routledge and Kegan Paul, 1978).

Webb, S. and B. *Soviet Communism: A New Civilization* (London: Gollancz, Second edition 1932).

West, E.G. *Economics, Education and the Politician* (London: Institute of Economic Affairs, 1968).

Williams, B., 1962, 'The Idea of Equality', in his *Problems of the Self* (Cambridge: CUP, 1973). This article was first published in Laslett and Runciman.

Wills, G. *Inventing America* (New York: Doubleday, 1978).

Index of Names

Abzug, B. 189
Acton, H.B. 93
Adams, A. 37
Albertus Magnus 154
Allende, S. 119, 181
Andreski, S. 135
Aquinas, T. 148
Aristides, A. 9
Aristophanes 102
Aristotle 65, 67-9, 79, 116, 136, 148-50, 152-4, 191
Arthur, T. 191
Atkinson, A.B. 71, 87-9
Attlee, C.R. 17
Austin, J.D. 37, 138, 175-6

Babeuf, G. 21, 76, 109
Balzac, H. de 147
Bambrough, R. 124
Bane, M.J. 58
Bannister, R. 111
Barry, B. 80, 94, 125, 154
Bauer, P.T. 78
Bay, C. 121
Becker, L.C. 193
Beloff, M. 156
Benn, S. 36
Bentham, J. 25, 36, 39
Berki, R.N. 181-2
Berlin, I. 69, 87-9, 134
Blackburn, R. 128
Bosanquet, N. 183-5
Boudon, R. 50-1
Brittan, S. 81, 96, 141
Broadway, F. 159
Bruce-Gardyne, J. 159
Burgess, T. 23
Burke, E. 71, 192
Burton, J. 169
Butler, E.F. 191

Cabet, E. 191
Callaghan, J. 14-5, 191
Camara, H. 145-7
Carr, E.H. 119
Carroll, L. 113
Chamberlin, E.H. 190
Chaplin, C. 168
Chernyshevsky, N.G. 130
Chomsky, N. 119
Churchill, W.S. 56
Cicero, M.T. 189
Clark, E. 57
Cobb, J. 33-5
Cohen, R.S. 194
Cole, G.D.H. 156-7, 166-7
Cole, M. 13-14, 156-7
Coleman, J. 51-2, 54-7
Condorcet, M. de 37-9
Confucius (K'ung Fu-Tzu) 40, 49
Conquest, R. 156-7
Cox, B. 55
Cranston, M. 39, 109
Crosland, C.A.R. 17-8, 28-9, 45, 66, 83, 188

Darwin, C. 170
Dearden, R. 123
Descartes, R. 176-7
Director, A. 91
Donnison, D.V. 31, 59-63, 71, 190-2
Dostoievsky, F. 155
Durkheim, E. 50, 171
Dworkin, R. 36
Dylan, R. 97
Dyson, A.E. 55

Edwards, P. 13, 40
Einstein, A. 138-9
Eltis, W. 159

Index of Notions